The Squatters' Movement in Europe

Commons and Autonomy as Alternatives to Capitalism

Squatting Europe Kollective

Edited by Claudio Cattaneo
and Miguel A. Martínez

PlutoPress
www.plutobooks.com

First published 2014 by Pluto Press
345 Archway Road, London N6 5AA

www.plutobooks.com

Distributed in the United States of America exclusively by
Palgrave Macmillan, a division of St. Martin's Press LLC,
175 Fifth Avenue, New York, NY 10010

British Library Cataloguing in Publication Data
A catalogue record for this book is available from the British Library

ISBN 978 0 7453 3396 0 Hardback
ISBN 978 0 7453 3395 3 Paperback
ISBN 978 1 8496 4930 8 PDF eBook
ISBN 978 1 7837 1042 3 Kindle eBook
ISBN 978 1 7837 1041 6 EPUB eBook

Library of Congress Cataloging in Publication Data applied for

This book is printed on paper suitable for recycling and made from fully managed and
sustained forest sources. Logging, pulping and manufacturing processes are expected to
conform to the environmental standards of the country of origin.

10 9 8 7 6 5 4 3 2 1

Typeset by Curran Publishing Services
Simultaneously printed digitally by CPI Antony Rowe, Chippenham, UK
and
Edwards Bros in the United States of America

Contents

Acknowledgements   *vii*

Introduction: Squatting as an Alternative to Capitalism   1
Claudio Cattaneo and Miguel A. Martínez
   Box 0.1 Some Notes about SqEK's Activist-Research
   Perspective   17
   Miguel A. Martínez
   Box 0.2 SqEK Processes as an Alternative to Capitalism   22
   Claudio Cattaneo, Baptiste Colin and Elisabeth Lorenzi

1 **Squatting as a Response to Social Needs, the Housing
  Question and the Crisis of Capitalism**   26
  Miguel A. Martínez and Claudio Cattaneo
   Box 1.1 The Environmental Basis of the Political
   Economy of Squatting   52

PART I CASE STUDIES   59

2 **'The Fallow Lands of the Possible': An Enquiry into the
  Enacted Criticism of Capitalism in Geneva's Squats**   60
  Luca Pattaroni
   Box 2.1 Anti-Capitalist Communes Remaining Despite
   Legalisation: The Case of House Projects in Berlin   81
   Lucrezia Lennert

3 **The Right to Decent Housing and a Whole Lot More
  Besides: Examining the Modern English Squatters
  Movement**   85
  E. T. C. Dee
   Box 3.1 Criminalisation One Year On   104
   Needle Collective

4 **The Power of the Magic Key: The Scalability of Squatting in
  the Netherlands and the United States**   110
  Hans Pruijt
   Box 4.1 Provo   113
   Alan Smart
   Box 4.2 My Personal Experience as a NYC Neighbour   131
   Frank Morales

Contents

5   'Ogni Sfratto Sarà una Barricata': Squatting for Housing
     and Social Conflict in Rome   136
     Pierpaolo Mudu
       Box 5.1 The French Housing Movement: Squatting as a
       Mode of Action Among Other Tools   159
       Thomas Aguilera

PART II SPECIFIC ISSUES   165

6   Squats in Urban Ecosystems: Overcoming the Social and
     Ecological Catastrophes of the Capitalist City   166
     Salvatore Engel Di Mauro and Claudio Cattaneo

7   Squatting and Diversity: Gender and Patriarchy in Berlin,
     Madrid and Barcelona   189
     Azozomox
       Box 7.1 Some Examples of the Great Variety and Diversity
       within the Berlin Squatting Environment   206

8   Unavoidable Dilemmas: Squatters Dealing with the Law   211
     Miguel A. Martínez, Azozomox and Javier Gil
       Box 8.1 The interaction between Spheres of Morality
       and of Legality   230
       Claudio Cattaneo
       Box 8.2 'Your Laws are Not Ours': Squatting in Amsterdam   232
       Deanna Dadusc

Conclusions   237
Miguel A. Martínez and Claudio Cattaneo

Appendix: The Story of SqEK and the Production
Process of This Book   250
Claudio Cattaneo, Baptiste Colin and Elisabeth Lorenzi

Notes on Contributors   255
Index   259

Acknowledgments

This book owes a debt, first, to all the SqEK members who participated in the meetings and online debates. Most of our ideas became more fruitful thanks to this collective way of combining our local and personal work, with the critical sharing of our perspectives.

Second, nonactive SqEK members but activists within the different squatting scenes of the cities where we met, who attended some of our meetings or hosted us, or guided our visits to particular squats, also contributed to our reflections with their valuable insights and experiences.

Also, in different stages of the production of this book the editors have been helped, specially regarding the language supervision, by some SqEK participants beyond or independently from their individual contributions to the chapters and boxes. Above all, E. T. C. Dee was in charge of the final style overview, but we are also very grateful to Alan Moore, Nathan Eisenstad, Matt, Frank Morales, Jake Smith and Lucrezia Lennert.

Finally, we are grateful to David Castle from Pluto Press for his advice and support.

Part of the research in which the book is based and some of the expenses involved were possible due to the funds supplied by the MOVOKEUR research project # CSO2011-23079 ('The Squatters Movement in Spain and Europe: Contexts, Cycles, Identities and Institutionalization': Spanish Ministry of Science and Innovation 2012–14).

Squatting as an Alternative to Capitalism: An Introduction

Claudio Cattaneo and Miguel A. Martínez

This book is about how the squatters' movement has emerged and how it represents a comprehensive alternative to capitalism. Capitalism is a broad phenomenon, so given its hegemonic nature, the squatters' alternative must be understood at the local level first. Given the multiple scales upon which the interactions between the global and the local take place, a starting point of analysis refers to how and to what extent the practices of squatting scale up from a local attachment. This implies the necessity of understanding whether the formal and substantial features of the squatters' movement are reproduced and expanded at a wider level, or to put it another way, how they change and adapt to a broader social reality.

In the following chapters, we focus on the potential and actual alternatives to capitalism put in practice by squatters. Sometimes, the actions appear to be immediate reactions to certain needs, without much concern about their further implications for most of the participants – at least at the outset. The power of squatters seems to increase when the squats are connected to other similar anti-capitalist practices and are consciously promoted as part of broader anti-capitalist movements. Since the capitalist system is narrowly supported by most state agencies, the radical orientation of squatting may be also distinguished in any oppositional action against those public policies that are deemed to fuel the reproduction of capitalism and social inequalities. The different forms of squatting – either urban or rural, social or political – are also relevant to anti-capitalist struggles because they offer positive means for the development of many other alternative initiatives beyond squatting itself, be they communal house projects, self-managed social centres or the defence of other common goods.

Above all, we need to clarify what we mean when we refer to 'squatting', 'capitalism' and 'anti-capitalist alternatives'.

What Kind of Squatting?

Generally speaking, squatting is about the illegal occupation of property, used without the previous consent of its owner, which could be a public institution, a particular individual, a private corporation or any sort of organisation. Although there are many forms of squatting worldwide, in this book we do not deal with all of them. It is said that one billion people are squatting in houses or on land worldwide (Neuwirth, 2004). This is an amazing figure, accounting for one person out of seven. But we do not focus on such a broad dimension, and we stay put in Europe and North-America, in post-industrial and widely urbanised countries. In such a context, most cities are experiencing radical transformations in the use of space. In particular, in the last four decades the implementation of neoliberal policies, gentrification and other processes of social displacement and segregation, the shrinking stock of social housing, the privatisation of public services and spaces, and the commodification of larger aspects of our lives, seriously threaten any aspiration to a just city (Fainstein, 2010; Harvey, 1973) or to fulfil the 'right to the city' (Lefebvre, 1968).

As will be verified in this book, our approach has little to do with the illegal character of squatting. In spite of the central role that legal issues and processes can play in explaining the life of a squat, we rather prefer to focus on the context in which squatting emerges and its impacts. Therefore, our second remark about the definition of squatting leads us to the political features of squatting as an urban movement. Although 'political squatting' is a very fuzzy category because there are different political dimensions involved in each configuration of squatting (Martinez, 2012; Pruijt, 2012), a specific typology may help to distinguish the most significant diversity within the movement, notwithstanding the fact that some squatters may remain isolated from any sort of political coordination and mutual aid.

In Western European cities many squats are inhabited by immigrants, ethnic minorities such as the Roma, people homeless as a result of different social and personal conditions and so on. As long as these people do not pay rent, they are excluded from the housing market, and therefore their actions in squatting represent a practical and direct way to satisfy their housing need. This is an overtly alternative means of being housed apart from the options offered by capitalist markets or state supply, if any. However, their actions are almost exclusively intended to satisfy an immediate need in response to a desperate situation. The squat is considered as a temporary lodging solution, and if possible, the occupants aim for better conditions of dwelling – more permanent and legal. Moreover, they tend to squat in isolation and not as part of any political movement, either spontaneously self-organised or in relation to self-help and pro-housing rights activism. Behind this type of squatting there is often no other motivation than to remedy a desperate situation, secretly and in silence. Such a reason for action has little to do with what is usually called 'political squatting'.

Certainly, the principal argument which emerges from the heart of the political squatters' movement is the practical defence of the right to decent and affordable housing. This is in line with the practice of direct illegal occupation which nonpolitical squatters adopt to satisfy their immediate needs, although they are not always able to express such a justification. The striking point is that political squatting offers a broader rationale for going beyond material housing need. First of all, political squatters criticise the dominant relationship between existing need and the way this can be satisfied in present Western European societies. The usual targets of their critique are the neoliberal forces of the late capitalistic stages: financial speculators, real estate developers, and the policy makers that favour them and exclude the worst-off from access to affordable housing.

Criminalisation and repression of squatting is considered as an abuse of the penal laws, since the right to a shelter is a fundamental one. Thus, the 'political' here also refers to the pretended public visibility of both the practice of squatting and the aforementioned criticisms. The aim of political squatters is to prefigure ways of living beyond capitalist society, implying the need loudly to express this message. On the one hand, political squatters address economic, social and political elites in order to let them know the desperate and precarious economic situation of those who cannot enjoy the right to housing. On the other hand, political squatters critique the society at large and make manifest with practical examples the kinds of problems, arguments and prospects that squatting suggests. In the end, it is basically about sustaining the legitimation of an act of social disobedience confronting the housing question.

Furthermore, as the emergence of social centres attests, the issue of housing is not the only one to be embraced by political squatters. Self-produced and creative commons culture opposing intellectual property rights; space required for holding political meetings and campaigns; alternative exchanges of goods, foods and beverages; social interactions and debates without the pressure of paying with money, and similar phenomena are possible thanks to the availability, accessibility and openness of many buildings which have previously been occupied illegally. Regardless of the kind of social needs behind squatting, political squatters argue that is not legitimate to leave private property abandoned. The right of use should be prior to the defence of absolute private property. Making profit from private property does not justify social inequalities regarding access to housing or social spaces. As a consequence, such an explicit criticism becomes manifest through direct action, public campaigns, the production of visual and written documents, political debates, press releases, confrontation with institutional powers and other forms of active or passive resistance. This book provides diverse accounts of the political squatters' movement, although other expressions of squatting are frequently intertwined with it.

In the recent years we have also witnessed cases of fascist squatted social centres, like Casa Pound in Rome, for instance (Kington, 2011). The name is inspired by the figure of Ezra Pound, an American poet and essayist who lived in Italy and embraced fascism. He was strongly anti-capitalist, condemning finance as the driver of the economy, seeing usury as evil and pointing at corporate banks as responsible for the First World War. Casa Pound was the name of a building squatted in 2003 for housing citizens of Italian nationality. Although the inhabitants were evicted, it gave space to the birth of Casa Pound Italia, an active political organisation, now present throughout the Italian territory. There is a neo-Fascist inspiration behind some of those who – against speculative corporate interests – are engaged in squatting actions. Their squats are part of a wider political programme which aims at the reconstitution of a strong central state, is strongly anti-global and anti-capitalist, and promotes social mortgages for home property, birth policies favouring Italians but not immigrants living in Italy, and strict public control of strategic economic sectors such as finance, energy, transport and primary resources. Other aims are to promote social and economic autocracy, a revision of the Schengen Agreement in an even more strict manner, a nationalist-based defence of the Italian identity and a clear-cut separation from minority identities. Casa Pound Italia uses squatting as a tool to implement some ideas from its very controversial programme.

This is a quite delicate issue. Although it is somehow ambiguously anti-capitalist, far-right political squatting is not part of our analysis, while left-wing or left-libertarian squatting is here considered as an alternative to the capitalist society at large. In these forms of squatting, a wide social diversity and different cultural minorities are included. In contrast, far-right squatters violently oppose migrants, ethnic minorities and lesbian, bisexual, gay, transgender and questioning (LBGTQ) individuals and organisations. Leftist squatters, however, are active in the provision of resources for deprived people, and apart from help in housing them, are generally involved in campaigns opposing restrictive and repressive migration policies, or the persecution of unconventional gender identities. Again, from a political leftist perspective of squatting, rallying around these issues, and doing so in squats, is felt to be more legitimate than obeying the laws that protect the right to maintain vacant private property.

A final form of squatting which is not directly incorporated in the present research refers to the occasional and temporary occupations of places as tactical protests, without claiming them for housing or social centre purposes. Sit-ins, occupations of open squares and parks, 'reclaim the streets' festivals, workplace occupations during a strike, and famously the Occupy movements, may be ideologically connected and also incorporate squatters, but do not necessarily share most of the claims, practices and forms of self-organisation that the squatters' movement develops (Hakim, 1991; Notes from Nowhere, 2003; Shepard and Smithsimon, 2011).

Thus, this book aims at a deeper understanding of the political squatters' movement as a direct answer to housing deprivation and other social problems inherent to the dynamics of neoliberal capitalism in Europe and North America. The scholarly literature on the topic of squatting is highly fragmented and not easily accessible. The intention of this book is to contribute to the knowledge of squatting across Europe and North America, and not only in one country or city. By collecting research made through different scholarly perspectives, we seek to analyse squatting beyond the sole issue of housing. The cultural dimension of living in common, the historical emergence of the movement, the bonds and connection with society at large, the inclusion of social diversity, the regular dilemmas concerning legalisation and criminalisation processes, the critique of consumerism, the alternative ways of life, the environmental dimension and the rural squatting phenomenon fall within the scope of our gaze.

In sum, we approach squatting as a heterogeneous phenomenon, specific to the local urban context in which it is formed and developed. While prior to the current systemic crises squatting was related mainly and almost uniquely – at least, in the eyes of mass media – to a sort of counter-cultural critique of the consumerist city, for us squatting is now more heterogeneous than ever. It can be intended either as a means towards something else – the institution of a right, through for instance the legalisation of a squatted house, or the cancellation of an urban plan that could cause irreversible social and environmental damage – or as an end: the maintenance of a threatening space against capitalist dynamics from positions of the radical autonomist and libertarian left (Mudu, 2012). The diverse cases of squatting dealt with by the authors offer original reactions against the commodification of housing and urban spaces for

5

the sake of their exchange value. When possible, the analysis takes in a historical examination of particular squatters' movements, and also a reflection of how significant squatting is within the local context, and the wider contexts of the financial crisis and, to some extent, environmental devastation.

Capitalism: Discontents and Alternatives

It is far beyond our present goal to define what capitalism is, but we cannot avoid highlighting a few crucial aspects tightly connected to the illegal occupation of empty buildings. Having expanded throughout the world with increasingly diminished barriers, deregulated capitalist modes of production, exchange and consumption, and the liberal assumptions underlying their hegemony (De Angelis, 2007; Harvey, 2005; Polanyi 1944), have provoked an enormous earthquake.

Very briefly, capitalism starts with a social contract between unequal individuals that allows the exploitation of labour and the accumulation of surplus value in the pockets of capitalists. But this was not historically possible without the help of different legal regulations and the massive mobilisation of peasants who were obliged to move to industrial settlements. Capitalism means the domination of a particular economic system over the whole society, including both its political and cultural frameworks. Exchange value replaces use value, and every single social relationship and natural resource becomes commodified, subject to being bought and sold. Private ownership of the means of production (land, minerals, energy supply, machinery, capital and so on) and reproduction (shelter, food, leisure, education, culture and so on) is a part of the whole complex of social relationships which is colonised by capitalism. Economic inequalities and, in particular, the existence of an 'underclass' which threatens workers' wages and conditions of work, are equally necessary to the continuation of such a system.

Workers' organisations and struggles may change some of those conditions if they operate within the limits of liberal (or even authoritarian) political regimes. And noncapitalist forms of making profits such as rent extraction and slavery may also coexist relatively peacefully if the tensions with the dominant ideology do not overflow, leading to uprisings out of the elites' control.

Hence, we need to ask what is the relationship between capitalism and squatting.

In principle, squatters take over spaces that have been abandoned by their wealthy owners because they are rich enough to have no urgent need for them, or because they are waiting for better opportunities to make use of them. Proprietors, thus, are full capitalists if they dispose of these vacant spaces for productive (under exploitative relationships) or speculative purposes. In either case, squatters can stop, at least partially, the process of making profit from the estate. But this is not always the case. Some proprietors may be part of the working and middle classes who followed an individual or family strategy of saving and investing in the real estate sector. Some capitalists do not have any plan in the short run for their empty properties, so in the meantime they do not really care about occupation by squatters. At most, the act of squatting is an interference with the capitalist and noncapitalist operations of economic accumulation given the prevailing rules of the housing and urban markets. However, squatters strive for the decommodification of houses and buildings while embracing the use value of any urban good. The vacant spaces serve, then, to secure housing needs, to create housing communes of mutual sharing, and sometimes to open social centres where a range of creative, political and even productive initiatives are unleashed. The interference turns into an anti-capitalist experiment. The experiment may be replicated somewhere else, and subsequently many more can escape from the capitalist logic.

Political squatters are anti-capitalist: speculation using housing stock is considered one of the worst legal behaviours within a capitalist society, since it is the origin of housing exclusion and other social inequalities. Monetary speculation is considered to be an even worse business. Social relationships based on labour exploitation under economic compensation are also normally absent in squats. But being anti-capitalist does not mean rejecting the use of money and of free markets. In fact many squats are established informal businesses – see for instance Pruijt's (2012) typology of entrepreneurial squatting – that, although freely playing in the market arena, are internally constituted as horizontal and self-organised entities and run through cooperative and often voluntary work. All this makes them radically different from other market players like capitalist corporations. For their individual income some squatters also participate in small economic projects outside the squats (often in cooperatives, sometimes in the informal economy) while others cannot avoid participating in the labour market, and work in salaried jobs for capitalist enterprises.

Capitalism is a perverse system guided by an addiction to profit with disregard to the needs of the rest of humanity. People no less than spaces are judged by their capacity to produce profits. They can be employed or discarded depending on the capitalists' calculations and aspirations. Empty houses and unemployed people are both dismissed until a use can be found for them. Otherwise, it is the rest of the society that has to deal with the problems that capitalists can cause. On the capitalists' side, abandonment and destruction of the built environment does not entail any social or environmental trouble if the foreseen economic benefits are good enough. Private ownership of land and buildings provides a higher degree of direct control than is found in the relationship between capitalists and their workforce. Although there are legal restrictions to the degree of urban speculation, they are ineffective and cannot constrain the whole process of urban development based on the predominance of exchange values. Given such a context, real estate developers and speculators may also fail. Rational calculations also have to take into account the general cycles of economic boom and bust, and properties are not always easily sold or rented when and how the owners wish them to be. That is to say, vacancy is both a tool and a side-consequence of urban capitalism. Squatters are never completely sure whether they are interrupting the speculative engine or just taking advantage of the malfunctioning of the urban growth machine.

In this book we want to emphasise that urban and political squatting has lasted for more than three decades in Europe and North America. Over this long period of time an abundance of evidence has emerged about the practical achievements and the potentialities of squatting as an anti-capitalist struggle. Beyond the influence of every specific squat, there is a large network of mutual learning, connections and mutual help: that is, squatting has become a transnational urban movement. Squatters resist the commodification of housing, cities and their own lives. They embrace cooperation and social justice while satisfying basic human needs. Squatting is the most salient symbol of opposition against the damages caused by an unjust distribution of wealth and rampant urban speculation. Living with others without exploitation and being efficient about the preservation of collective needs by making use of the dark holes in urban capitalism (the vacant spaces), squatters offer a political example which is easy to imitate. If the actual circumstances of vacancy and squatting cannot always define a frontal and decisive alternative to capitalism, in most of the cases political squatters, their multiple practices and their critical discourses represent a valuable symptom and indication of how to overcome capitalist society.

Our perspective also takes into account the contradictions and failures that squatters have experienced. An excessive generalisation might ignore, for example, the cases of squatters who sublet rooms. If squatting becomes just a way of saving the rent when you are a student while preparing yourself to compete in the market, to participate in the exploitative relations of labour or to buy a home, then the anti-capitalist effects of

8

squatting are just limited to the existence of every particular squat, and not always to all the processes taking place inside. Living in a squat does not necessarily entail an anti-capitalist attitude, or work out if no other personal transformations and political involvements occur. Meant in such a narrow sense, squatting risks being of no use for overcoming capitalism: no capitalist regime has been destroyed by one social group alone, and even less so by individualistic dynamics such as living rent-free. Within sectors of the squatters' movement, blind tactics regarding the salvation of one particular squat without considering the effects of repression on the rest erode the movement's consistency and capability to spread. Beyond the movement, it would be a failure to miss out on the opportunity to tie in with other urban and environmental struggles.

The current crisis is founded upon huge financial speculation which includes housing, the built environment and natural resources as fields of investment. Public services, food and knowledge come next. No matter the devastating effects of these processes over millions of people and a limited Earth, global and imperial capitalism follows a never-ending path of accumulation. From this perspective, squatting defines a field of urban contention with one of the dimensions of capitalism. However, many squatters and activists in related social movements also try to look forward to wider ways of autonomous and sustainable living. Their criticisms concerning the urban ground of the present economic crisis have shown that common people have sufficient power to resist the most adverse situations such as lack of affordable housing and accessible social spaces. These are the shared threads, open questions and concerns underlying the stories told by the authors of this book.

The Authors

SqEK (Squatting Europe Kollective) is the name of an activist-research network that was born in 2009. Since then, more than 100 people have joined the electronic mailing list and many regular events have been held in different cities. All the contributions to this book are authored by SqEK members who decided to join this process through the email list and the latest SqEK meeting. For us – the coordinators and individual authors of the book – this collective project has been a source of reflection, dialogue and cooperation. The texts we have produced aim at in-depth analysis of a diverse range of issues about squatting, as well as providing activists with systematic data and original interpretations. Most of us are based in different universities across Europe and North America, but some are more involved in their local squatters' movement than in research institutions. In addition to our different academic backgrounds, one of the strengths of this group of authors, and of SqEK in general, is the gathering of committed scholars who are actively participating in and researching into the squatters' movement. We seek to provide first-hand information rarely made visible by mass media and external social scientists.

The relationship between SqEK, the present group of authors – which constitutes a collective within SqEK – and each individual is a nested one. The context in which the book emerged as an idea is the broad one of the SqEK network, its meetings and the SqEK email list; within it, the group of contributors has been formed and evolved, and worked and cooperated in the realisation of the book. At the individual level, several people have put their activist or scholarly expertise into each of the chapters and boxes, and two editors have coordinated the entire work. However SqEK has also been involved as a whole, via the list or in meetings, in the completion of the book. More details of this process are given in the Appendix, which clarifies how this book is a production of SqEK with explicit authors, some of whom have proven expertise in their field.

Contents of the Book

Having seen that not all typologies of squatting can be represented, we acknowledge that not all perspectives around squatting can be undertaken. Hence, we have emphasised case studies and empirical evidence about different aspects of the squatters' movement, while attempting to keep a balance with our theoretical foundations, the core topic of this book and also our real-life experience within the squatters scenes.

The question we as editors have suggested to all the authors is whether or not squatting has displayed specific alternatives to capitalism. Our aim is to contextualise the squatters' movements, to see to what extent squatting is either a local or a global alternative, to what degree squatters manage to do without, and survive at the margin of capitalism. We take on board the idea of a critique to capitalism, expressed in how squatters live in everyday communes and how they create spaces where the impossible becomes possible. Thus, we draw on both past experiences and recent events in order to assess the potential conditions under which squatting could be scaled up to provide a larger alternative to capitalism.

The chapters are organised as follows. Below are two boxes, one from Miguel A. Martínez, which offers a presentation of SqEK as a research collective and of the methodological debates about being activist researchers, and one from Claudio Cattaneo, Baptiste Colin and Elisabeth Lorenzi, offering insights into how both our horizontal processes for decision making and the way our meetings take place constitute alternatives to capitalism. Then follows a chapter that sets the wider framework of this book, that of capitalist dynamics and the crisis, the housing question and the kind of reactions and resistance that squatters propose. The rest of the book is divided into two main parts where we further develop the guiding ideas we presented above, and in particular, provide more contextual insights about the historical, economic, political and environmental constraints within a capitalist society.

The first part, 'Case Studies' – Chapters 2 to 5 – comprises city case studies which engage in a historical presentation of how the squatters' movement has emerged, flourished and at times declined. Common to all experiences is the centrality of the housing issue. However, we learn that while in some cities and contexts more radical experiences around the squat as an alternative commune have flourished, in other situations or moments in time the squatting phenomenon has been more focused on reclaiming housing rights. The cases presented are samples of a complex spatial-temporal reality represented by the experiences of Amsterdam, New York, London, Brighton, Berlin, Geneva, Barcelona, Rome and Paris.

In particular, Part I begins presenting a case for fomenting a genuine alternative to capitalism, rooted in a criticism of the consumerist society. Here squatting is the justification for engaging in the lifestyles that such a counter-cultural alternative entails. This radical approach has characterised in many cities the emergence of what could be understood as the squatters' movement. This part further develops by presenting other city case studies which show the political approach of reclaiming housing rights. This movement, contextual to the present housing crisis, is best characterised in the last chapter of this series, with the cases of Rome and Paris, which are witnessing the emergence of large squatters' movements for housing. Extending beyond the traditional counter-cultural identity that emerges in the preceding chapters, these housing movements constitute another potential alternative to capitalism.

The second part of the book, 'Specific Issues' (Chapters 6 to 8) is structured across three specific themes: the relationship between the city, its environment and the movement's ecological dimension; the inclusion of diversity and gender minorities; and problems related to legalisation, criminalisation and institutionalisation of the movement. Beyond the housing issue, our experience tells that these are three facets of the phenomenon that better constitute challenging alternatives to the capitalist system.

These alternatives manifest themselves in very different ways, which are visible in the comparative nature of these chapters, in each of which information from at least two cities is presented. Far from being uniform blocks, environmentalism, consideration for minorities and institutionalisation processes have been presented in very different manners, so we can learn from these comparative case studies that the squatters' movement can at best constitute many alternatives to capitalism, which are local, context-specific and never hegemonic. In each city and context the movement emerges with its own characteristics.

Moreover, we find that these issues have a broader reach than the squatters' movement as a whole. Throughout Europe and North America they have been present in sociopolitical debates across local, regional and national contexts, and independently from the existence of a squatters' movement, society at large often acknowledges the importance of environmental, minorities and criminalisation problems. We argue that although they give marginal and very localised examples, the cases in these chapters deal with cutting-edge issues which show how the squatters' movement takes the ambivalent position of engaging in illegal experiences which have been introducing and promoting progressive sociopolitical practices which have often anticipated new legislation.

The book follows a structure where city case studies are presented in thematic chapters, so that particular characteristics of the squatters' movement of a city can appear across several chapters. Table 0.1 shows for each city that has been included in this work, the chapters that offer a particular analysis.[1]

Let us summarise each specific chapter.

Miguel A. Martinez and **Claudio Cattaneo** set out in Chapter 1 the context in which squatting practices take place today, in the midst of the deepest capitalist crisis in nearly a century. This context is important not only because housing is a reason for squatting, but also because this is a serious crisis of capitalism and alternatives are required. In this respect, the practice of squatting is well placed to provide an answer to such a stringent issue. The main argument of the chapter is that squatting represents an opposition not just to private property but to many facets of capitalism. It is more appropriate to say that squatting is a practical critique of urban speculation, but this would be to leave aside the fact that there are many other forms of economic speculation that are equally contested. Squatting is a multidimensional way of living that pursues the collective satisfaction of human needs through autonomous, participative and horizontal means of direct democracy. Otherwise, neoliberal policies,

Table 0.1 Structure of the book according to cities analysed

Part	Context	I Case studies				II Specific issues		
Chapter/City	1	2	3	4	5	6 Ecosystems	7 Minorities	8 Legalisation
Geneva		X						
Berlin		X					X	X
London	UK		X					
Brighton			X					
Amsterdam				X				X
New York	USA			X		X		
Rome					X			
Paris					X			
Barcelona	Spain					X	X	
Madrid							X	X

the rule of capitalist market, the housing bubbles and the exhausting oil transactions will reproduce existing social inequalities.

In Chapter 2 **Luca Pattaroni** presents the case of Geneva, a city with a powerful squatter movement which in the 1990s managed to get to the core of city politics. Not just campaigning for the right to housing, the Geneva squatters' movement represented a colourful diversity of attitudes, behaviours and lifestyles which flourished in opposition to the grey of the capitalist city. Pattaroni makes the case that since the idealistic surge of May 1968, a new-left political vision centred around self-management, solidarity, conviviality and creativity has emerged. People started to squat in order to live differently, not just to satisfy a 'need'. The chapter is a narration of an intimate journey into the stages that shape a squat's cycle: occupation, installation, habitation, eviction and perpetuation. It shows how the criticism of capitalism is applied in practice in the lifecycle of a squat. Also, it shows the power of the movement which stretched through the 1980s, growing a wide political consensus against housing speculation which favoured its existence and got sympathisers to adopt the squatters' festive conceptions of political struggle. In an intriguing manner, Pattaroni shows how squats are not only places of contestation, but also drivers of a rich and alternative life which eventually succumbed to the revenge of the market, the conception of the city as a commodity and zero-tolerance policies. The resurrection elsewhere proves how the phenomenon is mainly that of a network movement. **Lucrezia Lennert's** comments (in Box 2.1) reinforce the sense that house projects, which are quite common in Berlin, promote alternative lifestyles and help people manage personal lives largely apart from the dominant capitalist ways of living.

In Chapter 3 **E. T. C. Dee** provides an account of the Brighton and London history of the squatters' movement, both how it originated and how it appears today, decades later. The issue of criminalisation pending upon illegal occupations in residential premises is a central one in that story. Although not much has been written about it, the criminalisation of squatting in England and Wales since 2012 is a crucial landmark which might seriously challenge the future existence of the movement in these countries. The author argues how important squatting was for housing during the 1970s and 1980s, an importance which is also related to the political activity undertaken by activist groups who reinforced the right to housing through their squatting actions. The amount of empty properties, a number always much larger than the number of homeless families, fostered a shared understanding of the existence of a housing crisis that resulted in a certain societal approval of squatting.

The concept of 'political squatting' is closely related to the refusal to accept urban speculation in real estate – whether it leads to housing shortages, the construction of commercial superstores or the contested use of public urban space – but is also analysed in relation to the declarations that politicians and activists offer about the issue. These explain the shift in public opinion and perception of a once well-accepted phenomenon, although as the author notes, the combination of empty buildings and economic crisis will mean that squatting persists, despite its criminalisation. Box 3.1 by the **Needle Collective** explains how the squatting phenomenon has been evolving one year after criminalisation.

In Chapter 4 **Hans Pruijt** elaborates on the history of the squatters' movement in Amsterdam and New York City (NYC). In particular, he focuses on how it became large-scale, and how it had the power and the organisation to manage the adaptation of top-down public plans in Amsterdam – including the Olympic Games – while it did not succeed so much in NYC. Pruijt observes that the case of NYC verifies a prevailing notion of squatting as merely a means to be housed, instead of also being considered an end itself. This prevented the maintenance of the movement over long periods of time as part of a larger plan of political activism at the city scale, as occurred in Amsterdam, where more combinations of squatting types have occurred. On the contrary, NYC squatters mainly focused on squatting as a deprivation-based and alternative housing strategy. A few comments made by **Alan Smart** (in Box 4.1) introduce the contribution of the Provos as pioneers of the Dutch squatting movement. In addition, **Frank Morales** (Box 4.2) tells a brief personal story of the Lower East Side squatters' movement, which sheds new light on how a repressive institutional context made the survival of the movement extremely hard, a situation that did not occur in the Amsterdam context.

In Chapter 5 **Pierpaolo Mudu** explores the context of squatting for housing in Rome, as a political claim to the right to housing. The stronger the crisis of capitalism, the bigger the rescaling of the squatting phenomenon. Here we observe the capacity of its reach and its heterogeneity. The first part of the chapter begins with elements of a cultural critique present in the lifestyle of people who choose to live differently, under communitarian principles, and who find in squatting an open window to make the jump towards an alternative life. It ends by presenting an almost forced choice for people in need of decent housing who find a practical solution in the occupation of houses, given the cul de sac down which the present neoliberal capitalism is driving them. This does not occur only in Rome. Paris is an example of a large wave of political squatting for housing, as *Thomas Aguilera* reports (Box 5.1), with organisations that are active in providing shelter for those in most need. A similar typology of squatting is spreading widely in Spain too, as an extension over the last two years of the direct actions and campaigns launched by the Platform of the People Affected by Mortgages (PAH).

At the start of Part II, in Chapter 6 **Salvatore Engel-Di Mauro** and **Claudio Cattaneo** see the city from the environmental perspective. Cities being both socially and environmentally unsustainable, the authors analyse local alternatives from Barcelona and NYC that, within the squatters' movement and in response to capitalist devastation, develop their ecological conversion through setting up urban gardens, bicycle workshops or rural-urban (rurban) communes. They claim that these examples form part of a more general process among the squatters' movement which has begun to recognise how anti-capitalist autonomy must be founded not only on issues of social justice, but also on the supply and production of sustainable resources, and access to the means of primary production. However, far from arguing a simple case for greening the city through more urban gardens and pro-bicycle policies, squatters criticise the (green) neoliberal city. In rurban communes a whole lifestyle is built around the principles of mutualism, ecologism and social justice.

In Chapter 7 **Azozomox** engages in a comparison between Berlin, Madrid and Barcelona, aiming at studying the issue of social diversity within the squatters' movement. In particular, the author deals with gender relationships. LBGTQ identities, the critical perspective of non-white and migrant women, everyday sexism and the division of labour in the reproduction of life are all controversial issues within the squats discussed. Although the relationship between capitalism and social domination in the field of gender relationships would deserve a larger discussion, the chapter provides evidence of the narrow connection – and sometimes clashes – between anti-capitalist and gender-emancipatory struggles. A strong self-criticism has arisen from inside the squatters' movement about the real contradictions and limits that political squatting has in terms of gender relations. Thus, Azozomox explains why some squats preferred to devote their political initiatives to those specific issues.

In Chapter 8 **Miguel A. Martinez**, **Azozomox** and **Javier Gil** propose a way of understanding the legal issues of squatting by reflecting on strategies of resistance, the challenge of criminalisation and the controversies around the options of squats converted into a legal status. The authors deal with the different legal regulations in some European countries, and the evolution of the legal and political treatments of squatting over the years and according to the state authorities concerned. They focus on the cities of Madrid and Berlin in order to understand how squatters face the overall criminalisation of squatting and particular threats of eviction.

Other European cases are also considered for comparative purposes, and in Box 8.2 Deanna Dadusc presents the case from Amsterdam, which has been affected by the new Dutch legislation that seeks to criminalise the movement. As the authors argue, squatters' resistance to the law may take place inside or outside legal institutions, so that the legalisation of some squats should not be regarded as the major outcome of the legal dilemmas faced by squatters. Various other strategies, benefits, side-effects and contextual explanations also need to be included in the analysis, as is shown by the examples mentioned in the chapter. Claudio Cattaneo (in Box 8.1) offers an explanation of squatters' illegal behaviour grounded on the pursuit of their moral principles independently from respect of the law and combined with the movement's capacity to resist oppression.

In the final chapter of this book we use the cases and arguments of the previous chapters in order to offer some answers to the original questions that motivated us. We also recall the ideas and remarks given by other SqEK members in the last debates we held in Paris (March, 2013).

Summing up, we claim that squatting does not represent a complete alternative to capitalism. Mainly, squatting provides a strong local alternative, with various branches of critical discourse, small-scale behaviours and autonomous practices directly connected with other anti-capitalist and emancipatory social movements. In addition, there are many hindrances and internal contradictions which squatters' movements need to face if they want to scale up to a level at which they become powerful enough to challenge the hegemony of capitalism.

Box 0.1 *Some Notes about SqEK's Activist-Research Perspective*

Miguel A. Martínez

We could define SqEK as an information and social network of activist-researchers. This should be distinguished from a formal organisation; it is neither an institutionalised research group nor a research institute. Instead of formal externally imposed regulation, SqEK members reach consensus decisions which are valid until the next face-to-face meeting. Decisions are usually based on previous debates which have arisen through the email list or during one of the regular encounters. Just as with squatting itself, no university, state agency, non-governmental organisation (NGO) or private company was behind the origin and development of SqEK, although members may use the resources of the institutions to which they belong in the course of participating in this activist-research network.

Membership in the network is also quite open and flexible. The first call to meet in Madrid in 2009 was addressed to researchers all over Europe who had published books or academic articles about squatting (the members are mainly from Western Europe), but it was an open call that also appealed to students researching into this or related topics. Later meetings were even more public, with the aim of inviting activists and people interested in squatting and other researchers, like those from North America. New scholars, students, squatters and activists attended the presentations and discussions, although only a few remained involved in SqEK. Those who did joined the email list, or later wrote a short letter of introduction and motivation, and asked to join. Most of those who approached SqEK via the internet participated in the regular exchange of messages and in the upcoming meetings. Beyond the internal mailing list, there is also a website: sqek.squat.net

While the name chosen refers to the existence of a 'collective', this is a specific and variable outcome of the activities that all the members perform through the network. Every time we meet, gather in order to write a book (like we have done for this one in our last two meetings) or a special issue of a journal, or form a group in order to research a particular topic, we produce collectives. All are part of SqEK. The unitary name might be misleading. The way of working is as a 'collective of collectives', that is, as an active network producing research activities with a collective dimension. The general collective entity, then, has looser boundaries than the subgroups. However, these would not be possible without the general umbrella, and the flows of information which are constantly underway within the network.

At the end of the second meeting SqEK held in Milan in 2009, a manifesto and research agenda was written collectively, and published soon after in *ACME* (an e-journal of critical geography) and the ISA-RC-21 (International Sociological Association-Research Committee) newsletter. This text emphasised that

> Critical engagement, transdisciplinarity and comparative approaches are the bases of our project .... Self-funded research in different countries, internal meetings of the research group and public events are, at the present, our main activities. Diverse methods of research and theoretical frames are also remarkable aspects of our methodology.

At first glance, this declaration does not suggest any exclusive method or theory within SqEK. Nonetheless, there are some approaches that are strongly endorsed within this network (and which could be described as the SqEK research agenda).

SqEK encourages methodological approaches in which the researcher is critically engaged in squatting. This is an open and not uncontroversial issue, but at least explicitly, invites self-reflection on the researcher's involvement with the practices and struggles carried on by squatters. There are different ways to express that engagement, from researchers who live as squatters themselves, to their availability to offer advice and information to squatters who request it. To make this commitment clear, we decided to hold public talks and debates with squatters in each of the cities where SqEK met. The same heterogeneity we observe within the squatters' scenes is also present within SqEK. There is no canonical model of the kind of activist-researcher that SqEK promotes, but the common ground is to consider this relationship crucial, and one which should be debated explicitly. We take it for granted that most who are affiliated with SqEK are sympathetic with squatting, or even joined this network due to their previous experiences as squatters. However this does not exclude critical perspectives regarding, for instance, squatters' contradictions, failures and unintended effects.

> SqEK will seek to critically analyse the squatters' movement in its relevant contexts (historical, cultural, spatial, political, and economic), trying to involve the activists in the research practices, and sharing the knowledge thus produced with them and society. ... Furthermore, in view of the diverse composition of our network we seek to challenge the traditional dichotomy between researchers and their subjects/ objects of knowledge. Whenever possible, we would like to involve squatters and activists in our research practices, thus favouring a collaborative and dialogical approach to knowledge production in the belief that social movement activists, just as any other social actor, are themselves producers of knowledge
>
> (SqEK research agenda)

Therefore, SqEK is a means for researching *about* squatting, for making collaborative research *with* squatters, and advancing public understanding *of* squatting. Cooperation, horizontality and direct democracy within SqEK are procedures of self-organising that stem from our past [or that of many members'] experiences in squatting groups. When possible, SqEK members have supported squats under threat of eviction, or disseminated information about different cases of squatting, autonomous social centres and other urban struggles. Activists' networks and squats have been important for hosting attendees to SqEK meetings, without restricting this mutual aid to the squatting scene.

In comparison with most conventional academic conferences, time limits for debates were more flexible in the SqEK meetings. It was familiarly assumed that the group would try to reach consensus concerning the organisational affairs of the network. Intellectual controversies were always welcome if they were able to shed light on the topics under examination. The depth of the discussions also varied according to the type of participants in each given situation. SqEK also learned from the activist style of do-it-yourself, launching research projects funded at a very low scale. Not least, it has been a relief for activist-researchers to discover that hundreds of European squatters are also 'shadow researchers'. Activists may not be entirely aware of their contributions to the public knowledge of squatting, but many are highly educated and involved in the kinds of debates, publications, talks, video making and campaigns which inform a research process. SqEK members feel themselves very tied to those kinds of self-research processes, although they also remain connected with academic debates, bibliographic references and theoretical discussions which may also interest activists. In addition, several proposals of publication in a nonacademic language, accessible to a wider audience, emerged within the SqEK meetings in order to popularise this collaborative production of knowledge about squatting.

Indeed, activist or militant research suggests that the boundaries between activists and researchers are blurred. This also means conflicts. Activists may consider some information secret, or sensitive for political reasons. Some activists do not want to help individuals in their academic careers. Some researchers only see activism as an academic subject from a distant point of view, and are heedless of activists' concerns. There is great diversity among activists, researchers and activists-researchers, so stereotypes tend to play a harmful role. In general, whether activist or researcher, nobody likes to be treated as an abstract, simplified and static research object. Thus, the main challenge for all the people involved in a project of activist research is to agree on the terms of the interactions, the means and goals of the cooperation, and the specific combination of subjective and objective analysis. Whatever form of work is adopted, there is also an unavoidable political debate about public access to the knowledge produced, and about the intended and unintended effects of spreading the knowledge. Accordingly SqEK decided to promote, as much as possible, copy-left licences and practices (that is, following the open source /creative commons culture which opposes intellectual property rights) in our publications. Still, some arrangements and concessions need to be made when dealing with corporate journals, since these are the institutional requirements imposed on an individual engaged in an academic career. To ignore this would be detrimental to the stability of the institutional researcher.

Further, while transdisciplinarity has conventionally been claimed for the social sciences since the 1970s, it is not so often brought into practice. Since the beginning of SqEK there has been a common concern about how sociologists, political scientists, geographers, anthropologists, historians, economists and others with many different intellectual backgrounds can work together. The initial measures adopted consisted of a collective listing of research questions according to each member's ways of thinking. These questions were grouped into five general dimensions:

- long and medium-term structural factors that make squatting possible
- analysis of 'conflicts' and 'dynamics'
- networks of social centres/squats, their politics and culture
- empirical case studies
- squatting in comparative perspective.

Then two subgroups of SqEK members were formed in order to work on two research topics according to that general research agenda. These groups produced articles by combining the different disciplinary contributions of their members. Transdisciplinarity was also manifested in the critiques during the SqEK meetings, when research developed from a particular social science was subject to comments and criticisms coming from different social sciences. Therefore, these transdisciplinary debates had a relevant influence in the individual writings in spite of the authors apparently belonging to a single scientific domain.

Finally, the comparative approach has been strongly supported by all researchers involved since the network was first launched as a means of connecting people from different European cities and countries. Some of them had also sought to compare squatting in two or more cities. All of us sought to obtain and share a deeper knowledge of all European countries as a way of assessing the transnational urban movement. Systematic comparisons point a way to overcome both local and descriptive stories about squatting. Comparisons are therefore conceived as a means to discover cross-national patterns and similar phenomena in different urban settings. In addition, the comparative perspective obliged SqEK members to collect empirical data in each place according to the variables agreed upon by all the researchers involved. While these intentions framed the whole activity of the SqEK in the long run, some of the publications were only able to collect articles with a national or local scope, leaving readers with the task of attempting the comparison on their own.

Box 0.2 *SqEK Processes as an Alternative to Capitalism*

Claudio Cattaneo, Baptiste Colin and Elisabeth Lorenzi

The SqEK meetings have provided the opportunity for face-to-face interaction between researchers, most of them coming from established academic centres, but also many independent and freelance activist-researchers. This mix of participants already occurs in academic conferences but in the case of SqEK conferences, the main difference and novelty refers to the venues where they are held: not only university institutions, but autonomous social centres both legal and squatted.

The open and closed modalities of the different SqEK meetings imply that the group works as a research group – when doors are closed – and as a provider of a service from a social centre – when the doors are open. With reference to the first, we note that SqEK meetings use horizontal organising processes developed by contemporary social movements. This is also a heritage of some claims formulated during the 1968 students' movements, and is still present in some workshops organised in academic institutions. This is the way a collaborative methodology is shaped. With reference to the second, an open door implies that, to the eyes of the external person, the event is not offered by an academic institution or by its research groups, but by a network within the squatters' movement, and in particular, one dedicated to scholarly research. In this way SqEK first appears to the public as part of a social movement, and only then it can be said that it contributes to the production of scientific knowledge. From a methodological perspective, it implies a step beyond 'participant observation', into 'participant observing', so that the main position shifts from that of observation to that of participation; from participatory research to activist research. As more than an external observer – albeit many members are engaged in participation – SqEK stands as a participant in the production of scholarly knowledge, as another activist within the movement. The research carried out in this book is original insomuch as it is participative, activist and collective.

In parallel with the meetings – which can be seen as catalysts of initiatives and collaborating projects – the SqEK email list offers a platform out of which proposals and agreements of the meetings are developed and more projects are proposed, such as the offer to publish this book, a process that is detailed in the Appendix, or to compete for EU or national grants.

Some unresolved contradictions still remain on the table, not only inside SqEK but also as a matter related to any activist research process. How do we combine academic meritocracy – which often seeks principal and leading authors – with the social and collective production of knowledge? In the Appendix we also explain how this contradiction forms part of a learning process, with its obvious limitations. And with reference to the relationship between squatted social centres and knowledge production, what do squatted and collective places have to offer for scholarship? What can be scientifically produced that stems out of their premises and processes? And what is there that academic and formal research centres cannot offer? How do we avoid the exclusive dichotomy of activist versus academic production of knowledge? We see that there are grounds for combined activities and processes between the academic/scholar sphere and the activist/social centre sphere, and SqEK contributes by promoting horizontality in decision making, by acknowledging the impossibility of truly independent and objective research, by adopting nonindividualistic values and engaging in self-organised social and research processes. We see that as SqEK and through our meetings we are contributing to enhance this collaboration and to generate novel forms of scholar production.

Academic centres are increasingly becoming branches of the capitalist system through partnerships with the private corporate sector and similar processes of privatisation. But both the horizontal and consensus-based method that SqEK follows in the production of knowledge, and the practice of self-organising conferences within squatted social centres, are already enhancing an essential alternative to capitalism, and constitute a challenge to its hierarchical organisation.

Note

1   Given the high interconnectedness between the case studies and specific issues of the movement, each chapter relates to several other ones. As editors of the book we have inserted text in square brackets [like this] which explains the connection, continuity or divergence between arguments across chapters.

References

De Angelis, M. (2007) *The Beginning of History.* London: Pluto Press.
Fainstein, S. (2010) *The Just City.* Ithaca, N.Y.: Cornell University Press.
Hakim, B. (1991) *Temporary Autonomous Zone.* New York: Autonomedia.
Harvey, D. (1973) *Social Justice and the City.* Baltimore, Md.: Johns Hopkins University Press.
Harvey, D. (2005) *A Brief History of Neoliberalism.* Oxford: Oxford University Press.
Kington, T. (2011) 'Italy's fascists stay true to Mussolini's ideology.' *Guardian,* 6 November 2011. www.guardian.co.uk/world/2011/nov/06/italy-fascists-true-mussolini-ideology
Lefebvre, H. (1968) *Le droit à la ville* [*The Right to the City*]. Paris: Anthropos.
Martínez, M. A. (2012) 'The squatters' movement in Europe: a durable struggle for social autonomy in urban politics.' *Antipode* 45(4), 866–87.
Mudu, P. (2012) 'At the intersection of anarchists and autonomists: autogestioni and centri sociali.' *ACME* 1(3), 413–38.
Neuwirth, R. (2004) *Shadow Cities: A Billion Squatters, A New Urban World.* London: Routledge.
Notes from Nowhere (2003) *We Are Everywhere: The Irresistible Rise of Global Anticapitalism.* London: Verso.

Polanyi, K. (1944) *The Great Transformation: The Political and Economic Origins of Our Time*. Boston, Mass.: Beacon Press.

Pruijt, H. (2012) 'The logic of urban squatting.' *International Journal of Urban and Regional Research*, doi: 10.1111/j.1468-2427.2012.01116.x

Shepard, B. and Smithsimon, G. (2011) *The Beach Beneath the Streets. Contesting New York City's Public Spaces*. Albany, N.Y.: State University of New York Press.

1

Squatting as a Response to Social Needs, the Housing Question and the Crisis of Capitalism

Miguel A. Martínez and Claudio Cattaneo

Introduction

Is squatting a feasible alternative to housing problems in the capitalist system? Is squatting only a marginal activity undertaken by people in need who are motivated against the rule of capitalism? Is squatting no more than a temporary reaction to the unsolved 'housing question' in the current crisis caused by the malfunctioning of capitalist mechanisms?

These questions deserve a careful analysis. The capitalist system has experienced crucial shifts all over the world. Neoliberal policies and increasing global flows have been pervasive since the 1970s. The global elites and corporations have enjoyed new privileged and flexible ways to accumulate capital. In the meantime, the poor, the underpaid, occasional workers, undocumented migrants and the working classes have suffered new forms of dispossession. These have included cuts in public services and subsidies, looser regulation of working conditions, rising costs of living in urban settings, and police surveillance and repression in order to keep the wealthiest segregated from the deprived. Housing needs and other kinds of urban dwellers' social needs fall under that general umbrella. Therefore, the practice of squatting empty properties should not be dissociated from such an overall context.

In particular, we are now interested in understanding how different expressions of squatting are closely interconnected as a result of the constraints of the capitalist context in which they occur, although sometimes individual squatters or groups of squatters do not form an organised movement. The squatters' class position, the political ties between squatters and the urban value of the occupied buildings may be highlighted as three substantial aspects in order to distinguish the relationship between capitalism and types of squatting. We argue that 'social' and 'political' squatting is an extremely simple way of classification which obscures how social needs in general, and housing needs specifically, are determined by contentious interactions between those who rule the principal capitalist mechanisms of accumulation and those who are excluded from them. Any form of squatting, thus, is both 'social' and 'political'. What makes the difference, in our view, is why squatting is undertaken, what its different goals are, and how can they be understood in relation to prevailing capitalist ways of managing and allocating urban goods. In particular, in this chapter we analyse how the different types of squats, squatters and owners, on the one hand, and the ways that squatters take in order to satisfy their own and other social groups' needs, on the other hand, can contribute to understanding the most relevant reasons behind squatting.

Given the housing shortage, the lack of affordable and decent housing compared with available income, the stock of vacant buildings and the practices of real estate speculation, it is evident that squatting is a direct response to the failures of both capitalism and the welfare state. The key question is whether squatting is a sufficient and efficient response. If we consider the imaginary situation in which all the empty buildings are occupied, then the question would be: are there still housing and social needs to be satisfied? If so, squatting would not be the answer since all the built places would already be in use. The whole set would be divided into those occupied in conventional ways (by state or private owners, private tenants, housing cooperatives and so on) and those occupied in unconventional ones such as squatting (that is, the occupation of a property without the owner's permission). However, the size of the unconventional sector might be so limited that squatters and the homeless do not represent a threat to the whole real-estate system. Furthermore, in spite of the fact that the homeless and squatters may be self-housed, unacceptable social inequalities may remain within the conventional housing system, so these are not necessarily challenged by the persistence of squatting. The mere fact of occupying empty properties does not entail a change in the rules of the game, but only represents a partial transgression of some of them.

Squatters may solve their own housing dilemmas by exploring alternative or illegal practices, and they can also spread their example to others with similar concerns. Notwithstanding that, the core of the real estate market, whether under the rule of private agents or state managers, might not be touched by those who promote alternative ways of solving housing needs for a minority of the population. Squatting, lastly, could not be a useful alternative for the broader society unless all the housing stock was empty or all tenants stopped paying rent (assuming tenancy is the dominant mode of access to a home).

A different approach to our initial questions needs to take into account the specific historical periods and political-spatial opportunities. We observe that the numbers of squatters keep a narrow relationship with the most critical moments of the economic cycles in terms of unemployment rates, housing prices, privatisation, gentrification, urban renovation and industrial restructuring. There are also significant variations from one city and country to another. Squatters develop their own skills to explore these opportunities and to perform tactical means of action. Obviously, many of them are also encouraged by strategic views and anti-capitalist prospects coming from previous and contemporary social movements. Every local squatters' movement, then, covers a particular section of urban conflicts according to both the political coalitions in which it is embedded and the expressions of the capitalist crisis in everyday life.

Tradition states that where there is a need, there is a right. Each of these words – 'need' and 'right' – holds very controversial meanings, and to disentangle them would bring us too far from our present goals. In a rough manner we can conceive that housing needs are not restricted to having a roof over your head and having the money to pay for the acquisition of that roof, and for rent, maintenance, taxes and/or the regular costs of external supplies. A good life at home is connected with a good life in a social, urban and natural environment. It involves the spatial location of the house but also the available social resources at hand, beyond the domestic space. If squatting constitutes an essential claim to satisfy housing need as a right to housing, at the same time it is also a claim to satisfy social needs, which is linked to seeing housing need as a broad 'right to the city', in the Lefebvrian sense (Lefebvre, 1968).

Most squatters do not aspire to own the property they occupy. Neither do they define the practice of squatting as theft or usurpation, since they emphasise the right to use and occupy abandoned properties and keep them in a liveable condition. If anything, according to Proudhon, it is property which is based on a primal theft. Squatting, at its best, supposes a sort of symbolic and eventual expropriation of the property of owners who are perceived as illegitimate because of their excessive wealth compared with the dispossessed. It is not the right to private property that is reclaimed by most squatters, but the right to a more just and equal distribution of the resources that allow a decent life. Expropriation thus involves an exercise of turning private goods into common goods. Housing needs, therefore, are accomplished alongside social needs. Squatting becomes, in the end, a form of class struggle where the housing question is a crucial one, but not an exclusive one. In fact squatting is more than just living under a roof, because it is a collective process of self-organisation to get access to an affordable space, a cooperative way of repairing and preserving the building, an alternative way of living in the margins of the capitalist patterns, and a political experience of protesting and mobilising through direct action.

Squatters Strive for Housing Needs and Social Justice

Every human need involves subjective aspirations and a lack of material resources according to conventional or underlying social agreements about the basic conditions for enjoying a decent life (Leal and Cortés, 1995: 4–12). Homeless people need a home, above all. Home seekers in contrast are those who need a new or a better home, such as young people, residents in substandard houses, families that grow in size, divorced couples, those who demand space for working at home, as well as migrant newcomers (Bouillon, 2009; Leal, 2010). People who aspire to live in communes or in co-housing initiatives, for instance, may also contribute to the expression of housing needs in the form of a demand.

Homes are not exactly the primary need, but they represent a way to satisfy many basic human needs such as protection, shelter, identity, affection and subsistence (Max-Neef, 1994: 58–9). There are other means to satisfy basic human needs, but without the satisfaction of at least the need for physical health and personal autonomy, it is quite difficult to participate in social life and to pursue your own goals (Doyal and Gough, 1991; Gough, 2004). Adequate shelter may be conceived, then, as an 'intermediate need' or a 'cultural satisfier' that helps other needs to be fulfilled. [This becomes evident in Chapter 2, which analyses how squatters' counter-cultural critique to capitalism is made possible in the special relationships that are developed within communes, like the Berlin house projects, or in the way well-being is achieved by the freedom to refurbish a home according to the different and evolving needs of its members, or even by the services that the existence of a house can offer to activists.]

As has been frequently noted, these processes addressing the satisfaction of needs involve an exercise of social power (capabilities) because there are observable and implicit conflicts between individuals and groups trying to influence, shape and determine others' needs and desires (Lukes, 1974: 23). This opens the door to political action in the field of housing and social needs. Squatters exercise their *power*, their capabilities, in aiming at satisfying their own needs, and also support the struggles of those who are excluded from the dominant housing system. Solidarity with the homeless, the substandardly housed, the poor and young people who cannot afford a decent and well-serviced house, is also a political aim of all kinds of squatters, those who self-house themselves and those who run squatted social centres. This is another substantial reason for not separating housing and social needs, and pro-housing and pro-social-centres squatters.

The satisfaction of human needs depends on many factors. Squatters, for example, can only *represent* the interests of those excluded from the capitalist housing system (although they often deny the politics of representation and prefer the politics of autonomy, direct democracy and self-representation). However there are environmental limits to the size of the population to be housed and the materials and energy employed in the construction of houses (Riechmann, 1998: 310). Squatters can only operate within the already built stock, regardless of its inherent environmental sustainability. They leave aside the claim for housing all the excluded by demanding new constructions. In both cases, there are also social, political and normative principles to deal with. Who has a priority right to be housed? What are the criteria used in practice to produce an equal and just access to a squatted place? How do we overcome the barriers faced by particular social groups as a result of their gender, class, ethnicity or abilities (Nussbaum, 2003)?

These aspects have received some criticism from outside the squatters' movement since the very beginning (Lowe, 1986). Priemus (1983), for example, argued that only 'bona fide squatters' could contribute to adding empty dwellings to the housing stock by improving their premises. They also 'place the housing shortage on the political agenda, expose abuse of ownership and increase the pressure on the authorities to tackle speculation in real estate effectively, to gear the programming of house-building better to the demand and to improve housing distribution policy' (Priemus, 1983: 418). These squatters practise self-help, help others to find accommodation and use squatting as a means of protest against housing shortages, vacancy, speculation and housing policies. However, there are many squatters who occupy social housing at the expense of the groups who have priority of access according to the official regulations. For instance, squatters typically house young people, single persons and (in the case Priemus is discussing) Dutch nationals, a clientele that is different from the deprived social categories like families with children that are supposedly favoured by the state agencies (ibid.). Among the responses to this criticism, some argued that 'the largest part of the houses occupied were taken from private owners who preferred, for motives of profit, to speculate with empty dwellings, or to turn houses into offices' (Draaisma and Hoogstraten, 1983: 410). Also, 'squatters rarely prevented people in greater need from being housed because most squatted houses were not intended for immediate use' (Wates and Wolmar, 1980: 61).

There are many autonomous groups which deliberate, fix norms and take their own decisions about where to squat according to the location, the type of building and their knowledge about the owner. They also recruit members or back other potential squatters by relying on trust, political affinity, needs, opportunity, capacities, skills, information and so on (Adell and Martinez, 2004; Bailey, 1973; Corr, 1999; Sabaté, 2012; SQUASH, 2011; Thörn, Wasshede and Nilson, 2011). [The Netherlands, particularly Amsterdam, is a clear case where the articulation of the squatters' movement reached a high level of complexity and organisation, as Hans Pruijt presents in Chapter 4.] Therefore, the controversy about the squatters' awareness of the social, urban and environmental context leads to the internal diversity of the movement and the single initiatives that any group takes. The issue of social justice, then, needs to be debated according to each autonomous group of squatters, since there is no central organisation that can impose general normative criteria. Nonetheless, it cannot be skipped because it affects the core argument about the legitimation of squatting to satisfy housing and social needs.

Another source of the legitimation of squatting has to do with the type of owner and the features of the empty properties that are taken over. The final decision to occupy a specific building depends on a limited amount of information. Whether the owner is a large corporation, a small company or a private proprietor, the major issue at stake is the owner's class situation, which can be measured here in terms of their economic power and also according to the speculative operations they develop. The more distant the owner is from the squatters' class situation, income and ideological principles, the greater the legitimation of the conflict as a class struggle. However, this does not mean an immediate confrontation, because the owner's reaction after the occupation may follow different strategies. Sometimes, for example, the owner avoids a direct confronta-tion for a certain period of time while preparing documents for launching a judicial attack or while negotiating with interested buyers. If the legal owner belongs to the middle classes (or, in some exceptional cases, to the working class) and the property is crucial to their own economic survival in terms of simple class reproduction, the conflict with the squatters tends to be more direct, and is usually quickly channelled through the courts. The class dimension of the conflict thus plays a secondary role compared with the rest of the dimensions concerning the value given to the eventual speculative actions and the specific condition of the building.

The same applies to state-owned properties, with the addition of the squatters' assessment of the policies carried on by political authorities and state officials. The squatted building is considered as a public resource and the justification of its occupation must address the particular sector of public policy in which that building is managed. Less clear is the case of private associations, foundations, religious and political organisations and the like. The legitimacy of these groups may vary greatly in the squatters' eyes, so a combination of the previous arguments and new ones related to the particular organisation can be used to justify the occupation.

The last classification we can introduce here relates to vacant stock. Following Leal and Cortés (1995: 16–17), we can distinguish three general cases:

- Empty properties subjected to an active exercise ('with an actual project') of rehabilitation, sale, rent, change of use or prompt occupation. The main problem with these 'active' purposes is that the action can be delayed for a very long time and in the meanwhile the property remains vacant. Dutch legislation, before the full criminalisation of squatting in 2010, required owners' 'active plans' for the building to be demonstrated in order to facilitate the eviction of squatters.
- Empty properties which are completely abandoned, closed and kept out of the market or from the public sector. There are many reasons to explain these cases 'without any actual plan' for the property, ranging from an intention to obtain a legal change in the planning classification of the building and the speculative goal of waiting for a situation when a profit can be made, to the absence of any decision about the management of the property, and the existence of conflicts between different owners and/or managers.
- Vacant properties that are considered as a 'long-run family project', and could belong to individuals of any social class. In this case, the acquisition of the house or building was made in order to transfer it to a son or daughter in the future, to use it later when the owner is retired, or to keep it as an investment which will provide an income which would be needed should the owner confront unemployment, a low level of pension or a financial crisis. These owners do not sell or rent these properties because they do not need the possible revenue urgently, or

because they expect a change in their personal situation which will oblige them to transform this asset into money or into their primary home.

Given all the above elements at play, we argue that squatting is more than just a simple challenge to private property.

Sometimes squatting consists simply of unconventional forms of getting accommodation, but more frequently squatting challenges capitalism as a whole: the uneven distribution of private property, the labour exploitation, the commodification of housing and urban life, the functional tendency of state powers to favour the elites' and capitalists' accumulation, and so on. The legal preservation, inheritance and reproduction of private property is only one of the foundations of capitalism and social injustice, but capitalism works thanks to many other mechanisms and social relations which change from time to time. Speculation in the housing market, for example, may develop through expensive, scarce and expanded forms of tenancy instead of access to home ownership. Socio-spatial displacement of the poor may also contribute to opening new business opportunities for the elites in the city centre. In spite of the limited impacts of the squatters in altering these capitalist mechanisms and the urban growth machine, the squatters' movements are able to shift them to the foreground and make them visible.

Housing Deprivation at the Core of the Financial Crisis

The phrase 'the housing question' recalls Engels' seminal contributions in 1872 and 1887 to the analysis of urban problems from the point of view of working-class interests (the 'social question') and by imagining a post-revolutionary society. Engels (1975[1872]: 587) disputed Proudhon's embracement of the right to home ownership in a more egalitarian society. On the contrary, Engels advocated state control over the whole built stock and a just distribution according to everyone's needs. The practice of squatting is situated in an intermediate territory. Although most squatters reject private property as it is now because it is considered an obstacle to the satisfaction of the housing needs of large numbers of people, they consider that once a building is occupied, only some people have the right to use and manage the space. This does not usually mean that squatters claim the right to a legal title as private owners (although this sometimes happens), but only that they claim the right to take care of the building and of the life inside according to their own collectively agreed rules

(Martínez, 2002: 189–92). This can be called a right to *partially private possession*, rather than to private property. The interesting lesson about these analyses is that they urge us to focus on the major shifts within the history of capitalism and the role played by the housing question. This endeavour exceeds our present purposes, although a few illustrations may help us to understand how squatting emerges as a reaction against this overall context, and is fuelled by more than the exclusion of access to a home.

More than just focusing on the issue of private property, the squatting of empty buildings provides a public critique of capitalist speculation. Profit rates have been falling since the 1970s, and the capitalist reconversion from industrial production to financial markets has been the way to keep profits alive. In particular, financial markets have been oriented increasingly towards the housing sector. Urban speculation is thus only one of the expressions of broad speculative operations within capitalism. These consist of credits, debts, mortgages, pension funds, patents and all sorts of financial deals with legal titles and money, which fuel the capacity for accumulation of capital regardless of the commodities, services, work, natural resources and background information (López and Rodríguez, 2010: 76–81).

After the expansive period of capital accumulation through the central role played by the heavy Fordist industries (1945–73), during the following years of crisis a combination of different means were used to recover the rates of profit for the global elites. Neoliberal policies, for example, involved the retrenchment of the state in most areas from national industries and the delivering of services and subsidies to all who needed them (Harvey, 2007). Monetary policies were dissociated from the amount of gold actually held, and direct foreign investments were allowed to move worldwide almost without national controls. The privatisation of common goods, lands, natural resources (minerals, oil, water, fisheries and so on), public services (health, education, transport, planning and so on), software and knowledge, created new forms of scarcity and appealing markets for investors. The new technologies of communication, computing and transport were able to provide tools for the quick movement of capital and goods, although the flows of people remained strongly restricted. Fordist and post-Fordist industries as well as the increasingly more industrialised and mechanised food production were displaced to new emerging regions of the world such as Asia and Latin America, while the wide sector of services occupied much of the workforce of the richest countries. Financial institutions like the banks, the International Monetary Fund (IMF), the World Bank and hedge funds were able to dictate the policies of indebted countries, but also to control our present and future lives through student loans, housing mortgages, consumption credits, retirement funds and so on (Harvey, 2007). These forms of financial speculation are not completely new since they are based on old forms of tributes, enjoying rents and the primitive destruction of commons, but their novelty is in the accelerated rhythm of expansion and colonisation of all the spheres of life, including in particular, in recent times, the sphere of housing. This highly developed and sophisticated means of capital accumulation through financial instruments has provoked severe economic crises such the one in 1998 and the latest one which started in 2008.

Empty apartments and office buildings, abandoned factories or schools, destruction of public parks and arable lands, commodification of music and theatre spectacles, or renovation of old urban areas, are some of the material aspects resulting from the pressure of speculative forces in tight connection with the political institutions that favour them. Real-estate speculation, then, is part of a wider engine of a mobile capitalist speculation which can jump from the promotion of urban mega-events to the hoarding of cereal crops, and can intervene in the international exchanges of national currencies and debts.

No squatters' movement was strong enough to stop these ongoing financial processes, but the occupation of some empty spaces at least made them visible. In spite of the material and economic benefits which squatters can hold by keeping themselves apart from the pervasive flows of economic speculation in most dimensions of our personal and social life, their struggle is mostly symbolic and political, calling for others to join the cause against urban speculation. The real estate sector also suffers internal contradictions: while some agents want to accelerate the cycle of construction, others tend to decrease the pace at which they put their assets in the market (López and Rodríguez, 2010: 118). State policies may oscillate between favouring some real-estate developers in the housing sector, for example by building roads and other infrastructure, and freezing state support for private urban projects. These contradictions and variations open different opportunities for squatting from time to time, and from place to place. Urban speculation is quite variable, and may be affected by interest rates, the wages paid to employees, the duration and costs of education, and not least by strikes, fair-trade movements and campaigns to preserve social commons. Squatters therefore take advantage of the available cracks which those contradictory economic flows are producing.

Obviously, this implies that their struggle goes beyond opposition to the concentration of private property in a few hands. Rather, squatters question how private property is managed by either financial speculators or the state authorities. Squatters also try to stop the artificial circulation of money by placing themselves as (temporary) obstacles to the tactic of making profit through the built environment. Finally, squatters open opportunities and offer practical examples to those who wish to extract themselves, at least partially, from growth and the speculative urban machine. There is no mechanical adaptation to the economic crisis because the squatters' movement follows its own social and political logics of self-reproduction, which have to do with their achievements, organisation, media representation and their interactions with state authorities. However, the empty holes left behind by urban speculation are a crucial source and motivation for squatting practices in particular places. The squatters' movements did not start to develop in Europe and the United States in the 1970s by chance: this was the time when the previous wave of capitalist expansion was reaching an end.

Urban Speculation and Financial Crisis: Lessons from Spain

The Spanish case is quite significant for understanding these processes. In the last four decades there have been phases of economic expansion and recession. The major economic indicators such as gross national product (GNP) changed sharply. The first economic crisis began during the period of transition from dictatorship to liberal democracy, from 1975 onwards. This heyday for social movements – involving citizens and workers above all – was not able to transform the power of the elites, the crisis persisted, and a profound industrial restructuring gave rise to a high percentage of unemployment (Castells, 1983; Pérez and Sánchez, 2008). After the decline of those movements, squatters who broadly followed the practices seen elsewhere in Europe appeared around 1984, although there were some individual cases from 1977 (Martínez, 2002). Spain was incorporated into the European Union in 1986. This inaugurated a new wave of urban speculation which lasted until 1992. In 1995, squatting became a criminal offence following a substantive change in the Penal Code. However, the squatters' movement was experiencing a strong expansion, wide media coverage and increasing public attention.

After a few critical years and alongside the emergence of many more protest movements, another phase of economic prosperity for the elites was initiated around 1996. Apart from the traditional tourist industry and the economic concentration of power in a few groups of large corporations which took advantage of the liberalisation of strategic sectors, the economic boom until 2008 was based on the construction of houses, major infrastructure and often unnecessary large public buildings (López and Rodríguez, 2010; Naredo, 2011). Intensive flows of incoming migrants and several reforms of employment regulations contributed to keeping salaries very low, and work temporary and precarious. Housing prices, however, rose continuously. Anti-globalisation movements and squatters (Martínez, 2007) remained very active and critical about these massive mobilisations of workforce, land and oil (and also about the state's involvement of Spain in the Iraq war) but their voices were not loud enough to warn society at large about the greatest urban process of speculation and political corruption ever. Among the tentative uprisings of those years, it is worth noting the Movement for Decent Housing, active between 2006 and 2009, in which some squatters also participated (Blanco, 2011).

Figure 1.1 shows how six indicators related to finance and housing shifted sharply from before the bubble (up to the 1990s) to the time of the bubble (until 2007):

1 The availability of houses for rent decreased dramatically, from 40 per cent of all housing in 1960 to 10 per cent in 2005.
2 The proportion of construction that was social housing (VPO in Spanish, which covers privately owned houses enjoying different state subsidies) reduced from 34 per cent in 1973 to 4 per cent in 2005.
3 While in 1997 credit granted to industry was 3.3 times higher than loans for real estate, in 2005 loans to the real estate market became higher than the those to industry.
4 Homeowners became increasing indebted, with the proportion of the house cost they owed growing from an average 45 per cent in 1990 to 60 per cent in 2004.
5 Housing prices increased relative to wages, so the average time someone needed to work to earn the equivalent of the price of a house grew from 14 months in 1980 to 14 years in 2005.
6 There was increasing speculation over the value of housing plots, with the proportion of the cost of the average house that was attributable to cost of the land growing from 25 per cent in 1985 to 55 per cent in 2005.

The bursting of the financial bubble brought about the highest ever historical rates of unemployment (up to 27 per cent at the middle of 2013) and foreclosures on people who could not pay their mortgages (with an average of almost 100,000 foreclosures per year between 2008 and 2012, although this figure includes both houses and commercial properties, according to the CGPJ, 2012). The bursting of the bubble, this time, was the worst

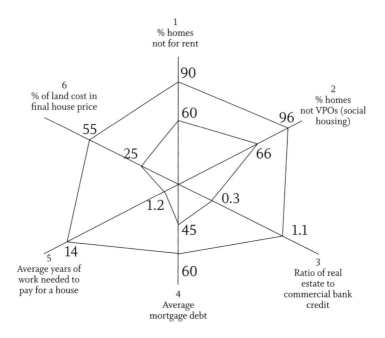

Figure 1.1 Evolution of major indicators about the 'housing bubble' in Spain, 1960–2007

Sources: Cattaneo (2008: 18) and VVAA (2007).

ever. On 15 May 2011 a popular autonomous movement occupied the squares of many cities. A few weeks later, local assemblies started to meet everywhere. A huge grassroots mobilisation aiming to stop the foreclosures followed next (PAH, an acronym for the Spanish for Platform of People Affected by Mortgages: Colau and Alemany, 2012, 2013). Squatters also took part in these movements, and new squats, unexpectedly, were launched by some of the activists who had recently been involved in these new types of autonomous politics (Martínez and García, 2013). In August 2011 the two principal political parties, the PP (conservatives and neoliberals) and PSOE (social democrats and liberals), agreed upon a change in the Constitution in order to concede supreme priority to the payment of state debt. All other public expenses needed to be reduced in order to meet the interest claimed by creditors. Cuts in salaries, subsidies, pensions and public services, the privatisation of state services and properties, the discovery of immense cases of corruption and fierce repression of social movements, became the regular agenda of the final years of this long neoliberal turn, which had been well prepared over the previous decades (López and Rodríguez, 2011). Concerning the housing question, some data may clarify the trends. First of all, the proportion of home ownership rose over the periods of both economic growth and decline. In 1950, 46 per cent of the housing stock was in the hands of private owner-occupiers and 54 per cent was occupied by tenants (although the proportion of tenants was 94 per cent in the city of Madrid and 95 per cent in Barcelona: Naredo, 2011: 30). By 1970 the proportions had been reversed, with 64 per cent of owner-occupiers and 32 per cent renting houses. This linear trend ended in 2001, when there was 82 per cent home-ownership and 11 per cent renting (Pareja, 2010: 112). The percentage of state-owned social housing for rent reduced from 3 per cent to 1 per cent between 1950 and 2001. These changes were not echoed in the rest of Europe, with the exception of some Eastern European countries such as Hungary (Naredo, 2011: 22).

Ownership meant stability, quality and also financial investment. In comparison with other European countries, the Spanish state barely offered state-owned housing or any other affordable alternatives. On the contrary, most of the housing policies during this period were aimed at removing obstacles to home ownership: direct aid to families who bought a house by subsidising the interest rates on mortgages, tax relief on mortgage interest payments, and subsidies on the purchase of standard houses for the middle and working classes with a very flexible control regime (Pareja, 2010: 119–20). There were almost no alternatives for those needing a home other than becoming a house owner. As a result, more and more social groups sought finance for house purchases. A whole society was obliged to take out mortgages from financial institutions if they did not want to become homeless.

Young people were among those who suffered the consequences of exclusion from the housing sector, because of their financial uncertainties, their high rates of precarious employment and unemployment, and the lack of public housing and other affordable alternatives to house ownership. This led to an extraordinary delay in the age at which they became independent from their parents. For example, in 1997 more than 80 per cent of the Spanish population aged between 18 and 29 years still lived with their parents, while in comparison, in Denmark the proportion was less than 30 per cent and in the Netherlands less than 40 per cent (Leal, 2010: 25). Of course, they were the first victims of the rising prices of housing, while the previous owners and the new investors made profits from their privileged situation. The first important housing bubble between 1986 and 1992 was mainly caused by incoming flows of foreign speculative capital (Naredo, 2011: 49). Tourism, international exhibitions and the Olympics, the so-called modernisation of the national infrastructure (high-speed trains, for instance) and explicit public policies and urban plans fuelling the construction of housing, paved the way for all kinds of speculative activity.

The almost 5 million migrants who came to live in Spain after 1996 also participated in this already well-established and very expensive housing market. For these and for other new home buyers, interest rates had fallen considerably compared with a decade earlier. In 1990 the average rate of interest on new mortgages was over 16 per cent. In 2006 it was around 4 per cent (Rodríguez, 2010: 59). However, this source of profit was not sufficient for the financial companies, and they tried to incorporate immigrants and young people into the dream of home ownership by extending the payback period for mortgages and using other tools to ensure that house prices continued to rise. The mortgage period reached an average of more than 28 years in 2007, but recent foreclosures have led to cases when people will be paying back their financial providers for up to 40 years. At the same time house prices never stopped increasing: at a yearly rate of 11 per cent, the accumulated rise in housing prices was 183.8 per cent between 1997 and 2007 (Rodríguez, 2010: 67). The major consequence was an extreme transfer of rents from individuals and families to the financial sector. While home owners spent on average less than 30 per cent of their income on housing up till 2000, in 2008 the average home owner was spending 51 per cent (Rodríguez, 2010: 71).

This huge amount of financial debt generated a lot of vulnerability, instability and hidden poverty for those following the mainstream way for accessing a house, which means the majority of the population. Local authorities and the central state fed this machine, and presented it as a new source of wealth and revenue for the government, and for local government in particular. However, there were natural and social limits to the never-ending construction boom ,which the authorities did not even attempt to foresee. The number of empty houses, for example, grew to an unbelievable high: more than 3 million were officially registered in 2001 (around 15 per cent of the total housing stock). This figure increased to 3.5 million in 2011, although this only represented 14 per cent of the increased stock of housing, according to the National Institute of Statistics (INE: www.ine.es). Once banks, developers and constructors could not sell all the newly built houses, the vicious circle of recession, unemployment and unpaid debts contaminated the whole economic life of the country. The credit crunch started primarily in the real estate sector, but immediately global financial corporations put pressure on the government to aid banks that had acquired debts to other international banks and financial agents. This game ended with the state underwriting the private load of debt, which drove the whole state financial system into a cul-de-sac. That the state could no longer afford to provide social services was the perfect scenario for the implementation of new neoliberal policies of privatisation.

Two salient aspects of this exemplary case of urban speculation are the overproduction of houses (and major infrastructure) and the discipline applied to the workforce. On the one hand, the 7 million housing units that were built in the decade from 1997 to 2007 did not respond at all to social needs. The demographic growth was much lower (with an absolute increase of 5.3 million inhabitants according to the INE). Wages and income did not grow substantially (they only increased from an average of €15,000 per year in 1997 to €18,700 per year in 2007: INE, see also a more detailed analysis in López and Rodríguez, 2010: 229–36). As López and Rodríguez (2011: 8) noted, 'after nearly 900,000 housing starts in 2006 – exceeding those of France, Germany and Italy put together – sales began to fall away. By the end of 2008 there were a million unsold homes on the market, while Spanish household indebtedness had risen to 84 per cent of GDP.' The highest rate in Europe of houses per inhabitant coexisted, para-doxically, with the worst rate of housing affordability. Simultaneously, the construction industry also created the highest European rates of empty, secondary-touristic and substandard houses (Naredo, 2011: 52). This had serious urban, environmental and political consequences. Urban sprawl, territorial polarisation (leaving abandoned immense rural areas) and the fast demolition of buildings which deserved rehabilitation, showed how urban planning was reduced to nothing more than a legal tool that backed new real estate developments. The local and regional banks, closely tied to the rich elites who started the first wave of vast urban development in the 1960s, contributed to the municipal corruption and reached unsustainable levels of risk after selling millions of subprime loans to indebted home owners (Naredo, 2011: 55–6).

On the other hand, it is worth recalling that home ownership was the solution to public order promoted by the dictatorship. The more people were indebted and attached to their property, the less they were prone to challenge the social order. The same disciplinary project continued over the democratic years, with the additional impulse of the destruction of social housing. The rising prices of houses in the period 1986–92 created an enormous social polarisation between those with access to a house and those excluded. The 1997–2007 boom turned that social cleavage into a new and overlapping one: indebted households versus financial investors.

Submission to debt was even a stronger discipline than that associated with the immobility created by house ownership. Moreover, the heyday of urban speculation came with many micro-instruments of 'housing and urban violence' (VVAA, 2007) such as forced displacements, frauds in financial or buying agreements, attacks against undesirable tenants and squatters who delayed the plans for prompt demolitions and reconstructions, the lack of public control on the rising rents, and the absence of public help to those who live in overcrowded households.

Once builders were not able to construct any more, and the banks were not able to get payment of the interest on their loans, and construction workers could not keep their jobs, and unemployment and debts were transmitted to other economic sectors, the collapse was unavoidable. First the social democratic government of Zapatero, then later the conservative one of Rajoy, decided that the middle and lower classes should pay the bill for the elites' losses. According to the European Commission (2012), between 2007 and 2011 the Spanish state aided the financial companies with a total of €90 billion, which represents 8.4 per cent of the Spanish GDP in 2010. It is already planned to increase the aid up to 32 per cent of GDP (equal to €337 billion). If this were not enough, the so called 'austerity measures' imposed by the Troika (the European Commission, the European Central Bank and the IMF) resulted in budget cuts, wage freezes and the dismantling of social programmes. External financial institutions and agents, then, obliged a whole population to pay the private debts of a few. The mirage of prosperity has disappeared. Social exclusion has become more visible once the veil of the financial mode of accumulation has been torn away. Personal freedom and national sovereignty, in the end, are just fictions under the domination of financial capital and the neoliberal policies that support their power.

As we mentioned above, the squatters' movement in many Spanish cities did not stop protesting against the vacancy levels and the speculative games behind the housing sector which caused great damage in all the public spheres. They just used one of the elements of that game, a few vacant properties, to call society's attention to urban speculation in particular, and financial speculation in general. Vacancy, rising prices and housing deprivation were just symptoms of the more intensive forms of job exploitation, rent extraction and capital accumulation. Squatting, therefore, represented an oblique way of challenging the final stages and complex mechanisms of the capitalist society. Only when the Movement for Decent Housing and the M15 movement tackled the political consciousness of broader parts of society – once it found itself deep inside the crisis – were squatters' claims considered more acceptable and useful to counterbalance the underlying crisis which had existed before the crash, and was ongoing and explicit at the end of the decade.

Why Do Squatters Oppose Home Ownership?

Some years ago, there was a passionate debate about the relationship between home ownership, social class position and political action. Saunders (1984), for example, argued that the class position in the sphere of production imposes limits to the social position in the sphere of consumption, but not an absolute determination. Thus, some crucial aspects of consumption, such as housing, open relevant lines of social cleavage and stratification which can overlap class relationships while keeping a certain degree of independence. The specific forms of capital accumulation that home ownership provides, the shared social interests of home buyers and their preferences regarding some state policies on urban planning and fiscal subsidies, for instance, are suggested as the basis of this type of social division. For Saunders, then, private property entails 'exclusivity in rights of control, benefit and disposal' (1984: 208) plus the rights of sale and inheritance which grant great power to the holder, although there are always specific legal regulations which constrain those rights to some extent.

Furthermore, in a context of continuous privatisation, he argues that first those excluded from ownership, and later those excluded from state provision (or 'collective consumption'), will behave:

> from relatively coherent communal self-help strategies on the part of those who enjoy cohesive social networks to sporadic and relatively unorganised outbreaks of civil unrest and attacks on private property on the part of those who lack either the patience or the resources necessary for the development of such a compensatory strategy.
>
> (Saunders, 1984: 215)

In the end, Saunders claims that individual rights to property or private consumption should be preserved in a socialist society, but the state should avoid any possible market 'exploitation' (that is, rent extraction and speculation) exerted by the holders over the rest.

From this perspective, we could consider squatters as either those who develop self-help strategies in order to counterbalance both the dominant tendency to privatisation and the social exclusion which that engenders, or those who just attack private property as a desperate gesture against the icon of their social exclusion. However, Saunders did not distinguish clearly between property (legal title) and possession (effective use). Individual and collective rights to use private property do not necessarily imply either a claim of the right of private property, or its extension to the whole society. In addition, the kind of collective possession that squatters practise can be considered a useful measure to exert social control over actual and potential real estate speculative deals, at least for a while. This would agree with both Saunders' proposals and Proudhon's endorsement of the right of workers to be small owners if there is equality and mutual cooperation, a sort of market under the workers' control. If this argument is true, squatters would not be exactly against private property but against social inequality caused by exclusive accumulation and the capitalist mechanisms of speculation. Squatters distrust both the unique alternative of a solid state provision of housing to hinder the trend of privatisation, and the rule of the wealthiest within a free market. Given the starting point of already vacant property and homes occupied in different forms, squatters add their specific claim of autonomous housing tenure to that diversity, while at the same time they criticise the bureaucratic modes of social housing, try to discourage workers' wish to buy, and spread the call for the abolition of private property as a radical approach to opposing urban speculation.

Hodkinson (2012: 4) has classified squatting as a type of 'alternative-oppositional' challenge to the mainstream market provision of 'individual home ownership or private renting backed up by some form of state-regulated or funded safety net for those unable to access the private market'. Squatting, then, is conceived as a 'rival praxis' to the main-stream, an 'overtly politicised act of defying private property and creating (temporary) autonomous living spaces outside of market and state control as part of a squatting movement' (ibid.). Housing cooperatives, for example, will fall under the type of 'alternative-additional' because they would not be able to contest the dominant housing system as squatters do. Instead, housing co-ops and collective ownership would tend to add a choice to the private property system by reducing the costs of purchasing. However, collective ownership may be seen by squatters as a more feasible alternative to capitalism than squatting itself once they have been evicted several times. As Pruijt (2003: 135) notes, squatting combines a political opposition and an economic demand, and these two dimensions may diverge. The satisfaction of housing need may prevail over the opposition to private property if squatting is the last resort for those trying to be adequately housed. Once this option disappears and resistance is broken, squatters may accept other less oppositional forms of housing such as co-ops, self-construction and rental.

Therefore, in political terms squatting may be defined as 'an act of refusal and autonomy, a counter-cultural prefigurative alternative to the everyday dictates of state and capital' (Hodkinson, 2012: 4), while in economic and social terms squatting puts in practice a 'sustainable way to repair, heat and maintain buildings, and deal with owners, authorities and the community. Effective squatting also entails contributing to the push for a lively, low-income people friendly city' (Pruijt, 2003: 134). Although most squatters reject capitalism, they also reject statist solutions for the housing shortage because 'state housing within capitalism has been a disempowering and alienating experience for tenants through the top-down and paternalistic welfare relationship it has created between provider and client' (Hodkinson, 2012: 13).

Obviously, state housing no less than squatting may be available as an option for the most deprived social groups. The key question is which one is most efficient in setting up an alternative to the capitalist exchange-value of housing as a commodity and a financial investment. The answer resides in several aspects, all mutually intertwined, including the size and volume of the public and squatted stocks compared with dominant home ownership, long-term sustainability in terms of financing the maintenance of the buildings and basic services, the autonomous ways of collective management, and regulations that impede a complete reversal of the form of tenure. Other collective housing alternatives may erect barriers to the tide of capitalism and neoliberal policies, but sometimes they are not afford-able for the lowest-income groups, and these groups may be trapped in financial and speculative serfdom just as private home owners usually are.

The Pitfalls of Home Ownership in the United Kingdom, Japan and the United States

Recent analysis has emphasised the different context, timing and pace at play when neoliberal policies apply to the promotion of home ownership. The cases of the United Kingdom and Japan, for example, show how political authorities implement liberalism and push speculative dynamics according to those key aspects (Forrest and Hirayama, 2009). In the 1980s, Margaret Thatcher attacked a widespread welfare state, and in particular council housing, in order to get it dismantled and to favour owner-occupied dwellings. At that time the United Kingdom had around a third of households living in the state housing sector, while by 2000 this figure had shrunk to 12 per cent (Forrest and Hirayama, 2009:1002–3). A large proportion of state-owned housing was sold (that is, privatised) to the tenants. Deregulation of the financial market also fuelled competition between mortgage providers.

In contrast, Japan followed a slower pace in the implementation of neoliberal policies. The previous situation consists of a relatively small public rental sector targeted on the poor and special needs groups (Forrest and Hirayama, 2009: 1003). Similar to the US case, these groups were not able to purchase their homes even if they asked to do so. Thus, the level of home ownership in Japan was rarely high after the 1960s (averaging 64 per cent) compared with other industrialised countries. The explanation was a financial policy of subsidising low-interest mortgages up to 49 per cent of the loan in the 1990s. Once home ownership was the dominant pattern, those subsidies disappeared around the late 1990s. The neoliberal dogma of avoiding state intervention in social and economic affairs was applied following state intervention which favoured market forces. Financial agents found a new group of clients for their loans, and low interest rates encouraged the mortgage business.

However, after periods of housing inflation, prices went downwards between 1989 and 1993 in the United Kingdom and between 1990 and around 2005 in Japan. 'This implied the end of the era when home ownership was reliable in terms of property asset accumulation and, instead, the beginning of the new era in which property ownership is higher risk and less sustainable' (Forrest and Hirayama, 2009: 1004). The policy responses, then, differed. In the United Kingdom some programmes attempted to incorporate low-income groups in those able to access home ownership, while in Japan subsidies to mortgage interest rates were implemented again and mass construction was also favoured. Therefore, when the market did not work, the neoliberal policies used the public budget to feed the pursuit of private profit. The promotion of home ownership was thus one of the key flagships of these policies, intertwined with other measures of privatisation and deregulation. In the periods of rising prices it was younger households who could not afford to enter the home ownership market. They had to opt for renting from private landlords, who also took advantage of the 'buy to let' market. First-home seekers, whether young or immigrants (as happened in Spain) are the first losers from this dominant housing system.

As a consequence, it is evident that the waves of inflation and decline (involving mortgage defaults), backed by neoliberal policies, created instability, uncertainty and severe social divisions. In illustration:

> The current situation in the British housing market is a potent and toxic mix of sharply increased borrowing costs, a shortage of loan finance, rising

numbers of empty and unsaleable properties, a rising number of bad loans
and waning confidence in the entire financial system. … Growing job insecurity, rising debt and a generally less supportive social security system have
also been key ingredients in delaying departure from the parental home and
restricting access to home ownership. Here, however, there are differences.
In the UK, education-related debt is an important new factor. The growing
costs of higher education mean that more students choose to stay at home
during university years and also that more young people leave university or
college with a large debt. In Japan, however, the key factor is the growth of
irregular employment among a younger generation.

(Forrest and Hirayama, 2009: 1009–10)

In addition, housing deflation was also at the core of the periods of
economic recession, which means that housing bubbles in the institutional context of neoliberalism form a greater threat to the rest of social
and economic life.

In the United States, a recent report about the housing system in NYC
pointed out that there is a housing shortage and a housing surplus at the
same time (Butler, 2012). In this city, around 70 per cent of the population live in rental housing. However, rents rise to extremely high levels all
over the boroughs, and above all at the core of Manhattan. The New York
City Housing Authority (NYCHA) has not built public housing since the
mid-1990s (Shwartz, 1999), and around 161,000 home seekers who cannot
afford the market prices are still registered on its waiting lists. According to
official data, the total estimated vacancy level in NYC in 2011 was around
8 per cent of the housing stock, although 165,500 vacant units (5 per cent
of the total stock) were not available for rent or sale because they were
dilapidated, under renovation or used for recreational purposes (HVS,
2011: 11). The median contract rent–income ratio was 31 per cent in 2011,
but three in ten of renter households in the city (30 per cent) paid 50 per
cent or more of their income for contract rent, excluding the costs of fuel
and utilities (HVS, 2011: 7).

Butler (2012: 2) provides two arguments regarding this situation.
First, the public housing stock was not affordable for the working classes,
although it was built thanks to the state subsidies and thus using the contributions of taxpayers. Second, construction workers were among those
who could not afford to pay for decent housing because in the residential
projects the wages were below the current union scales. These sharp social
cleavages occurred in a context of neoliberal policies. Since 1947, a Rent
Control Law had controlled rental costs and made houses affordable for
most residents. The NYCHA also provided affordable dwellings all over
the city, Manhattan included. Many labour unions also developed their

own housing projects. In those decades, black people and latinos were the most excluded social groups regarding access to a home. Nevertheless, small landlords and real estate lobbies, such as the Realty Advisory Board, the Real Estate Board of New York and the New York Building Congress, fought for the abolition of the Rent Control Law in order to 'either force out poor, working class or lower middle class tenants and replace them with upper middle class or wealthy tenants that could pay higher rents, or outright destroy their units' (Butler, 2012: 5). The first battle was won by the elites' lobbies, and a new Rent Stabilization Law in 1971 replaced the Rent Control Law. This provided for rents to increase every one or two years. Afterwards, private landlords started a second battle:

> In Manhattan's Lower East Side, West Side and Upper West Side and in the downtown areas of Brooklyn, many landlords tried to force tenants out by denial of services like heat, hot water, repairs and locked exterior doors. Some even encouraged criminals to come into their buildings and prey on tenants or even hired them for that purpose. Those areas were predominantly White neighborhoods that were close to Manhattan's two main business districts, Midtown and Downtown. The goal was to 'gentrify' those areas – to drive out working class tenants and replace them with upper middle class and rich folks who could pay higher rents. In some cases, this meant driving tenants out of existing buildings, doing modest renovations, collecting a J51 Major Capital Improvement tax credit and then renting out the building at the new higher Rent Stabilization Law rents. In other cases, it meant driving out the tenants, tearing down the existing building and using that city low interest loan and tax credit program to build luxury high-rise apartment buildings in the place of the older buildings.
>
> (Butler, 2012: 7)

In other areas that were not so attractive to gentrifiers, landlords used the strategy of burning down their buildings to collect the insurance money (Marcuse, 1985).

Subsidies to private companies to renovate housing stock, the increasingly precarious nature of work and irregular low wages, plus the raising of rents every year, contributed to housing inflation. Home ownership was even promoted by landlords, who turned their properties into cooperatives and condominiums where the new owners had to pay high 'maintenance fees' in addition to mortgages. This was an easy way to avoid the constraints of the Rent Stabilization Law. After the early 1980s, the building boom caused rents to soar. The numbers of homeless or badly housed people also went up rapidly.

After the decline of 1989, authorities, developers, landlords and workers agreed upon new investments, subsidies and regulations to help the construction sector recover. In 1994, for example, the landlords' and constructors' lobbies won a new battle. Rents over $2,000 per month were made exempt from the Rent Stabilization Law. This deregulation had a side effect:

> This so called 'luxury decontrol' encouraged landlords to raise up rents as much as possible to get them over the $2,000 a month limit. The new rules also encouraged 'churning' apartments – encouraging rapid tenant turnover because every time a landlord gets a new tenant, that's a new lease and a new chance to raise the rent.
>
> (Butler, 2012: 13)

In parallel, the NYC Department of Housing Preservation and Development (HPD), launched by the Koch administration, had implemented a policy of allowing not-for-profit housing associations (community-based organisations) to deal with the renovation of the most ruined stock (Gould et al., 2001: 188). In other words, a neoliberal policy was fully developed. Deregulation in favour of elites' interests, reduced state intervention, public subsidies to mega-developments (Fainstein, 2008), and privatisation of the few 'public housing' initiatives, paved the way for generating one of the biggest housing bubbles in the world throughout the 2000s. While employment conditions worsened for the working classes and ethnic discrimination overlapped with housing exclusion, the flow of public funds aimed at helping the construction industry built dwellings for the affluent upper and global classes.

The most significant squatters' movement in New York took place from the early 1980s in the Lower East Side (Manhattan). This neighbourhood was under pressure from gentrification, demolition and renovations. Initially, around 500 squatters lived in 20 buildings, some of the most dilapidated ones in the area (Pruijt, 2003: 139), but the figures grew to around 3,000 squatters or people involved in the movement, and 25–30 buildings occupied in the mid-1990s. The occupation of vacant lands in order to promote community gardens was also linked to squatters' activities from the very beginning. Solidarity with homeless organisations and campaigns was also a central claim of this movement. Most of the squatted properties belonged to the City, and 200 squatters living in 11 buildings were able to sign an agreement with the Giuliani administration (through the mediation of a federal agency: Pruijt, 2003 :142), between 1998 and 2002, in order to acquire legal status. Although most of the squatters opposed the housing policy of the HPD, finally they faced the dilemma of being immediately evicted or entering into the plans for privatising the public housing with the help of community organisations. The legalisation process obliged squatters to borrow money from the banks, but some of them still are ineligible to take out mortgages.

After the bursting of the housing bubble in 2007, new organisations such as O4O (Organize4Occupation) and Picture the Homeless launched new squats and helped people to take over empty buildings (Martínez, 2012). [O4O activist Frank Morales presents a more detailed account of squatting in the Lower East Side in Chapter 4: the gentrification suffered by the poorest and the privatisation of the housing sector analysed here are complemented by his personal account of how wild repression can be contrasted by the strategic coalition of squatters in solidarity with their neighbours.]

Conclusions

Hodkinson suggests that anti-capitalist housing alternatives may adopt three strategic perspectives:

- prefigurative ones (or 'living-in-common') as people 'try to meet our housing needs and desires through the creation of non-hierarchical, small-scale, directly democratic, egalitarian and collective forms of housing in our everyday lives' (Hodkinson, 2012: 16) while they express 'life despite capitalism' and 'the pragmatic anarchist approach of solving our housing conditions in the here and now through the extension of dweller control and mutual aid' (ibid.)
- defensive ones (or 'housing-as-commons'), with the preservation of public housing from privatisation, and even the defence of home owners from repossessions, evictions, demolitions, commodification and displacement as a result of the speculative attacks against housing as a use-value, and crucial bonds with other social groups
- (counter-)hegemonic ones as a development of a 'common housing movement' where creation (prefigurative experiences) and resistance (defensive struggles) coexist, expand, proliferate and diversify.

Squatters work with the prefigurative forces of autonomous and self-help housing alternatives. However, squatters will not get rid of capitalism if they only oppose home ownership and private property. Instead, Hodkinson proposes alliances with residents in public housing and with weak home owners threatened by foreclosures and gentrification, for example. Since home ownership and state housing in the present capitalist system are quite functional to the elites' interests, any anti-capitalist strategy should also focus on viable ways to transform these regimes into more collectively owned and self-managed ones. [The recent developments of squatting for housing rights show how a counter-hegemonic force is likely to emerge, with the case from Rome discussed in Chapter 5 being an excellent example. Similarly, the coalitions that are now occurring between parts of the Barcelona squatters' movement and the platform of People Affected by Mortgages – which has recently started squatting empty blocks owned by banks – show the beginning of a similar case.]

Squatting opposes private property as one of the bases of the social inequalities in the dominant capitalist system. In addition, as we have argued before, squatting also opposes other essential mechanisms of capitalism, mainly commodification, urban speculation, unbearable financial debts and the inflation of housing prices. Most squats combine a broad critique of the capitalist system as a whole and a practical solution to some of its major contradictions in the real estate sector. Squatters thus contribute with practical solutions to the housing needs of those involved in the squatters' movement, and those who self-house themselves taking advantage of the vacant stock of houses and buildings. Although these direct actions are often temporary and fragile, they offer an accessible, affordable and efficient alternative to the failures of both the housing market and public policies on housing matters. These failures become evident with the bursting of financial bubbles and the increasing poverty it entails.

Squatting cannot provide housing for all and it is not able to challenge the whole capitalist system, but it can serve to help some of those excluded by capitalism and those who wish to change the system by their involvement in an alternative way of living, political campaigns, other social movements and so on. This is the reason we do not see a big gap between so-called 'social' and 'political' squatting, or between squatting just for housing and squatted social centres. Different types of squatting, along with other urban struggles ('defensive' ones, for example), may be combined in order to increase their anti-capitalist (or 'counter-hegemonic') effects, if this is the case. The local political, economic and environmental context suggests that the crises of capitalism vary significantly, and so do the specific reactions against them, such as the squatters' movement. [The reach and effects of this antagonistic relationship between capitalist forces and squatters' movements will be more deeply analysed in the Conclusion, after the presentation of case studies and specific squatting issues in the following chapters.]

Box 1.1 *The environmental basis of the political economy of squatting*

The fate of financial capitalism, the regular and devastating housing bubbles and the continuous depletion of natural resources are all interlinked. In particular, the environmental dimension of squatting has rarely been pointed out. Above all, the occupation of vacant buildings implies a wise and efficient use of natural resources since it diminishes the pressure to construct new buildings. Therefore, already occupied land and all the energy and materials that were employed in the construction are effectively used by someone, regardless of the legal title they hold.

We should not analyse the housing bubble and the inherent dynamics of post-industrial capitalism in isolation from the decreasing availability of natural resources (oil in particular). As much as they have been considered as bubbles that later explode, the nature at the base of speculative processes is not only formed by thin air. As Martinez-Alier (2008) argues, the economy is made of three levels. At the top we find the speculators contributing to the financial dimension of the economy, who are only interested in the infinite growth of monetary (M) value, of accumulation for accumulation's sake, M–M' processes, Below, at the factory floor, lies the productive economy, made of material processes of commodity (C) production, distribution and consumption, which also contribute to the capitalist process of accumulation. This goes through a material process: M–C–M'. Most factories are now increasingly displaced to emerging economies, such as China, the Far East and Latin America, while European and North American economies are specialised in the service sector and dematerialised economies dependent on real production elsewhere. Finally, at the very bottom level and deep underground in the mines, there are the physical resources which are used as inputs to the processes of commodity production This is not by chance known as the primary sector, which includes extractive industries, fisheries, livestock and agriculture production. They are only finite resources on a limited planet, and the economic growth imperative has meant that key natural resources are now less available, such as the atmospheric carrying capacity of anthropogenic carbon dioxide emissions (one of the most salient outputs of the economic process) and the availability of cheap oil (one of the most basic inputs that fuels the current production). 'Peak oil', for example, will soon determine, if it is not already doing so, economic turbulences and sharp changes in energy supplies. The construction and the housing sectors are obviously deeply affected by these natural constraints.

Not only does the building sector require materials and energy from the natural world in order to produce, but all capitalist dynamics, since although they tend towards pure speculation, depend on real processes made of real resources. As Nafeez Mosaddeq Ahmed remarks (2010), between 2005 and 2010 oil production first reached a peak and then stabilised on a plateau, while the price per barrel hit the record of $147. As a consequence, speculation over global food raised prices in 2008, leaving many in desperate hunger, and the real estate bubble exploded in many countries simultaneously.

If an economy is compelled to grow at an ever-increasing rate but scarcity of natural resources fails to provide adequate material input, the tendency will be to substitute material with immaterial growth, as has occurred through the processes of dematerialisation of post-industrial economies and through the consequent rise in the GDP relevance of the service and financial sector. This post-industrial transformation has contributed to maintaining certain levels of economic growth, but at the cost of rising levels of indebtedness. This is known as 'debt-fuelled growth'.

Evidence of reduced oil consumption leading to a long-term drop in profit rates and economic growth and in less capacity for debt repayment is explained by Tverberg (2012). Although it might appear as a chicken-and-egg problem, he shows the ties of the financial crisis to the oil crisis in 2008. As peak oil expert Richard Heinberg (2011) claims, by also connecting the present financial crisis with a crisis in energy resources, society will not be able to get back to growth. Since the abandonment of the Gold Standard, the supply of money is not any longer related to a physical resource. This implies that the amount of financial debt is not naturally limited, and in the last few decades it has experienced a J-shaped exponential growth curve, a debt growth not backed by a similar growth in the production capacity of the real economy which in turn was limited by the increasing scarcity of cheap fuels. Douthwaite (2012) finds an explanation of the financial-energy link by looking at the international flows of debt and fossil energy, particularly involving the rich post-industrial nations, and provides an account of how these advanced economies in the past ten years have been increasingly borrowing capital from developing countries, such as the exporters of fossil energy. However, the money was borrowed rather than being invested in real production, and was spent in consumption (mostly consumer spending on mortgages). The debt/ GDP ratio increased well beyond 100 per cent, meaning that for each euro or dollar borrowed, less than one was contributing to the national GDP (paying salaries and resources). As a corollary, any GDP increase of one euro or dollar has been fuelled by more than a euro or dollar borrowed from abroad.

References

Adell, R. and Martínez, M. A. (eds) (2004) ¿Dónde están las llaves? El movimiento okupa: prácticas y contextos sociales [*Where are the Keys? The Squatter Movement: Practical Issues and Social Context*]. Madrid: Catarata.

Bailey, R. (1973) *The Squatters*. Harmondsworth: Penguin.

Blanco, R. (2011) ¿Qué pasa? Que aún no tenemos casa [*What's Going On? We Still Don't Have a House*]. Madrid: Fundación Aurora Intermitente.

Bouillon F (2009) *Squats. Un Autre Point de Vue sur les Migrants* [*Squats: Another Point of View on Migrants*]. Paris: Alternatives.

Butler, G. A. (2012) 'No vacancy: why New York City has a housing shortage and a housing surplus at the same time.' http://nyc.indymedia.org/en/2012/09/120520.html

Castells, M. (1983) *The City and the Grassroots. A Cross-Cultural Theory of Urban Social Movements*. Berkeley, Calif.: University of California Press.

Cattaneo, C. (2008) *The Ecological Economics of Urban Squatters in Barcelona*. PhD thesis, Universitat Autònoma de Barcelona.

Colau, A. and Alemany, A. (2012) *Vidas hipotecadas. De la burbuja inmobiliaria al derecho a la vivienda* [*Mortgaged Lives: From the Housing Bubble to the Right to Housing*]. Barcelona: Cuadrilátero de Libros.

–– (2013) ¡Sí se puede! Crónica de una pequeña gran victoria [*Yes, We Can! Chronicle of a Small Great Victory*]. Barcelona, Spain: Destino.

Corr, A. (1999) *No Trespassing: Squatting, Rent Strikes and Land Struggles Worldwide*. Cambridge, Mass.: South End.

CGPJ (Consejo General del Poder Judicial) (2012) 'Datos sobre el efecto de la crisis en los órganos judiciales' ['Data on the effect of the crisis on judicial institutions']. www.poderjudicial.es/cgpj/es/Temas/Estadistica_Judicial/Informes_estadisticos/Informes_periodicos/

Douthwaite, R. (2012) 'Degrowth and the supply of money in an energy-scarce world.' *Ecological Economics* 84(1), 187–93.

Doyal, L. and Gough, I. (1991) *A Theory of Human Need*. New York: Palgrave Macmillan.

Draaisma, J. and van Hoogstraten, P. (1983) 'The squatter movement in Amsterdam.' *International Journal of Urban and Regional Research* 7: 406–16.

Engels, F. (1975 [1872–87]) *Contribución al problema de la vivienda* [*Contribution to the Housing Problem*]. In K. Marx and F. Engels, *Obras escogidas* [*Collected Works*]. Madrid: Akal.

European Commission (2012) State aid in the context of the financial and economic crisis. http://ec.europa.eu/competition/state_aid/studies_reports/expenditure.html#II

Fainstein, S. (2008) 'Mega-projects in New York, London and Amsterdam.' *International Journal of Urban and Regional Research* 32(4), 768–85.

Forrest, R. and Hirayama, Y. (2009) 'The uneven impact of neoliberalism on housing opportunities.' *International Journal of Urban and Regional Research* 33(4), 998–1013.

Gough, I. (2004) 'Human well-being and social structures: relating the universal and the local.' *Global Social Policy* 4(3), 289–311.

Gould, I., Schill, M. H., Susin, S. and Schwartz, A. E. (2001) 'Building homes, reviving neighborhoods: spillovers from subsidized construction of owner-occupied housing in New York City.' *Journal of Housing Research* 12(2), 185–216.

Harvey, D. (2007) 'Neoliberalism as creative destruction.' *Annals of the American Academy of Political and Social Science* 610(1), 21–44.

Heinberg, R. (2011) *The End of Growth: Adapting to Our New Economic Reality.* Gabriola Island: New Society Publishers.

Hodkinson, S. (2012) 'The return of the housing question.' *Ephemera* 12(4), 1–21.

Leal, J. and Cortés, L. (1995) *La dimensión de la ciudad* [*The City Dimension*]. Madrid: CIS.

Leal, J. (2010) 'La formación de las necesidades de vivienda en la España actual' [The creation of the housing need in the Spain of today], in J. Leal (ed.), *La política de vivienda en España* [*The Politics of Housing in Spain*]. Madrid: Pablo Iglesias.

Lefebvre, H. (1968) *Le droit à la ville* [*The Right to the City*]. Paris: Anthropos.

López, I. and Rodríguez, E. (2010) *Fin de ciclo. Financiarización, territorio y sociedad de propietarios en la onda larga del capitalismo hispano (1959–2010)* [*The End of the Cycle: Financialisation, Land and Society of the owners in the Long Wave of Spanish Capitalism*]. Madrid: Traficantes de Sueños.

—— (2011) 'The Spanish model.' *New Left Review* 69, 1–15.

Lowe, S. (1986) *Urban Social Movements: The City after Castells.* London: Macmillan.

Lukes, S. (1974) *Power. A Radical View.* London: Macmillan.

Marcuse, P. (1985) 'Gentrification, abandonment, and displacement: connections, causes, and policy responses in New York City.' *Journal of Urban and Contemporary Law* 28, 195–240.

Martinez-Alier, J. (2008) 'Languages of valuation.' *Economic and Political Weekly* 43(48).

Martínez, M. A. (2002) *Okupaciones de viviendas y de centros sociales. Autogestión, contracultura y conflictos urbanos* [*Squatting and Social Centres: Self-management, Counterculture and Urban Conflict*]. Barcelona: Virus.

—— (2007) 'The squatters' movement: urban counter-culture and alter-globalization dynamics.' *South European Society and Politics* 12(3), 379–98.

—— (2012) 'Tras las huellas de las okupaciones en New York City (2): legal-izaciones en Loisaida' [Following the trails of squatting in New York City (2): legalization processes in Loisaida]. www.miguelangelmartinez.net/?Tras-las-huellas-de-las,180 (accessed 3 February 2014).

Martínez, M. A. and García, A. (2013) 'The occupation of squares and the squatting of buildings: lessons from the convergence of two social movements', in B. Tejerina and I. Perugorría (eds), *Crisis and Social Mobilization in Contemporary Spain: The M15 Movement*. Surrey: Ashgate.

Max-Neef, M. (1994) *Desarrollo a escala humana* [*Human-Scale Development*]. Barcelona: Nordan-Icaria.

Mosaddeq, A. N. (2011) *A User's Guide to the Crisis of Civilisation: And How to Save It*. London: Pluto Press.

Naredo, J. M. (2011) 'El modelo inmobiliario español y sus consecuencias' ['The Spanish housing model and its consequences'], in J. M. Naredo and A. Montiel (eds), *El modelo inmobiliario español y su culminación en el caso valenciano* [*The Spanish Housing Model and its Culmination in the Case of Valencia*]. Barcelona: Icaria.

Nussbaum, M. C. (2003) 'Capabilities as fundamental entitlements: Sen and social justice.' *Feminist Economics* 9(2–3): 33–59.

Pareja, M. (2010) 'El régimen de tenencia de la vivienda en España' ['The housing tenancy system in Spain'], in J. Leal (ed.), *La política de vivienda en España* [*The Politics of Housing in Spain*]. Madrid: Pablo Iglesias.

Pérez, V. and Sánchez, P. (eds.) (2008) *Memoria ciudadana y movimiento vecinal. Madrid 1968–2008* [*Civic Memory and Neighbourhood Movements*]. Madrid: Catarata.

Priemus, H. (1983) 'Squatters in Amsterdam: urban social movement, urban managers or something else?' *International Journal of Urban and Regional Research* 7, 417–27.

Pruijt, H. (2003) 'Is the institutionalization of urban movements inevitable? A comparison of the opportunities for sustained squatting in New York City and Amsterdam.' *International Journal of Urban and Regional Research* 27(1), 133–57.

Riechmann, J. (1998) 'Necesidades humanas frente a límites ecológicos y sociales' ['Human needs and socio-ecological limits'], in J. Riechmann (ed.), *Necesitar, desear, vivir* [*To Need, To Wish, To Live*]. Madrid: Catarata.

Rodríguez, J. (2010) 'La demanda de vivienda y el esfuerzo económico' ['Housing demand and economic effort'], in J. Leal (ed.), *La política de vivienda en España* [*The Politics of Housing in Spain*]. Madrid: Pablo Iglesias.

Sabaté, I. (2012) *Habitar detrás del muro. La cuestión de la vivienda en el Este de Berlín* [*Living Behind the Wall: The Housing Question in East Berlin*]. Barcelona: Icaria.

Saunders, P. (1984) 'Beyond housing classes: the sociological significance of private property rights in means of consumption.' *International Journal of Urban and Regional Research* 8(2), 202–27.

Schwartz, A. (1999) 'New York City and subsidized housing: impacts and lessons of the city's $5 billion capital budget housing plan.' *Housing Policy Debate* 10(4), 839–77.

SQUASH (Squatters' Action for Secure Homes) (2011) 'Criminalising the

vulnerable: why we can't criminalise our way out of a housing crisis. A parliamentary briefing.' www.squashcampaign.org (accessed 1 October 2012).

Thörn, H., Wasshede, C. and Nilson, T. (2011) *Space for Urban Alternatives? Christiania 1971–2011*. Vilnius: Gidlunds.

Tverberg, G. E. (2012) 'Oil supply limits and the continuing financial crisis.' *Energy* 37 (27–34).

VVAA (various authors) (2007) *El cielo está enladrillado. Entre el mobbing y la violencia inmobiliaria y urbanística* [*The Sky is Bricked Up: From Mobbing to Urban and Real-Estate Violence*]. Barcelona, Spain: Bellaterra.

Wates, N. and Wolmar, C. (eds) (1980) *Squatting: The Real Story*. London: Bay Leaf.

Part I

Case Studies

2

'The Fallow Lands of the Possible': An Enquiry into the Enacted Criticism of Capitalism in Geneva's Squats

Luca Pattaroni

With more than 150 squats, in the 1990s the city of Geneva hosted one of the larger squatters' movements in Europe. The story of this social movement goes back to the 1970s, and it had almost completely disappeared by the end of the first decade of the 21st century. This movement was not concerned only with the sole question of housing – particularly social housing – but it constituted a more radical challenge to the way social life is organised within the modern capitalist city. Indeed, as I shall try to show in this chapter, squatters have repeatedly given birth to an enacted and embedded critique of capitalism. They opened up 'fallow lands of the possible' within the capitalist city, where frail and experimental processes took place through which different lifestyles could express themselves and alternative worlds were invented.

Essential Heterotopias

The squatting movement in Geneva, particularly in its heyday in the 1990s, can be described as the irruption of a pluralist, burgeoning, slightly off-beat world in the highly ordered universe that is the city of Geneva. By violating the established order, squatters opened a whole world of possibilities, wherein the wildest, most fragile projects could be dreamed up and tested. This was no utopia, but rather a 'heterotopia', to use the term coined by philosopher Michel Foucault to describe 'those different spaces, those other places, a kind of both mythical and real contestation of the space in which we live' (Foucault, 2009). These 'other places' – from gardens to monasteries to the parental bed where children invent an imaginary world – are necessary to society as a whole because they are spaces where the established order and all its demands of conformity are kept in check, so as to welcome and protect the vulnerable processes (learning, creation, sociability and meditation to name a few) which forge our humanity.

The Invention of the Squat

Before entering the world of squats and revisiting its major milestones (occupation, installation, habitation, evacuation and perpetuation), we must briefly go back and look at the history of squatting and squatters. Squatting, understood as illegally occupying land or a building, fits into the larger context of different forms of revindication and protest against private property, whose objectives and modalities were extremely divergent. As Cécile Péchu suggests, the invention of squatting[1] as a form of political action can be traced, at least in France, back to the end of the 19th century (Péchu, 2010: 21–35), It started with the *déménagements à la cloche de bois* organized collectively by anarchists as early as the 1880s. This consisted in quickly and quietly moving families who were behind several months on their rent so that bailiffs could not seize their furniture. In 1911, the Trade Union of Worker and Employee Tenants, under the leadership of union secretary George Cochon, took to using this practice as a form of political protest, along with other measures such as rent strikes. The relocations were public and accompanied by a 'racket' in front of the homes of bad landlords. By 1912, in the wake of all this, emerged the practice of 'reoccupying' empty apartments to house families in need. Thus did forms of direct action aimed at both meeting a need and providing 'propaganda of the deed' come to exist (Péchu, 2010: 35).

The period following the Second World War saw a proliferation of squatting activities to accommodate needy families with children. Abbé Pierre's 1954 appeal led to the birth of associations to help the homeless, whose activities resulted in the creation of shelters 'squatted' in vacant buildings. As such, squatting is above all a response to distress. Nowadays, associations like Droit au Logement (Right to Housing) carry on this humanitarian tradition of squatting by occupying empty buildings to house families in need [For a more detailed presentation of this collective, Thomas Aguilera in Chapter 5 deals on the widespread emergence of squatting movements for the right of housing as a response to the crisis, and how they are criticised by more radical Paris squatters.] The mediatisation of occupations also makes it possible to denounce the injustices of housing policies and promote veritable 'housing rights' that guarantee decent living conditions for everyone.

In addition to this first squatting tradition – while closely linked to it – the 1960s, with its critical movements that culminated in the events of May 1968, saw the emergence of another facet of the squatting movement. In the wake of community experiences and calls for a change of lifestyle, illegal occupations became an opportunity to experiment with other ways of organizing daily life. Now, people squatted in order to live differently, not just to satisfy a 'need'. It became a question of challenging the right to property and, more generally, capitalist forms of organising society.

The different squatting experiences we can observe in Europe oscillate between those two horizons (a more humanitarian one and a more critical one). More specifically, squats are used, to varying degrees, as shelters, as platforms from which to decry certain injustices and as places to live differently.[2] Some seek legal recognition, while others are more radical and avoid all forms of compromise. Others still are 'clandestine' and serve only as a refuge for particularly vulnerable populations. That said, to a certain extent they are all places where the logic of the market is attenuated, or even temporarily suspended. Thus do they contribute to promotion of non-market spaces needed to accommodate fragile populations and/or processes such as the pursuit of alternative ways of living, the establishment of convivial relations, artistic experimentation and not-for-profit projects, or the chance for less affluent populations to appropriate the spaces necessary to live well. These spaces are all the more necessary as the modes of capitalist development of contemporary cities gradually subsume all places and activities into the snares of market logic. In other words, no money means no social life, fun, creativity or pleasure.

As such, the now-defunct policy of tolerance implemented in Geneva starting in the mid-1980s can be seen as a kind of hard-won shield which allowed different types of squats to exist and coexist peacefully for several decades. These spaces took turns and even collaborated in offering refuge to the poor, sheltering the experiences of collective living that challenge how we relate to the world and others, and enriching the quality of the city's night-life and art scene.

The large majority of Geneva squats belonged in varying degrees to the critical tradition, wherein it was not simply a question of providing shelter for the poor, but of creating alternative spaces that questioned dominant lifestyles in our society and the market system that frames them.

How can we be blamed for dissenting, for adopting a logic of refusal with regard to this appalling representation of life? Squatting is not a response to a need for housing; it is creating situations that break with this representation. Invest in new spaces. Enjoy.

(anonymous leaflet, Geneva)

By questioning the framework of everyday life, criticism of speculation and the right of ownership blended with more practical issues, such as improvising a kitchen in an old empty building, repainting shutters in bright colours, shared toilet facilities or creating a wood-fired heating system. It also combined with the excitement of occupations and collective work, laughter, times of sharing, and the fears that arise when the threat of expulsion is imminent, or outbursts of anger that happen when the burden of cohabitation becomes too great. Here we touch on experiences where the political was intrinsically tied to the intimate, the personal – the essential conditions for rethinking boundaries and the way we live together.

The time has come to delve into both the history of the movement and the daily life of squatters. Our journey will follow the five steps that mark the life of all squats: occupation, installation, habitation, evacuation and perpetuation.

Occupation

The first phase which describes both the history of squats and the movement itself is *occupation*. During occupation, squatters violate the order of the city and, in so doing, one of the founding principles of liberal society – the right to ownership. In this phase, their critique of the status quo and demands for a new social order can be heard loud and clear. What matters is not only making your convictions heard, but also finding the political and popular support needed to organise a true power struggle with the state and the police. Above and beyond the strictly illegal nature of occupations, here it is a question of the legitimacy of occupations. A brief detour through the history of the squatters' movement in Geneva will help us grasp the motives and justification behind its birth, as well as the hopes and desires that lead to occupying and living in a squat.

The squatters' movement in Geneva was born, in the mid-1970s, of organised resistance to the plan to demolish and rebuild a little neighbourhood called Les Grottes, situated right behind the main train station and left partially abandoned for decades. In its place was to be built a denser area of 'modern' high rises. As in many countries at that time, this plan for so-called 'functionalist' urbanism received harsh criticism, since in it could be seen the negating of the traditional urban fabric, the strengthening of the movement to expel working-class people from downtown areas, and more broadly, the consecrating of a rationalist and capitalist logic of production of the territory.

Extreme leftist militants supported the neighbourhood's traditionally working-class population (artisans and workers) and its nascent residents association by occupying the numerous apartments left vacant in preparation for the demolition. With these occupations, squatters and their supporters wanted to show that these units were still habitable (contrary to the authorities' assertions), and should be renovated rather than destroyed.

These occupations and the direct actions that took place surrounding them (organized tumult in the streets, festive interventions at official gatherings and so on) are in keeping with the emergence of a new left that was at odds with social democracy and communism, and for whom social justice resulted from technological progress and the rationalisation of society. Significant in this respect was support for the demolition of Les Grottes by a portion of the socialist party (with the idea of providing quality social housing based on the model of new housing developments, typical of the French 'Grand Ensembles'). This new left – the product of the critiques and ideals of the May 1968 movement – advocated self-management and entertained a certain distrust of technology and the standards associated with the development of a state capitalism that not only strengthened inequalities but also, in its view, impoverished the human experience.

More precisely, the occupations themselves created the encounter and the dialogue between two contrasted segments of the new left (Gros, 1987). On one side we had the so-called 'gauchistes', who were usually small radical groups based either on a Maoist or a Trotskyist ideology (calling for an armed insurrection and workers' self-management). Those groups were illustrative of a radicalisation of what Boltanski and Chiapello have called the tradition of the 'social criticism' of capitalism, in other words a criticism of it as a source of inequalities and domination (Boltanski and Chiapello, 1999). On the other side, we had the so-called 'marginaux' who were promoting an ideal of self-emancipation from the convention of the bourgeoisie, through social and cultural experimentation (living theatre, communitarian life, drugs, sexual emancipation and so on). Inspired by the writing of the Situationists, they were anchored in the second main tradition of the criticism of the capitalism, 'artist criticism', rooted in the bohemian ideals of the 19th century, criticising the dehumanising and oppressing effects of capitalist society (Boltanski and Chiapello, 1999).

By allowing participants to organise collectively on a daily basis, the occupations made it possible not only to resist the plans for demolition and keep workers downtown, but to bring about another social world in the here and now, coupling the social and the artistic critique of capitalism. They allowed individuals to regain control over their environment, and gave an opportunity for less individualistic social relationships. This encounter – within the walls and everyday life of the squats – of those contrasted militant trends gave birth in the 1980s to what has been called 'alternative culture'.

Criticisms raised by the squat movement thus varied, pointing equally at policies of normalisation and standardisation, the lack of dialogue between authorities, the logics of the market and the individualisation of society. We can find them stated ironically on this 2001 wall newspaper:

> The Grottes were a disgrace for Geneva. What? A city so rich, so international, that it hasn't stopped standardising itself? What! A Western European city that hasn't pushed all of its working-class neighbourhoods to the outskirts yet …. Get rid of this filthy fungus, this strange, incongruous space that is all askew, alive and full of squats …. Paint those facades – so clumsily painted by those living behind them – all the same colour. Evict the squatters and raise the rents. Nothing should be left up to improvisation, or to residents. The urban planning service is much more capable of choosing the right living standards for everyone (especially for the city's image) than anyone else …. The same cleanliness, aseptic conditions, security and drought will cover all the sidewalks …. Our whole city … will be completely dead.
>
> (*Le Grottesque*, wall newspaper, no. 2, September 2001)

These critiques call for an alternative social universe in which principles like solidarity (versus the spread of market logics), conviviality (versus individualistic withdrawal), creativity (versus standardisation) and self-management (versus authoritarian policies) should prevail.

These principles are in line with the ideal of a right to the city as described by Henri Lefebvre in 1967. By 'right to the city' Lefebvre meant the right to use the city as a place of meeting and enjoyment. As a good Marxist, he contrasted the city's 'use value' with its 'exchange value', in which it is reduced to a place of 'gain and profit' and in which commodity exchange (spaces bought and sold, product consumerism and so on) is paramount. Faced with a city that seemed to be increasingly governed by the laws of the market, it was crucial to defend the idea that a city can be conceived, designed and used by those who live there rather than by those who own it financially.

Then I learned that these buildings were empty because they were making money. The call was even stronger. Not only can I reclaim an empty space and create a temporary autonomous area – a breach in the city's control – but I also hinder the nonperforming benefits of the rich, I diminish the building's financial value – its invented value, its *petit mort* – to give it real value: inhabitants. I refuse one world – that of ownership on paper and bank figures – and affirm another: that of the ownership by use.

(squatter's anonymous pamphlet, 1999)

These criticisms and the defence of an alternative notion of urban life based on solidarity, self-management, conviviality and creativity helped legitimise the occupations in the eyes of some of the population. This public legitimacy, which allied the squatters with some of the unions and left-wing parties, was indispensable in forging the counter movement needed to withstand repression.

Thus, toward the end of the 1970s, the movement gradually spread throughout the city. The occupations were presented as a means of fighting against speculation and the reduction of housing to a market object. This theme of the fight against speculation helped strengthen political alliances around the squatting movement. During the 1980s, occupations were more and more carefully staged and politically supported.

In the mid-1980s, this power struggle led to a policy shift by the authorities. In 1985 Claude Haegi, a city magistrate belonging to a centre right political party, signed the first 'trust contract' giving squatters the right to use an empty apartment building that belonged to the city. The magistrate's idea – very liberal, all things considered – was to temporarily remedy the lack of housing, and at the same time give more responsibility to the squatters via a contract. This solution was not supposed to cost the state anything. A portion of the squatters, however, refused this institutional solution, seeing it (not without reason) as a form of recuperation that would weaken the occupations' critical momentum. Nevertheless, these same squatters would, to a certain extent, benefit from the policy of relative tolerance[3] established subsequent to the first 'trust contract'. Indeed, the expulsions were gradually suspended (including those from private property and even instances wherein there was no trust contract) with the idea that it was better to put up with the occupation of property wrongfully left empty than to heighten social conflicts through the use of oppressive measures. [The way authorities and society respond to squatting is a key variable for the success of the movement, which in turn depends on the movement's capacity to influence them. In the next two chapters too we can see how across time squatting in England, the Netherlands and New York has been more or less successful and has managed to consolidate to varying degrees as a consequence of different social perceptions, legislation and state regimes, ranging between social democratic, paternalistic and neoliberal.]

This tolerance policy resulted in the proliferation of occupations, with a record number in the mid-1990s (between 150 and 200 spaces occupied at one time, depending on the source and counting method). During this time, a true power struggle was no longer needed to occupy a space; many of the occupations took place discreetly, without public demonstrations of support or even a clear indication of the nature of the occupation (no banners stating immediate demands on the façade or the like). Nonetheless, this period was also marked by more militant and radical occupations – inscribed within a libertarian ideology – where the finger was pointed at both the speculative logic of the real estate market and the need to create environments of self-determination.

> As this society does not offer us the right to live according to our desires and rhythms, we give ourselves permission to take it without asking.
>
> (ManiFeste Apacheria, 1998)

The face of the occupations of the 1990s and early 2000s was therefore multifaceted, like the occupied premises themselves (community houses, large multicoloured buildings, apartment-shelters and so on). This diversity of places allowed many people – and not only militants – to enter squats and even frequent them (they provided bars, theatres, concert halls and so on) on a more or less regular basis, sometimes even going so far as to move into them. Spaces of confrontation, as well as dialogues with authorities and neighbours, led to various learning processes.

Some who initially sought to live in squats simply for financial reasons gradually became militant activists. Others, wary of squatters, gradually discovered that they were ordinary people after all. The authorities, for their part, also learned how to deal with these demanding residents, and conversely, the squatters discovered the virtues of negotiating and learned to deal – critically, of course – with the requirements of building to a common order at the scale of the city (Breviglieri, 2009).

However, as we shall see, the 2000s were marked by the return of a more repressive policy that destroyed the slow learning process and most innovative compromises. Along with the strong-arm occupations resulting from the radicalisation of a faction of the movement in response to the oppression, the 2000s likewise saw the return of a game of alliances surrounding highly publicised occupations.

Above and beyond the different motives and forms of occupation, we still see a shared ideal in this militant tradition of squatting – which was interpreted more or less radically depending on the squat – of an alternative conception of living together based, it has been suggested, on such principles as solidarity and collectivisation, hospitality and conviviality, participation and self-management, and finally of creativity and spontaneity. In some ways, the squatting movement defies all logic – state or market-related – that could potentially impede plans of self-determination of space and lifestyle choice. Squats must therefore be places where these alternative notions of living together are carried out every day in the dynamic of social relationships and the materiality of shared spaces. As we shall see, it is through this material and social embeddedness in daily life of alternative principles of togetherness that squats open up an enacted critique of capitalism.

Another hallmark of the squatting movement is its specific 'repertory' of collective action (Tilly, 1978) embedded in a festive conception of political struggle, which derived partly from the artistic experiments of the 1960s and the 1970s (situationism, living theatre and so on). Thus, actions and events often took on an entertaining air. Among the many examples can be cited the satirical Calvin's Pride demonstration condemning the cold and austere nature of Geneva politics, and a nude parade protesting against expulsions in the 1990s. More entertaining and subversive still were actions such as 50-person impromptu soccer games in large retail stores or in the streets, inspired by the Reclaim the Streets movement of the 1990s and its famous 'critical mass' philosophy ('spontaneous' groupings of a large number of cyclists to occupy the streets). Present-day 'flashmobs' are a depoliticised version of this.

As we can see, occupation does not only concern housing in the narrow sense of the word, but also reclaiming public spaces in general and on a daily basis, removing them from both market logic and a separation of functions which is more or less intolerant of festive expressions and eccentricity.

> The resident should be able to manage not only his home but also his street, where he may want to plant palm trees, raise yaks or make bonfires out of cars.
>
> (anonymous flyer, 1990s)

Installation

Beyond the moment of occupation itself, the real challenge lies in taking possession of the premises and its surroundings to implement the ideals of self-management and community life. Thus, upon entering a building, squatters try to make the space habitable. This starts with urgent solutions (for sleeping, washing, cooking), followed by more specific adjustments which gradually define the burgeoning community's material comfort. It is during this second phase of the installation process that the political plans for collective living (as opposed to more individualistic models) take shape. This entails setting up living spaces that bear the marks of these ideals: spaces that allow for living together on a daily basis. Then do we see the walls that draw clear boundaries between the public and private – so characteristic of rental properties – come down. Former apartments are thus unified to create larger common areas. Doors are removed or left open.

At the heart of these renovations is the 'common room', an essential part of any squat, representing the political ideal of self-management (a meeting space) and conviviality (a shared, festive space). These common areas are often readily open to casual visitors (for relaxing, sleeping and so on). In the wake of such spaces we see the emergence of other spaces emblematic of squatters' ideals, such as 'sleep-ins' (room/dormitory accommodation for people passing through), or other spaces open to the public (underground bars, experimental art galleries, theatres and so on). At the same time, the setting-up also included the delicate task of assigning each person a sleeping place, an intimate space vital to any lasting cohabitation.

These new arrangements – from the most private to the most shared – are in general discussed by all of the occupants. Group meetings are at the heart of squat life, somewhere between the individuals' desires and plans for collective living. In more radical squats, decisions are made not on a majority basis but – following an anarchist inspiration (Graeber, 2004) – unanimously, which involves long, sometimes heated meetings, the idea being not to avoid conflict, but rather to generate it so as to gradually arrive at a consensus.

The installation phase is also a time of jubilation and enthusiasm that results from the basic pleasure of jointly appropriating a living space and setting it up according to people's desires. In surveys on private property, it has been shown that one of the main reasons for wanting to become a home owner is to be able to set up a space as you please (Thalmann and Favarger, 2002). This is one of the fundamental conditions of being able to truly appropriate your own home, above and beyond the formal dimensions of occupancy status.

In fact, there are two key aspects with regard to the right to ownership: security and appropriation. The legislation in Switzerland on the protection of tenancy rights has to some degree extended housing security to tenants. However, this happened at the expense of being able to take control of your home in a meaningful way, with tenants in Geneva hardly daring to paint their walls. Squatters, on the other hand, have incredible freedom in the first regard, but little security.

And thus, in a city where tenants – amounting to 85 per cent of the population – are afraid to so much as stick a nail in the wall, there is something deeply exhilarating about being able to get rid of things, or simply get up and knock down a wall because it clashes with your ideals. With these acts of reappropriation, squatters reinstill a sense of excitement and pride in their living place, and, in consequence, the material possibility of living differently – outside of the norms and rhythms imposed by society.

> It is not every day that we have the chance to live the way we want to, without constraints or the presence of conventions imposed by the system and those holding its reins…Having a space we manage ourselves, where we can do what we want: paint, make music, eat herring, celebrate, laugh, talk, share the fridge, sleep, cry, wash socks, walk barefoot or naked, be ugly or beautiful – it is this, and much more, we are seeking.
>
> (ManiFeste Apacheria, 1990s)

The first months of a squat's life are thus marked by intense physical and emotional investment. Squatting is not an easy task, especially when people occupy a space that has been long abandoned. Another relationship to this new dwelling, based not on the regular payment of rent but rather the effort spent reappropriating it and rendering it habitable, is thus forged. In other words, for squatters, it is a question of working less to earn a salary that, at the end of the day, will only make the landlord richer, and working more to maintain the premises.

> Art. 5: The choice of the Freundler house instead of a ready-to-use squat was intentional. It results from a willingness to invest time, money and energy in the definitive improvement and maintenance of the premises and openness with the adjacent park.
>
> Art. 6: As such, the relationship between inhabitant and habitat is not based on rent.
>
> (The Villa Freundler Convention, proposed to the City of Geneva, 1990s)

In this joint effort, occupants become close and forge lasting ties, demonstrating resourcefulness and creativity in their renovations. DIY is elevated to a veritable art form, contributing (along with recycling) to the daily struggle against an environment perceived as standardised and consumerist. Thus are walls and shutters given colour, an old bathtub lords it over the middle of a room, parking spaces become impromptu gardens, and so on. Gradually, objects and individuals spill over the narrow frames of order which govern the modern city.

But the squat is not only overflow; it is also the framework that has made other ways of living and consuming possible. Throughout the 1990s, the bars, restaurants and workshops set up on squat premises contributed to the development of veritable alternative cultures and economies. Collection systems allowed for the circulation of objects and food. Self-run daycare centres welcomed children of squatters as well as those of their neighbours. People could also drink and dance in the evening for a modest price (often the price is 'open', allowing each consumer to contribute to the extent of their means). They could exhibit or pursue new artistic projects without grants. Certain dance or theatre troupes born in squats have known later success even at the European level (Omar Porras's Théâtre Malandro, for example). The squat network was also the venue for many other supportive and festive events. 'Boulans' for instance – free meals alternately offered by different squats – assembled up to a hundred people at a time. The famous 'raft race' each year still sees the most unusual boats imaginable defying the laws of flotation. Inter-squat soccer tournaments brought squatters from all over Europe together around a football.

> By restoring 5 bd Emile-Jacques-Dalcroze to activity and turning it into housing, we have taken it out of the state of neglect into which speculators have put it, and are giving it new life by living in it, rehousing an evicted day care, setting up a library, and proposing various workshops, talks, screenings and concerts .... These different activities are open to everyone. Spread the word. Our response is one possibility among many, and we encourage everyone to react in his or her own way, collectively and supportively. We, the reappropriators of free living spaces, only 'sponge off' the Geneva that dreams of the money-king, those exploiters who live off the backs of those who work for them, the rich heirs who preach, who'd rather make virtual money with habitable spaces than house real people.
>
> (Occupation of 5 bd Emile-Jacques-Dalcroze, 25 August 2007)

By providing alternative spaces, squats opened a world of possibilities, especially for young and vulnerable populations who suffer the brunt of the market's demands. However, by taking place in the city and offering people a different way of relating to others in a materialistic world, the squat movement simultaneously ran headlong into the established frameworks and norms that govern community life at the city-wide scale, eliciting a variety of responses – from negotiations to evictions.

In this perspective, squatters truly constitute what the French philosopher Rancière calls a 'dissensual subject', that is, a political subject who breaks the consensus of the established order (1998). This dissensual subject is not only a discursive one – who criticises society orally – but one who makes manifest the 'difference of the society to itself' by empirically shaking the 'distribution of the sensible' (ibid.: 251). Indeed, for Rancière, the establishment of a given order is made possible by the 'hierarchic distribution of places and functions' for each person taken into consideration within that specific order. This distributing work – that operates a practical and visible delimitation of the place of each person in the society (a 'distribution of the sensible') – is what he calls a *police* (Rancière, 1998: 112). By physically and symbolically delimiting the right ways to engage in the society, each order inevitably produces a remainder, that is, excluded people and modes of living. The politic ('*la politique*') appears when such an established and reproduced order is challenged and new subjects call for recognition and a place to exist (ibid.: 16). The politic is therefore a call to transform the distribution of the sensible, to organise society differently in order to open it up to the excluded.

The story of the Geneva squatters' movement – and any squatters' movement – can be seen as truly political moment where the 'distribution of the sensible' of the capitalist order and its police are practically challenged. By turning small individual apartments into large collective ones, by opening up illegal bars without schedule and no fixed prices or by hosting illegal migrants, squats and squatters break the various normative settings which allowed the reproduction of a capitalist order based on negative individual autonomy, formal responsibilities and market regulations. Those experiences call for a renewed political work ('*le politique*' in Rancière's term) able to combine the building of a common world (police) and the call for emancipation and equality (politic). In effect, after years of reinvention of the 'distribution of the sensible', Geneva went back in the 1990s to repression, impoverishing the urban order of the city.

Before discussing the repression phase, let me look in a little more detail at the daily life of squats – a daily life that includes not only collective tasks, meetings and parties, but also rest and private routines. It is essential to understand this phase in order to grasp all the difficulty of a political action that is embedded in daily life.

Habitation

As I have emphatically pointed out, squats are places not only of struggle, but also of life. In this perspective, and in order for them to withstand the test of time, they must also make allowances for the individual habits and peculiarities of their inhabitants; in other words, they must allow each person to truly live in the occupied space. In this regard, the squat model could have been borrowed from philosopher Roland Barthes and his ideal of an 'idiorhythmic' community (Barthes, 1977). By this he meant a community wherein each person can live at their own pace. Such a community would diametrically oppose institutions like prisons, army barracks or monasteries, which operate by imposing a common rhythm. Contrarily, the idiorhythmic community must be able to make room for the desires and routines of each person. We find traces of such an ideal in squatter communities, where spontaneity is valued and any system of rules that is too formal arouses suspicion. At the same time, squats are often demanding communities in terms of individual contribution, whether it is maintaining or cleaning the site, making meals or settling financial matters in a joint manner. Here major tensions arise between the militant demands of collective life and each person's own need to dwell.

This need, or rather this 'inclination to dwell' as Marc Breviglieri calls it, refers to the individual's personal experience and how they gradually create a familiar world by appropriating it through personal use (Breviglieri, 2009). This is how each of us, little by little, weaves our routine and familiar world, from which we draw strength to face the outside world. By moving in, the person forges their singularity and pace, and keeps the injunctions of others – and the rules of social life in general – at arm's length.

Therefore, as any current or former squatter or roommate knows, living together (sharing your private world with others) is difficult, even more so if these 'others' are not friends or lovers. The militant context of the squat makes this even harder, as withdrawal in order to 'dwell' often is regarded as an abandonment of the collective project (Breviglieri and Pattaroni, 2005). How, then, do people organise a community at once militant and idiorythmic?

It is interesting to see how, over time, squatters learned to cope with this inclination to dwell. Gradually, walls are re-erected, and the formal privatisation of certain spaces is tolerated. More broadly, certain rules to help measure individual effort and responsibility emerge and are implemented to protect individuals from wearing themselves out by investing too much, as well as recognising their need to withdraw at times.

These changes are sometimes viewed as 'embourgeoisement' from the outside. However, this simplistic critique fails to take into account the challenges of creating a sustainable community that must also cope with these other aspects of our humanity. Experienced squatters understand these challenges and accept with irony their own contradictions as a guarantee of their human wealth. The issue is not to deny these other inclinations or wanting to eliminate personal paradoxes, but rather to find a fragile balance between the militant project and personal comfort, between a friendly, exuberant community and a more settled group. Squatters as such are caught between the need to regulate and institutionalise to ensure that their project is sustainable in the larger order of the city, and the need to carry on the objector tradition, that wellspring of life and upsurge.

Throughout the movement, squatters endeavoured to keep their political project alive and, through different events and activities, rekindle the enthusiasm of the early phases and militant vein. Collective works, the opening of new spaces, acts of protest, the changing of inhabitants, street parties, raft races and soccer tournaments were all opportunities for stimulating debate, and participation helped to maintain the ideal of a friendlier, more involved lifestyle. As we shall see, such moments were important because the movement's institutionalisation was both the guarantee of the survival of its ideals and the cause of its slow death. However, the disappearance of squats in Geneva was mainly the result of a political hardening caused by a major housing crisis and the return of property investment to cities.

Eviction

The last phase of a squat is *evacuation* or *eviction*. The event abruptly reminds squatters of their illegal occupant status, and makes a clean sweep of all efforts to devise innovative compromises. It solves the problems squatters raise by reaffirming the primacy of property and market logics. Out go the question about the limits of ownership and attempts to find new forms of collective housing.

Eviction, however, gives rise to new political and legal issues. Indeed, it is the state exercising the use of force, which must also be legally authorised and can be judged as legitimate or not.

From a legal perspective, many rules define the conditions for expulsion. While we cannot address them here, it is important to note that squatters are protected in their 'possession' of premises, and that it is therefore illegal for a landlord to remove them personally (or by using private security personnel). As people are not permitted to take the law into their own hands, landlords are forced to take legal measures to reclaim their property. For many years – at the instigation of the elected district attorney of Geneva, Bernard Bertossa – legal authorities weighed the benefit of owners recovering property that had been left more or less abandoned against that of maintaining public order. As a result there were no evictions – so as to not incite unruly demonstrations or other 'civil unrest' – so long as the property was destined to remain empty (in other words, there was no approved and funded project to demolish or renovate it). As we have seen, this doctrine allowed for the creation of the policy of relative tolerance that characterised the 1990s. However, this doctrine was more or less abandoned by the next district attorney Daniel Zappelli, who was elected in 2002 and instead instated a 'zero tolerance' policy with regard to squats.

However, debates surrounding the evictions went well beyond the question of their legality – like the occupations themselves – to that of their legitimacy. As such, the forceful evictions from the first squats in Les Grottes (and that of the Empeyta Street squat in 1975 in particular) resulted in large-scale protests against what appeared to be an illegitimate and disproportionate use of state force.

> Following the repressive events, I got involved in the neighbourhood's struggle for survival. There was a desire to share activities, to experience them together.
>
> (an occupant cited in *Collectif d'auteurs*, no. 96, 1979)

Similarly, 30 years later, the evacuation of one the most emblematic squat of Geneva – Rhino –sparked many demonstrations. In between those two repressive periods, evictions were not often as conflictive. Thus, during the 1990s, many evictions – like many occupations – took place quietly, often led by the squat brigade, which directed occupants to new empty spaces. Nonetheless, certain squats violently resisted eviction using barricades, or with squatters physically attaching themselves to the façades of the buildings. Such resistance was the policy of the movement's more militant wing, which continued to refuse to play the institutionalisation game and reduce the notion of squats to simple questions of housing for those in need (who were simply housed elsewhere).

Evictions are not a purely public problem; first and foremost, they concern those who end up in the street. In this respect, it is interesting to note that the diversity of backgrounds, which on the whole had little impact on daily life in the squats, played a significant role during evacuations. In fact, it was often the poorest – both financially and in terms of social networks, as is the case for foreigners (legal or illegal) in particular – who found themselves most greatly affected, whereas residents with strong local ties found temporary or permanent housing (with friends or family, finding a guarantor for a rental unit, and so on) more easily. The eviction phase thus brings us back to the harsh reality of the housing market, marked by crises and essentially governed by private actors looking to make a profit, in which all inhabitants are far from equal.

In this regard, with the virtual disappearance of the squat movement (barely a handful of squats remain in 2013), we can now more accurately measure its role, in both mitigating the impact of the market and real estate speculation on marginal populations, and more generally impacting on the city's social and artistic life. Evictions no longer concerned only squatters – almost all of who had been expelled at this point – but affected vulnerable populations in general. In 2009, 493 people were evicted from their accommodation, and this rose to 559 in 2010. Eviction processes are multiplying today, and at the heart of this process we find both an abusive hike in rent prices and an ever-increasing price per square metre, not only making the idea of tolerance towards squats illusory, but also making it more difficult to build social housing. [To this extent, the analysis of the previous chapter, which focused on Spain, the United Kingdom, Japan and the United States – showing how different processes have led to pretty similar results favouring neoliberal housing policies – can also apply to the case of Geneva and Switzerland.]

The increased pressure on Geneva's real estate market, due to strong demographic growth and the revival of the building market starting at the end of the 1990s (caused in particular by a drop in mortgage rates) most likely also played a key role in the ending of the exceptional tolerance with regard to squats. We see a sharp decrease in their numbers by the beginning of the 2000s (prior even to attorney Daniel Zappelli's election). The repressive policy introduced thereafter only accelerated the movement that the construction market – fuelled by the growth of the city's financial industry and multinationals – had launched. Very schematically, we can say that it was the growth of a 'winning' and 'global' city that bid on a wealthy population and the development of an increasingly luxurious real estate supply, with excessive rents[4] that not only pushed the popular fringes to the margins, but also stifled spaces that were favourable to experimentation and the development of non-market exchanges in the city. Thus began a return to the type of conflict that had ignited the urban struggles of the 1970s, between the city's use and exchange values. Apparently, it is the exchange value that has won out for the moment, with use gradually coming to take on a single expression – that of consumption (of land, culture, leisure and so on).

It must be said, however, that the splitting of the movement between a less militant fringe, which had become dominant during the 1990s, and one which had radicalised during the same period – refusing to compromise with political parties or even unions – played against it. Thus militants found themselves with neither political nor popular support against the repression. Removed from the collective struggle against the disenfranchisement of residents' power over their housing (especially that of tenants), they were unable to make the meaning of their struggle – which gradually appeared marginal and lacking solidarity – heard by the larger population.

Perpetuation

The squatting movement and the urban struggles of which it was born have nevertheless resulted in a number of institutional innovations which bear – however distantly – the marks of the militant principles the occupations defended.

The first which comes to mind is the so-called 'associative' cooperative, like CODHA, which was created by former squat movement activists. These housing cooperatives seek not only to ensure collective property for their members, but also to defend more participative modes of production and management. We find, for example, features such as common rooms (which also serve as meeting rooms – essential for collective management) in buildings built by these cooperatives.

More unusual still and very rare in Geneva are 'associative leases' – negotiated in former squats or occupations with the benefit of a 'trust contract' – which combine the mechanisms of social housing (typically constructed as an individual benefit) with aspirations towards a more collective way of living and self-management of the premises in question (Pattaroni and Togni, 2009). [The case of the house projects presented by Lucrezia Lennert in Box 2.1 is an example of this kind of lease, which became quite popular in Berlin after its squats had to be legalised. It shows how the anticapitalist critique can be perpetuated in other legal forms.] Under this type of lease, residents associations thus maintain an important say with regard to newcomers and building management. This solution offers great promise in terms of rethinking the balance between security and appropriation, as well as the larger issue of social ownership of housing.

Leaving these more institutional paths, we see a willingness to develop alternative lifestyles where control over people's environment and affirmation of a collective dimension in the production and management of daily life start to take precedence.

The choice of caravans as living spaces exemplifies the expansion of the field of possibilities. These caravans were originally nomadic when they first appeared on the lawn of a squat in the early 2000s, following the evacuation of a number of occupied spaces. Faced with the growing scarcity of housing and eager to push the limits of their freedom, some squatters decided to turn to a less-anchored living space, becoming part of a larger European movement toward a voluntary return to more nomadic habitats (of which the German *Wagenburgen* and English travellers were the precursors). Thus they asserted their determination to move away from the dominant models of ownership in our society to explore another relationship to housing and land. A series of migrations triggered by successive expulsions which ensued – affecting no longer squats themselves but rather their location – led these nomads farther and farther away from the downtown area. They were finally allowed to settle on a piece of land that was partly polluted and therefore of no use (or profit) to the host community.

In fact, the strategy of these squatters was more akin to that of colonisers (or American pioneers, who fled to occupy new lands) than a strategy of confrontation where people put up a fight to open up alternative possibilities in the heart of the city. To some extent, it symbolises the abandonment of inner cities to capitalist logic, where earlier urban struggles sought to regain a veritable right of use. This strategy nonetheless gave birth to an unprecedented collective living project, partly on the margins of the capitalist system (at least with regard to how to access and manage housing), which substantially increases self-determination of everyday living conditions. Should we then see them as a few leftover outsiders 'who couldn't let go' – as they are sometimes criticised for being – or the simple creation of a place 'apart' for those who do not want or cannot participate in neoliberal society? Or rather should we see in this an original and subversive exploration of different types of housing and lifestyles that is so characteristic of a post-industrial period? Indeed the themes of nomadism, and mobility more broadly, are at the heart of 'network capitalism' (Boltanski and Chiapello, 1999). New ways of organising production have resulted in a new relationship to territories marked by mobility: the massive increase in commuting, urban sprawl and the collapse of the relevancy of developed areas that structure the well-ordered territory of the Fordist economy (Du Pasquier and Marco, 2009).

In this perspective, caravans are perhaps a response (albeit marginal and provocative), an attempt to reappropriate the fringes of this world of mobilities that is a source both of empowerment and of suffering and unprecedented inequality.

Here we find ourselves facing the paradox of forms of resistance that, in a certain way, are also at the forefront of contemporary change. Similarly, the ideals that fuelled the squat movement (and the critiques of the 1960s before that) have permeated capitalist logic, where there is only a question now of autonomy, creativity and mobility. It is also not surprising that the institutionalisation of squats – starting with the first trust contracts – took place by commending the squatters' 'entrepreneurialism' and 'creativity'. Critiques at the heart of the urban struggles and the squatters' movement have been slowly integrated into political elites and the transformation of public action.

Many other institutional processes were also influenced by the critiques of the 1960s and 1970s. For instance, eco-districts are also the heirs of the social and ecological sensibilities of these movements. As with cooperatives, the institutionalisation of solution in this case led to unprecedented compromises with capitalist logics without, however, questioning them. The ideals of the urban struggle lost some of their subversive nature and edge in this process. What place is there, then, for real subversion? How does not only a discursive but an embedded critique of capitalism – that is, one able to open up real disruptive spaces and political claims – take place (Rancière, 1998)?

In this context, the future hope of militant factions, in which people voluntarily decide to be marginal (like the communities in Tarnac and those elsewhere in Europe) is to fuel the imagination of possibilities and at the same time sustain (through new technologies in particular) active networks of resistance. But it is not merely a retreat. Thus caravan dwellers are also active in Geneva's social scene, running bars at literature festivals or renovating old greenhouses in the heart of the city. By living in caravans, they are able – as was the case in former squats – to spend less time earning money because they do not pay rent. They therefore have more time to spend for collective work and projects. In this regard, the territories of urban struggle may be changing scale, and it is the relationship between living spaces and spaces of resistance that is evolving.

Similarly, within this shift of places of subversion and possibility, self-run communal and community gardening experiments can also be seen as an alternative response – less conventional and more removed from the logic of the market than certain 'organic' labels' – to the desire to promote locally based forms of consumption. [The environmentalist idea of creating these type of urban ecosystems through open-air squatting of abandoned urban spaces – and its broadening into the invention of 'rurban' squats – is a specific part of the squatters' movement's repertoire of issues which is becoming increasingly important and relevant.

This environmental dimension is analysed in Chapter 6 with the cases of New York and Barcelona.] More generally, the occupation of idle land (for vegetable crops and self-built dwelling) is a new strategy that directly questions land policy and, more broadly, the zoning system inherited from the 20th century. By promoting new forms of functional entanglement, these experiences naturally find themselves at the forefront of debates on urbanism. In particular the question of self-construction – of both straw huts and extensions to houses in residential areas – opens new avenues with regard to densification.

The spirit of squats therefore lives on in the exploration of possible alternatives, monitoring the market logic which so often makes more institutionalised projects lose much of their substance. It is always a question of playing against the established order – its distribution of places and functions – creating niches strong enough to accommodate other, more fragile, yet essential possibilities so that a true diversity of lifestyles and social relations can emerge. Will these experiments and the critique implicit therein succeed in gaining political strength, so as to find broader popular support, like in the 1970s and 1980s – the support necessary for undermining dominant forms of organisation and making room for new possibilities? This question is all the more relevant at a time when a relatively simplistic model of urban development is spreading that, day by day, is sandblasting the face of Geneva under the imperatives of international financial logics and policies 'by objectives' (Thévenot, 2013) aimed at creating competition between global cities.

Given these changes, it seems important to keep the memory of past experiences alive and to lend an ear (and a hand) to those to come; these are the conditions needed to maintain imagination of the possibilities and the heterotopias necessary to human life itself. In this regard, we could say that the last phase in the Geneva squat movement was also that of the conquest and invention of a city that, for a few decades, was a little more hospitable to its diverse populations and their ways of living – a city capable of making room for the most offbeat and fragile projects, a city where having no money does not automatically mean being ostracised. What has become of these wastelands, those real and imaginary heterotopias that give city dwellers a chance to dream and experience a better world?

Box 2.1 *Anti-capitalist communes remaining despite legalisation: the case of house projects in Berlin*

Lucrezia Lennert

House projects in Berlin are the legalised spaces which remain from the squatters' movement. Legalisation resulted from an intense period of struggle to defend squatted houses, and for many was the only alternative to eviction. As radical spaces, house projects have clearly compromised on their anti-capitalist politics through entering into the property market, and as such they can no longer claim to be part of a movement which challenges the capitalist commodification of housing. However, within the spaces themselves, forms of self-organised collective life are developed which continue to challenge capitalist economic and social relations. Legalisation, then, allowed for the establishment of an unusually stable radical urban infrastructure which provided spatial continuity for the development of anarchist, autonomous, feminist, anti-fascist, queer and other subversive forms of politics.

The fact that house projects remain spaces of radical political organising is made clear by the state repression they continuously face in the form of raids, evictions and police terrorising of inhabitants. One example is the house project Liebig 14 whose residents were evicted in February 2011 by several thousand police after it had existed for over 20 years as a collective living and autonomous cultural project. The threat of eviction faced by house projects in Berlin also demonstrates that even with legalisation, a collective house is not safe from the state forces which seek to destroy spaces of resistance and protect the sanctity of property ownership.

We can critically discern the extent to which a space is radical despite being legalised by asking to what extent the space is a commune: that is, a space of collective life in which the value form has no bearing.* House projects challenge capitalist relations through for example organizing non-commercial cultural events and dinners on a pay-as-you-can basis. House projects also practise organising the collective and the space of the building on a communal basis: the collective has a communal meeting and living room, and people can pass freely through the whole house. In many houses the rent of those who cannot afford to pay is supported by the rest of the collective. The communal structure of the houses allows for children to be raised by many people and thus break with traditional family unit structures. The space therefore remains radical to the extent to which life in the house and the materiality of the building is not privatised but remains an anti-commercial collective project in which resources, ideas and friendships are shared.

Whether a certain radicalism can survive legalisation therefore depends on the strength and coherence of the movement, and it necessitates that the members of a collective living together continue to develop ideas and practices which challenge capitalist logic.

* [There are places that, despite being squats, are not interested in developing alternative practices such as communal living, and also other places, not necessarily different from these, that use squatting as a mean to achieve better housing conditions, in the sense that they aim to obtain institutional support and eventually a legal status. The intersection of the diametrically opposed positions of anti-capitalist squatters interested in communal lifestyles and people oppressed by the neoliberal hegemony seeking help for better housing can be understood as an opportunity to set up a counter-hegemonic housing struggle, as envisaged in Chapter 1, and is also seen in the conflict between radical squatters and housing right activists such as Jeudi Noir in Paris, discussed in Chapter 5. A more detailed understanding of the Berlin case – and in particular of the dilemma between legalisation and the survival of radical spaces – is developed in Chapter 8.]

Notes

1   By 1800, the term 'to squat' was used to describe the activity of American pioneers who settled the land without any legal title (Péchu, 2010). It was only at the turn of the 20th century that the word was used to refer to the illegal occupation of a building. In French, the use of the masculine noun 'squat' appears only in the 1970s.

2   A more refined categorisation of the various logics of squatting can be found in Pruijt (2013).

3   This tolerance was relative, because even though they were not evicted, squatters without a contract of trust could still be punished. At the end of the 1990s in particular, squatters were convicted of crimes related to their residence and given various sentences, including prison terms.

4   I could cite many examples, but the most impressive is probably the 1 Gevray project to replace the former Hotel California, which was squatted and then used as student housing for two years, with luxury apartments sold for more

than CHF2 million for three rooms (more than CHF20,000 per square metre). Similarly, whereas a four-room apartment was rented for CHF1,000–1,500 four years ago, the same space now goes for CHF2,000–2,500. I recently saw an ad for a 96 square metre apartment for CHF5,000 a month on rue des Bains, which is emblematic of the gentrification of the Jonction neighbourhood.

References

Barthes, R. (1977) *Comment vivre ensemble* [*How to Live Together*], Lectures at the Collège de France.

Boltanski, L. and Chiapello, E. (1999) *Le nouvel esprit du capitalisme* [*The New Spirit of Capitalism*]. Paris: Gallimard.

Breviglieri, M. (2009) 'Les habitations d'un genre nouveau. Le squat urbain et la possibilité du "conflit négocié" sur la qualité de vie' ['New forms of habitation: urban squats and the possibility of "negotiated conflict" for the quality of life'], in L. Pattaroni, A. Rabinovich and V. Kaufmann (eds), *Habitat en devenir* [*The Habitat of the Future*]. Lausanne, Switzerland: Presses polytechniques et universitaires romandes.

Breviglieri, M. and Pattaroni, L. (2005) 'Le souci de propriété. Vie privée et déclin du militantisme dans un squat genevois' ['The hope of propriety: private life and the decline of militantism in a Genevan squat'] in A. Morel (ed.), *La société des voisins* [*The Society of Neighbours*]. Paris: Editions de la Maison des sciences de l'homme (Ethnologie de la France).

Du Pasquier, J. N. and Marco, D. (2009) *Le rapport territorial: essai de définition* [*Territorial Awareness: An Attempt at Definition*]. Paris: 3e forum de la régulation.

Foucault, M. (2009) *Le corps utopique suivi de Les hétérotopie* [*The Utopian Body Followed by the Heterotopia*]. Paris: Nouvelles Editions Lignes.

Graeber, D. (2004) *Fragments of an Anarchist Anthropology*. Chicago, Ill.: Prickly Paradigm Press.

Gros, D. (1987) *Dissidents du quotidien. La scène alternative genevoise* [*Everyday Dissidents: The Alternative Scene in Geneva*]. Lausanne, Switzerland: Ed. d'En Bas.

Pattaroni, L. (2007) 'La ville plurielle: quand les squatters ébranlent l'ordre urbain' ['The plural city: when squatters affect the urban order'], in M. Bassand, V. Kaufmann and D. Joye (eds), *Enjeux de la sociologie urbaine* [*Issues in Urban Sociology*]. Lausanne, Switzerland: Presses polytechniques et universitaires romandes.

Pattaroni, L. and Togni, L. (2009) 'Logement, autonomie et justice. du bail associatif et de quelques autres compromis en matière de logement social à Genève' ['Housing, autonomy and justice: associative leases and various other arrangements regarding social housing in Geneva'] in L. Pattaroni, V. Kaufmann and A. Rabinovich (eds), *Habitat en devenir: enjeux politiques, sociaux et territoriaux du logement en Suisse* [*The Habitat of the Future: Political, Social and Territorial Issues of Housing in Switzerland*]. Lausanne, Switzerland: PPUR.

Péchu, C. (2010) *Les squats [Squats]*. Paris: Les Presses de Sciences Po.

Pruijt, H. (2013) 'The logic of urban squatting', *International Journal of Urban and Regional Research* 37(1), 19–45.

Rancière, J. (1998) *Aux bords du politique [On the Edge of Politics]*. Paris: Edition La Fabrique.

Rossiaud, J. (2004) 'Le mouvement squat à Genève' ['The squatters' movement in Geneva'] in F. Ruegg (ed.), *La fabrique des cultures, Genève 1968–2000 [The Factory of Cultures: Geneva 1968–2000]* and previously in *Equinoxe* 24 (autumn 2004).

Thalmann, P. and Favarger, P. (eds) (2002) *Locataire ou propriétaire? Enjeux et mythes de l'accession à la propriété en Suisse [Tenant or Owner? Issues and Myths of Access to Property in Switzerland]*. Lausanne, Switzerland: Presses polytechniques et universitaires romandes.

Thévenot, L. (2013) 'Autorités à l'épreuve de la critique. Jusqu'aux oppressions du gouvernement par l'objectif' ['Authorities under the test of criticism up to the oppression of the government by the objective'], in B. Frère (ed.), *Quel présent pour la critique sociale? [What is the State of Social Critique?]*. Paris: Desclée de Brouwer.

Tilly, C. (1978) *From Mobilization to Revolution*. Reading, Mass.: Addison-Wesley.

3

The Right to Decent Housing and a Whole Lot More Besides: Examining the Modern English Squatters' Movement

E. T. C. Dee

Introduction

This chapter argues that squatting as a political tool began in England in its modern form with housing need, and quickly branched into other areas of protest, which continue to this day, with the right to decent housing remaining as a fundamental driving force. It focuses on political squatting for several reasons. Private residential squatting is of course much more common, but because of its underground nature it is almost impossible to track. Political squatting is open about its intentions as activism for social change and thus is easier to study. And paradoxically the political squatting movement, a vibrant social movement of over 40 years' standing, has been little theorised.

I concentrate on two important time frames: first the late 1960s and early 1970s, when the modern squatting movement began, and second the contemporary era (the late 2000s and early 2010s), when squatting has been criminalised in residential buildings and hence is ostensibly at an endpoint. Attempts were made to criminalise squatting previously in the late 1970s and mid-1990s, but for reasons of space I can only refer to those periods briefly (although these initiatives do in themselves indicate the continuance of squatting as a movement). I focus chiefly on Brighton and London, two places where the squatters' movement has existed and persisted since the late 1960s, perhaps in ebbs and flows, yet with a collective heritage (particularly in the Needle Collective). While there are land occupations and travellers living in Brighton and London (and the history of New Age travellers needs to be documented), I do not have space to cover them here. As we shall see, by far the largest number of squatters has always been in London. Brighton is included as a point of comparison, and many other UK metropolitan areas could also be studied, such as Bristol, Leeds and Manchester.

However, it is worth mentioning that statistics on numbers of squatters are few and far between. It is also worth noting that research on the squatters' movement in London is sadly deficient compared with work on other major European cities such as Amsterdam, Berlin and Copenhagen, which all also saw large political squatting movements in the 1970s (this is not to ignore the useful sources that do exist, such as Platt, 1999; Reeve, 2005, 2009; Wates, 1976, 1984; Wates and Wolmar, 1980). This chapter aims to contribute further to the beginnings of an analysis of the English squatters' movement. That squatting can be considered a social movement is becoming an increasingly uncontroversial notion, as this book itself indicates (see also Martinez, 2012; Mudu, 2004; Owens, 2009; Reeve, 2009).

My review of squatting in Brighton and London looks first at the beginnings of the modern wave, then moves forward into the present day.

The Beginnings of a Movement – London

The modern squatting movement started in the England in the late 1960s, in the midst of a severe housing crisis. In certain districts of London, slum housing was the norm and the arrangement of temporary accommodation for homeless families was a shambles, while many council-owned properties stood empty, awaiting demolition or even worse, simply stuck in bureaucratic limbo.

Cathy Come Home, a BBC film directed by Ken Loach and designed to highlight the problems experienced by many homeless people, was first shown in 1966 and caused questions to be asked in Parliament. It was subsequently shown on national television twice more, and this led directly to the foundation of Crisis (a homelessness charity) in 1967.

For Ron Bailey and other people working on tenancy rights and challenging recalcitrant local council policies with painfully little visible improvement to be seen, the possibility of squatting empty houses quickly became a more and more attractive option in order to break the deadlock. As Bailey writes in *The Squatters*, 'the immediate aim was of course, simply the rehousing of families from hostels or slums by means of squatting' (1973: 34). Although his book was written after the fact and nothing was stated at the time, his explanation of the further aims of the group is still worth quoting in full:

> Obviously we hoped that our action would spark off a squatting campaign on a mass scale, and that homeless people and slum dwellers would be inspired to squat in large numbers by small but successful actions. But the main purpose of the movement was even wider than this – we hoped to start an all-out attack on the housing authorities, with ordinary people taking action for themselves. Finally, and in close conjunction with this, we saw our campaign as having a radicalising effect on existing movements in the housing field – tenants associations, action committees, community project groups, etc. If these could be radicalised and linked together then we really would have achieved something.
>
> (Bailey, 1973: 34)

Thus, after some symbolic actions, the squatters began to occupy buildings in the borough of Redbridge in north-east London, which included the districts of Ilford, Redbridge and Wanstead. Bailey charts the legal steps used to keep the local councils from regaining possession, and also recounts the resistance employed against bailiffs. Some evictions were successfully prevented, but two of the most notorious incidents occurred on Monday 21 April 1969. The events of this day are not necessarily more meaningful than others but can be taken as emblematic of the struggle as a whole. The Beresford family, living at 18 Grosvenor Road in Redbridge, were evicted with their seven children in the early morning. They had not been presented with any legal documentation and indeed had not even been asked to leave before bailiffs and police broke into the house. These events were repeated at 43 Cleveland Road in Redbridge, where bailiffs smashed their way in and broke the jaw of a member of the London Squatters Campaign, David Jenkins. The family occupying the house, the Flemings, asked whether the bailiffs had a court order and were told, 'Are these your children? Keep your mouth shut if you know what's good for you and your family.' The family were evicted, all their furniture broken up and the house rendered uninhabitable.

However, this short-term defeat was miraculously converted into a long-term victory which contributed to the establishment of the 'right to squat' (that is to say, the actual pragmatic possibility as opposed to the legal justifications which were then being tested), when the London Squatters Campaign produced a pamphlet about the events of 21 April. As a direct result, an investigative journalist from the *Sunday Times* got involved and a television show, *Thames Today*, interviewed the families and David Jenkins (whose jaw had been wired up). The journalist was able to find out the name of the company of bailiffs, Southern Provincial Investigations (run by Barrie Quartermain). The squatters were then able to launch a prosecution against the bailiffs, and because of this legal action, plus a chain of other equally important squatting actions which involved more violent confrontations and mainly successful resistance to eviction, first Redbridge and then other local councils became reluctant to use violent methods in evictions. Two factors were key here for the squatters, public support and sympathetic mainstream media coverage.

From initial actions housing homeless families, squatting spread like wildfire. The London Squatters Campaign soon had to add 'East' to its name to distinguish itself from other London squatting groups, and later All London Squatters met as an umbrella organisation designed to allow the various groups to communicate. Adrian Franklin (1984: 16) gives figures of 1,000 licensed squats and 1,000 unlicensed in 1971, rising to 3,000 licensed and 35,000 unlicensed in 1974, and then exploding to 5,000 licensed and 48,000 unlicensed in 1975–6. In *Squatting: The Real Story*, Steve Platt gives an estimate of 40–50,000 squatters in the mid-1970s in the United Kingdom, mainly in London and also in Bristol, Portsmouth, Brighton, Swansea, Cambridge and Leicester (in Wates and Wolmar, 1980: 40).

At these numbers, squatters were of course bound to affect the society that they were part of; indeed it would be surprising if they had not. Franklin observes that 'we have to try to understand why some 30,000 people per year decided to live in squats'[1] (1984: 19). It seems clear from the literature that housing need was a principal driver for squatting, and once that was satisfied, squatters would pursue political, cultural and social aims (references for the United Kingdom are Bailey, 1973; Dee, 2012; Needle Collective, 2014; Platt, 1999; Reeve, 2005, 2009; Wates, 1976, 1984; Wates and Wolmar, 1980; for other countries see Martinez, 2012; Mudu, 2004; Owens, 2009; Pruijt, 2004). Two examples of later political interventions are the Centre Point occupation and the Tolmers Square resistance, both of which I touch on briefly below. Again, while these are both famous events, I want to make it clear that they are mentioned as representative of the movement, rather than being the only high points. Some other sites of struggle that are also representative were those at Elgin Avenue, Frestonia, Grosvenor Road, Prince of Wales Crescent, St. Agnes Place and Villa Road.

Centre Point was a 32-floor office building in central London at the crossroads of Tottenham Court Road and Oxford Street. Notoriously, it had been left empty since its construction was finished in 1966, since the owner was engaged in speculation and waiting for one tenant to take on the whole block. In a meticulously planned action, squatters occupied the building in January 1974 in order to highlight the crisis of homelessness in the capital. The action lasted three days, and opinion was ultimately split over whether the squatters should have remained barricaded in the building or not. In any event attention had been drawn to the issue.[2]

Buildings in Tolmers Square and its surroundings, also in central London, were largely squatted from 1973 until 1979.[3] Property developers intended to demolish a 12 acre area to make way for bland commercial offices, but were successfully resisted by the squatters, who reinvigorated a campaign against gentrification and speculation which linked tenants, community groups and political parties, with the ultimate support of Camden Council (Wates, 1976). Here we can see squatters taking action to house themselves, while at the same time battling to preserve an architecturally valuable square:

> Demolitions and threats to Georgian Bloomsbury and to Tolmers Square in Euston (the 'locus classicus of London's intellectual squatting movement'), succeeded anew in drawing public attention to the plight of the squares, and precipitated the initial stirrings of the movement for their preservation.
> (Longstaffe-Gowan, 2012: 270)

The fight over development had begun long before the squatters became involved, but local resistance had been worn down until the fresh energy arrived.[4] Nick Wates, one of the squatters, wrote that 'It was only by taking direct action that anyone could intervene. By occupying empty buildings, squatters were able to halt the decline, revive the community and revive leadership in the struggle against the developers' (Wates, 1976). All the squatters were eventually evicted and the square was partially demolished, yet as Wates comments in a later article:

> If it had not been for the campaigning, the office block would have been almost 3 times as large, there would have been far less and/or lower quality housing, many of the small streets with a wide range of thriving businesses would have been completely flattened and replaced with slabs of housing.
> (Wates, 1984: 1)

In terms of numbers the squatters' movement peaked in the 1980s, when many squats were legalised or formed into housing cooperatives. In following years, squatting as a social movement declined in force yet persisted in influence. Both the legal and pragmatic right to squat had been held almost up until the present day: squatting in residential buildings was criminalised on 1 September 2012. As Aufheben record:

By the mid 1980s, virtually every town in England and Wales had its squats
.... This scene was particularly well organized, and more politicized, in the
cities. On Bristol's Cheltenham Road, the Demolition Ballroom, Demolition
Diner, and Full Marx book shop provided a valuable organizational focus,
with the activities of the squatted venue and cafe supplemented by the
information and contact address of the lefty book shop. [In South London,]
Brixton squatters not only had their own squatted cafes, crèches and book
shop, but also Crowbar, their own Class War style squatting oriented paper.
Strong links were forged with the squatting movement on the continent,
particularly Germany, and draft dodgers from Italy were regularly
encountered. And with direct communication supplemented by the then
fortnightly Black Flag, a couple of phone calls and a short article could
mobilize numbers in solidarity with other struggles.

(Aufheben, 1995)

Tony Mahony was another member of the London Squatters Campaign.
Interviewed at the time by the Irish current affairs magazine *Nusight*,
Mahony stated that he could only talk of what he knew, namely struggles
in London, and formulated these particular struggles as 'an attempt
through direct action by homeless people to achieve their right to a decent
roof over their heads' (1969). He added that 'in England the groups are
local and autonomous which means there is no central strategy or single
ideology' (Mahony, 1969).

Looking at these events from today's vantage point, when squatters are
demonised and squatting in residential buildings has been criminalised, it
is fascinating to consider why the squatters were supported by the general
public. At least three reasons explain this. First, in a time of austerity,
people still remembered the post-war squatters occupying army camps in
1946 to provide housing for themselves, and respected the 'do it yourself'
attitude of squatters renovating derelict houses. Second, memories of
the Rachman scandal[5] were still fresh and slum landlords were generally
disliked. Third, and perhaps most importantly, the growing scandal of
homelessness and the vast amount of empty council properties gave a clear
moral justification to squatters who occupied houses and repaired them.

Mahony's reference to a 'roof over their heads' is an oft-repeated phrase
in the contemporary literature of the squatters themselves. Kesia Reeve
describes the UK squatters' movement as 'the embodiment of all that
the social movements of the 1960s and 1970s were said to be' while also
pointing out that it effectively refined the notion of a new social movement,
in that squatters showed willingness to compromise (sometimes engaging
in negotiation to legalise projects, for example) and wanted to satisfy their
housing need as well as working towards cultural or political aims (2009:

15). Crucially, Reeve sees the squatters' movement as also a 'movement of the materially disadvantaged, seeking to achieve social welfare goals in a context of housing need' (2009: 19).

On a crude reading of the evidence supplied so far, this might suggest that the squatters' movement was simply a combination of middle-class activists 'seeking autonomy and cultural expression' and working class people who 'wanted little more than somewhere to live', yet this is to ignore the complexities of the squatters' movement, in which people worked towards combined goals, as illustrated by the Tolmers Square example (Reeve, 2009). In order to explore this point further, let us look at the case of Brighton in the 1970s.

The Beginnings of a Movement – Brighton

Bailey states that 'outside London the longest and most determined squatting campaign took place in Brighton' (1973: 124). At this time Brighton had a large working-class population and terrible housing conditions, with slum landlords charging high rents and entire streets left derelict. A group called the Brighton Rents Project had been set up to campaign for tenants' rights. It was 'an alliance of socialists, Labour Party supporters and housing militants of all kinds' (Bailey, 1973: 125). Its first occupation was a token day-long squat of two council-owned properties at North Place on 10 May 1969. Six days later, the same houses were again occupied in order to prevent their demolition to make way for a car park. Following this success, the Project picketed a Brighton Council meeting on 22 May and attempted to deliver a petition of 2,000 signatures displaying 'public worry and concern about housing problems' (Platt, in Wates and Wolmar, 1980: 26). The mayor stopped the meeting and invited the police to clear the Town Hall, which resulted in 11 arrests. Clearly, the nascent squatters' movement was making an impact.

A Brighton squatters group was forming out of the May Day Manifesto group of socialists, young socialists, international socialists, anarchists and communists (some but not all of them students). A two-part article published by an anonymous author in issues 18 and 19 of the alternative newspaper the *Brighton Voice* recorded that group campaigned on homelessness, surveying rented accommodation, keeping lists of empty houses and supporting rent registration by tenants. Inspired by the success of the North Place actions, the Rents Project and its May Day associates decided to squat two empty council-owned properties on Terminus Road, on 14 June. The council quickly took them to court on 2 July and won possession after 28 days. However, in the meantime another four families had squatted houses on Terminus Road and the adjacent Railway Road. Before the council moved to evict any of the families, on 19 July the Project moved all six families to a row of empty houses at Wykeham Terrace, which had once housed army married couples (there is a resonance here with the waves of squatting following both world wars, when the Vigilantes group took action to house returning servicemen and their families). The houses were due to be auctioned off on 23 July, but the sale was cancelled and in August more families moved in, with other buildings owned by the council on the same block also being squatted.

Following the adverse publicity incurred at Redbridge and other places in London, Brighton Council was presumably reluctant to evict the squatters by force, but was handed a gift when some squatters from Wykeham Terrace were arrested for the bombing of the nearby Army Recruitment Office on 19 August. This action is listed on the *Angry Brigade Chronology* (it is the only Brighton event listed over the course of its four-year campaign) but is also alleged to have been committed by an undercover agent, later named in the *Voice* as Steven Prior (*Angry Brigade Chronology*, 1985; *Brighton Voice*, issue 19). Whatever the truth of the matter, it was a disaster for the squatters, and ructions quickly appeared among the broad coalition of varied political hues in the Rents Project. Three people were later jailed and all the families were evicted by court order in November 1969.

These initial events had put the option of squatting back on the political agenda, but public actions in subsequent years appear to have dropped off with the backlash over the Wykeham Terrace arrests. (Of course it is impossible to state what was occurring with private residential squats.) Moving into the 1970s, Steve Platt records in his contribution to *Squatting: The Real Story* that 'in November 1971 the Cyrenians, a charity for the single homeless which had become exasperated with Brighton Council, squatted three houses' (in Wates and Wolmar, 1980: 32).

The second issue (April 1973) of the *Brighton Voice* stated that the Mighell Street Commune was attempting to legalise a squat with the council, but its eventual fate was not recorded. It also noted that Eugenia Griffin squatted in 1973 after becoming fed up with waiting for a council house. At that time, there were 1,200 people on the housing waiting list and 2,000 empty properties; squatting had spread to nearby towns such as Newhaven and Lewes. The battles which would establish the right to squat and the significance of squatters as actors in society were being fought, just as they had been in London slightly earlier.

By 1974, the number of empty properties in Brighton was estimated at

3,000 (*Brighton Voice*, issue 13). The *Voice* reported that three people from South Avenue in Queens Park were evicted without a court order (Feb/March 1974). The same issue also recorded that squatters on Vere Road had been violently evicted by Nicholas van Hoogstraten. The notorious van Hoogstraten was the epitome of an uncaring landlord, who regularly sent thugs to intimidate tenants and attack squats. He was later imprisoned for authorising a grenade attack on an associate, and linked to the murder of Mohammed Raja in 1999.[6] Van Hoogstraten was convicted over the Vere Road incident and fined £2,000 (*Brighton Voice*, issue 20).

Frustrated at the inability of the council to house them despite the number of empty properties, the Flynn family (parents and four children) took action and squatted 32 Buller Road. They then squatted at Terminus Road, where a possession order was granted to the council and they successfully resisted eviction on 31 May. The Flynns were later evicted, but the action was claimed as a victory since Terminus Road was then renovated and the Flynns were finally housed by the council in Gloucester Road. At this time, the Hotel Aquarius was squatted by a group of 30 young people, including students. These squatters later went on to win licensed status for squats, where they lived for several years on brokered 'no rent' deals for derelict properties which they fixed up and maintained.

By 1975, an article in the *Voice* stated that 'the squatting movement has hit Brighton and this time it's here in a really big way' (issue 23). The Brighton and Hove Squatters Association was set up with two objectives – to provide instant accommodation for homeless people in Brighton and to publicise the property/housing situation. However, as more and more squats were opened, in September 1975, a crucial contestation occurred. Squatters at 2 Temple Gardens resisted six attempts at illegal eviction before a court order for possession was granted. In the subsequent eviction, three squatters were arrested for allegedly assaulting an unauthorised bailiff, who went to hospital, where he claimed he had been given stitches to close a wound, while the doctor who treated him said he had applied a sticking plaster. The owner, a Rolls-Royce driving millionaire called Joseph Norton, had arrived with a group of thugs and assaulted the residents of the squat (seven adults and two children). The *Voice* opined that 'as the week long trial dragged on it became obvious that the affair of 2 Temple Gardens was a side issue and that the men were really standing trial for being squatters' (issue 29). The three men (John Jordan, Paul Hayward and Peter McCabe) were each given sentences of six months suspended for two years and fined £25 or £50, despite another person, Tony Greenstein, standing up in court and admitting that it was he who had struck the thug in self-defence.

Three men had been found guilty, but this flashpoint served as an indication that squatters were now prepared to resist militantly. In addition to housing need, another motivation was emerging: the political will to occupy buildings simply because they were empty. As an anonymous article in the *Voice* stated:

> Of course squatting is an attack on private property: it should be. Not an attack on the houses themselves or a destruction of walls, windows or floors, but a principled attack on the iron law of property which rules our society, making it lawful for some people to have two, three or twenty houses and others to have none at all. It may be the law but it is not justice. squatting is one way of bringing a little bit of justice into this ruthless society. MORE PEOPLE SHOULD SQUAT.
>
> (*Brighton Voice,* issue 29, emphasis in original)

This new militancy, allied to the prior victories of the London Squatters Campaign, meant that the right to squat in Brighton had now been established. Legal means had been found to support squatters prepared to face up to the illegal tactics of bailiffs.

As with the case of London, the diverse squatters' movement had formed out of various needs, primarily for housing. The availability of empty property, coupled with the willingness of people to occupy it, had created fertile conditions for this movement to form. And it continued to grow, so much so that on the national scale, the criminalisation of squatting soon became an issue. Indeed, in 1976 a motion by Brighton Council calling on the government to criminalise squatting was passed by 39 votes to 12. The Campaign Against the Criminal Trespass Law fought an ultimately successful struggle to protect squatters rights, although the Criminal Law Act 1977 did introduce some changes in the law. At this time, the *Voice* quoted Colin Ward as estimating that the number of squatters in the United Kingdom was between 40,000 and 50,000, the same figure as Platt gave (*Brighton Voice,* issue 36; Platt in Wates and Wolmar, 1980: 40).

By the mid-1970s, squatters in Brighton had established the right to squat. They had highlighted the terrible conditions of many rented properties, they had intervened to house people failed by the council, they had won licensed squats and they had housed themselves rent-free, providing the possibility for them to pursue other interests instead of working to pay a high rent. The squatters formed a diverse movement of people with different class backgrounds, different from but with similarities in trajectory to the movement in London.

It is appropriate to end this brief examination of the beginning of the modern English squatters' movement with two quite similar quotations. The first is from Michael Elbro (Brighton Council's new housing manager), in 1978:

> I think that squatting is a symptom of the problem, it's not a problem in itself, it is only so because of the laws of our land. As squatting becomes more vociferous then we need to sit up and think that there's a lot wrong with the housing situation as it is.
>
> (*Brighton Voice*, issue 44)

The second is from an undated communique from the Elgin Avenue squatters in London:

> Squatting is not a 'problem' the problem is the housing crisis. Council and Government should be forced to provide decent housing for ALL.
>
> (Elgin Avenue Squatter, nd, emphasis in original)

Recent Events – Brighton

Moving into the present day, I would contend that political squatting continues to be a social movement affecting social and urban policies. In Brighton, not everyone feels this way. Councillor Maria Caulfield, the Cabinet member for housing for Brighton Council, commented in a letter to the *Argus* (a local tabloid newspaper) that 'Unfortunately, the romantic notion of the squatter who inhabits a property that would otherwise stand around empty, even makes improvements to the property and leaves for the next empty home without costing anyone anything, has long since disappeared' (2010).

Others disagree. Tony Greenstein, himself a squatter at the Aquarius Hotel in the early 1970s and subsequently resident at a licensed squat on Landsdowne Place in Hove (as well as a veteran of the Temple Gardens court case mentioned earlier), declared in a more recent *Argus* article that 'The housing crisis today is twice as bad. There is a need, and there are a large number of available properties' (quoted in B. Parsons, 2012). Also in this article, entitled 'Pressure mounting for licensed squats,' SNOB(AHA), or the Squatters Network of Brighton (And Hove Actually), the latest incarnation of a political mouthpiece for local squatters (formed to resist evictions, to aid coordination among squatters and to respond to inaccurate media stories about squatting), stated that 'To us, it seems morally wrong to leave properties empty and unused .... So here's our suggestion – the squatters stay on short term leases, maintaining the building through use. Then they leave when the building really is going to be demolished or redeveloped.'

The SNOB(AHA) statement referenced a Freedom of Information request which showed that in the previous year, the council had spent £161,000 in securing empty properties (in other words, employing companies such as Sitex Orbis to close off houses with metal sheeting and alarm systems, in order to discourage squatters and vandals). This figure did not include other costs incurred by leaving properties empty, such as renovation work and legal fees to evict squatters.

The squatters group has applied pressure on the council (which has a minority Green Party administration) to set up licensed squats along the same lines as those brokered in the 1970s, but observed that Green councillors, while sympathetic to squatting, were too afraid of a right-wing backlash led by local Conservative Members of Parliament such as Mike Weatherley (Hove) and Simon Kirby (Kemptown) to engage seriously with the idea. In email correspondence the squatters told me that they have a list of council-owned properties that have been left empty for years and often squatted, such as Brookmead on Albion Street, a house on Ditchling Road and two houses on Preston Road. Ironically, all of these properties had been used previously as temporary housing by the council (email from SNOB(AHA)).[7]

A success story of sorts for the squatters was Ainsworth House, another council-owned building previously used as sheltered housing, which had been left empty for three years while awaiting development. It was occupied by squatters in November 2011, who then resisted attempts at eviction before Christmas. The occupiers left peacefully in January, and work began to demolish the building and build eco-friendly flats (the first council housing to be built in Brighton for 30 years). Despite a dominant narrative in the local media which declared that the squatters had delayed the renovations, it appears that the occupation of the building had actually brought a forgotten project back onto the political agenda and had encouraged the local council to press forward with plans to work on it. When the building was first occupied, Stuart Gover, vice-chairman of the Brighton City Assembly, stated, 'It's been an open invitation for squatters for years. The Greens are simply not doing what they have committed to do .... They are showing no interest in pursuing the build at all' (quoted in Gardner, 2011).

Through its website and communications with the local and mainstream press, SNOB(AHA) has also worked to counter assertions by Mike Weatherley (a proponent of the criminalisation of squatting) that squatters are middle-class lifestylists, 'talented, web-savvy, legally-minded' and that there was no link 'whatsoever between the genuine homeless of my constituency – such as the rough sleepers on Church Road – and a typical squatter' (2012). In early 2012, squatters took action in response to a homeless shelter being shut down, and opened up a squat as the Autonomous Homeless Shelter. In its year-long lifespan it housed in the region of 60 individuals, giving a roof over their heads to those rough sleepers who wanted one, and allowing some of them, for whom the drug and alcohol-free space provided an address and a respite from the street, to gain temporary accommodation arrangements from the council.

Most damaging of all perhaps for Mike Weatherley was an article published by the activist newsletter *SchNews* (published weekly since its beginnings at the Courthouse squat in 1994), which sought to contest his statement, made on *BBC Newsnight*, that homelessness charities supported him in his pledge to criminalise squatting. Since all major homelessness charities (such as Shelter, Crisis and St Mungo's) had already made clear their opposition to the proposals, a *SchNews* journalist called Weatherley's office to enquire which groups he had been referring to, and was told that Off the Fence, a local charity based in Hove, supported Weatherley. However, the journalist then called Off the Fence and spoke to its managing director, Paul Young, who told him:

> Mike Weatherley has never talked to me or the Trustees about squatting. One million empty houses in the UK is criminal. Anyone saying that Off the Fence's position is to criminalise squatting would be wrong. ... In regards to squatting, the only criminal element is properties that are left empty, while people are freezing to death on the streets of this City.
>
> (*SchNews*, 2011)

Political squatting in Brighton still clearly focuses on housing need, but also acts as a means of protest regarding other issues in addition to protesting against criminalisation. [Hans Pruijt in Chapter 4 gives further evidence of a very similar role that Amsterdam political squatters played to stop city development plans.] For example, new supermarket developments are often resisted through site occupations as part of community struggles against the large supermarket chains such as Tesco, Sainsbury and Lidl. I list some of the occupations below.

In 2002, a May Day party followed by the Harvest Forestry squat on land below the station catalysed protests against the building of a Sainsbury supermarket and yuppie flats on land that had previously been owned by National Rail.

The Lewes Road Community Garden existed for just over a year (May

2009 until June 2010) before being evicted. Local residents had occupied a derelict lot previously used as a petrol station and put in various types of raised bed in order to grow vegetables and flowers. When eviction proceedings began and it became clear that developers wanted to build flats with a Tesco Metro supermarket on the ground floor, the users of the popular garden became even more keen to defend it, seeing off bailiffs and bulldozers on more than one occasion, until legal threats against named individuals led to the garden being relinquished.[8]

More recently, in 2011, the Sabotaj squat took occupation of a building at the Old Steine in central Brighton, where a local fruit and vegetable shop (Taj) had gone into receivership and the Sainsbury supermarket chain had taken on the lease. At a quickly called meeting, 100 people met in the former shop to discuss how to use the building. It became a centre for opposition to the 'clone town' effect in Brighton, in which all but identical shops owned by large companies dominate high streets and squeeze out independent retailers. A petition of 1,400 names was presented to the council urging it to 'keep Brighton unique', and the alcohol licence for the supermarket was refused. Local Green councillors were regular visitors to the occupation, and indeed one was even able to take action to prevent the police completing an illegal eviction, since he was on the board of the Sussex Police Authority. A local magazine commented:

> With banner branding that would make most multinationals jealous, SaboTaj occupied the much-loved ethnic supermarket, turning it into an art gallery, but the police arrived early one morning and it was all over. Despite Morrisons being just a few doors up, Kemptown had another new supermarket.
>
> (*Brighton Source*)

Acknowledging the tradition of political squatting in Brighton, the 2012 Brighton Photo Biennial took as its theme 'Agents of Change: Photography and the Politics of Space'. In a text written for the *Guardian*, the curator declared that 'not unlike the occupations that stretched from London to New York last year, or the activities of UK Uncut, political squats use strategic forms of creativity to transform privatised space into a commons', going on to state, 'we have defined political squats as empty buildings opened by squatters to the public as social centres, libraries, gardens and, in particular, places to make and show art' (quoted in Burbridge, 2012). The Biennial produced a colour pamphlet (spoofing a local property magazine) which discussed political squatting in Brighton from 1994 to the present.

Squatted social centres have also provided short-lived interventions into larger political debates. The Courthouse and Old Redhill Motors centres were set up to contest the Criminal Justice Bill and the Prevention of Terrorism Bill respectively. More recently, the Churchill Square occupation allied itself with anti-cuts protests in 2011, and other buildings have been utilised as residential spaces before conferences and demonstrations. In April 2012, a huge and long-term empty department store was occupied for an intersquat convergence by SNOB(AHA).

Thus, we can see that squatters in Brighton have affected social and urban policy in various ways, both by protesting and by taking affirmative action on political issues such as supermarket expansion, use of space, state legislation and local council housing policy. As mentioned earlier, squatters were also active in challenging the new law[9] which has criminalised squatting in residential buildings: SNOB(AHA) replied to the government consultation, published statements attacking the proposed bill and organised two marches in protest. The law came into force on 1 September 2012, and two days later three squatters were arrested at a building on London Road after a seven-hour stand-off. They were charged with the new offence of squatting in a residential building, obstructing the police and abstracting electricity. The latter charge has since been dropped and the other charges were scheduled to be heard in April 2013, providing an important test case in terms of setting a precedent for how the new law will be applied in future.

Recent Events – London

In London, the first person to be arrested and imprisoned under the new law was Alex Haigh, 21, arrested on 2 September 2012 when the police came to his squat because someone else had given the details as a bail address. Alongside two others (including the prior arrestee), Haigh was arrested, and after pleading guilty was jailed for three months.

When the possibility of criminalising squatting was debated again, SQUASH (Squatters Action for Secure Homes) was reformed. It was initially set up in the mid-1990s to fight the contemporary threat to criminalise squatting. As a campaigning group it published reports such as 'Criminalising the vulnerable' and 'Can we afford to criminalise squatting?', lobbied members of Parliament and participated in the government consultation on squatting. Ironically, while the Ministry of Justice (MoJ) response to the consultation (entitled *Options for Dealing with Squatting*: MoJ, 2012) did engage with some arguments put forward by SQUASH and other groups opposing criminalisation, including SNOB(AHA), it appears to have discounted the huge majority of responses to the consultation since they were against criminalisation.[10]

The squatter groups also worked to counteract a moral panic which arose in the mainstream media about criminal, foreign squatters who targeted decent home owners, pouncing to occupy places when they popped out to get a pint of milk. Ironically, it was again Redbridge in London that was at the centre of the storm, with the *Evening Standard* running stories about 'A community besieged by squatters' and a resident, Sarah Dixon, starting a petition to stop squatting in the neighbourhood (Blunden and Parsons, 2012). Another *Standard* article related the tale of Janice Mason, 'whose childhood home was taken over by Moldovan squatters', and who asked 'why should someone be able to go into your house and take it over?' (quoted in R. Parsons, 2012). However, it is interesting to note that even a politician such as Mike Weatherley, who has previously mobilised such arguments in support of criminalisation, now refers to the 'myth ... that people's actual homes – where they live every day – are getting invaded .... Such stories are rare and are not illustrative of the wider problem but they do happen' (2012).

Yet overall, public opinion appears to have shifted from the reportedly broad support in the 1970s for people occupying some of the many empty properties to an altogether different perspective on squatters as criminal, foreign scum. A YouGov poll which asked 'Do you think the law should be changed making squatting a criminal offence or should it be left as it currently is?' was answered 'yes' by 81 per cent, 'no' by 13 per cent and 'don't know' by 6 per cent (Campbell, 2011). According to the local detective chief superintendent and chair of the Community Safety Partnership in Redbridge, 'squatting is linked to Anti-Social Behaviour and can cause a great deal of nuisance and distress to local residents' (Williams, 2012), while the *Evening Standard* reported that:

> organised gangs of Eastern Europeans have occupied and trashed strings of empty neighbouring properties. One resident taking on the squatters in Ilford told how she returned home from work one day to find up to 30 of them in the four-bedroom house next door.
> (Blunden and Parsons, 2012)

We can observe here what critical discourse analysis would term a dominant ideological-discursive framework. This hegemonic discourse both informs and creates a stereotypical view of squatters (Dee, 2012). Steve Platt writes that negative discourses about squatters have been present in the media since the 1970s. Further:

homelessness, when it comes down to it, is a social problem, not an individual one. With the best will in the world, this presents a problem for the popular media, which is always better at telling an individual story rather than providing meaningful social analysis.

(Platt, 1999: 117)

He argues that 'for those who deal in straightforward heroes and villains – the deserving and undeserving – there is no dilemma here. For those who would try to represent nuance and complexity, it is much more of a problem' (Platt, 1999: 111), yet it is also very useful for politicians and others high in the hierarchy of credibility if squatters can be typecast in the role of 'undeserving' or 'bad'.

In the debate surrounding criminalisation, the narrative of the 'bad' squatter drowned out all other narratives, even if the vegetable-farming squatters of Grow Heathrow were often represented as 'good' squatters. Unmentioned in this debate was London's strong tradition of squatted social centres. Just a small selection of recent ones would include Ramparts, Ratstar, Belgrade Road, OffMarket, the Bank of Ideas, Colorama, the Cheese Factory, House of Brag, Palestine Place and the Cuts Cafe. These spaces provided venues for anti-capitalist organisation and local struggles. The first two lasted for years rather than months, which is quite unusual. OffMarket was a project which lasted for more than a year, but only by virtue of moving location several times, whereas the latter two projects were time-limited, in that they were declared from the very beginning to be happening for only two weeks, in order make the precariousness of the project a positive factor. As the names suggest, both these projects focused on specific political issues: solidarity with Palestine and mobilisation against economic austerity respectively.

There were several squats connected with the Occupy camps at St Paul's and Finsbury Square in the City of London, which included the Bank of Ideas, a large social centre in the old headquarters of UBS, a squatted courthouse in Old Street and a disused school (whose squatters were illegally evicted the same night as those at the St Paul's camp). These were followed by a homeless project in Holborn (the Hobo Hilton) and a squatted community library in Friern Barnet.

But how many people are actually squatting in the present day? It is clear that there are no exact figures available. Squatters themselves are not interested in the question: for example when I asked the opinion of members of SNOB(AHA) they responded (by email) that had no particular use for the precise number of squatters even within the Brighton area.

In its *Consultation: Options for Dealing with Squatters*, the MoJ stated that 'there is no data held by central Government about the number of people who squat or their reasons for doing so', and then proceeded to estimate the number of squatters nationally at 20,000 (MoJ, 2011). A Freedom of Information request revealed that the estimate had been reached after considering that there had been 216 interim possession orders and 531 ordinary possession orders granted against trespassers of all descriptions in UK courts in 2010, but the reasoning here is difficult to follow.

Coming from another angle, Kesia Reeve and other colleagues have written several papers for Crisis, which identify a link between home-lessness and squatting (a link which would seem self-evident to most). In *The Hidden Truth about Homelessness: Experiences of Single Homelessness in England* (Batty and Reeve, 2011), 437 single homeless people were surveyed in 11 towns and cities across the United Kingdom, and 142 claimed to have squatted previously (39 per cent of the total). In an earlier report, *Life in the Margins* (Reeve and Coward, 2004), 165 homeless people from three locations (London, Craven and Sheffield) were surveyed. Of these, 68 people had squatted previously (55 men and 13 women).

However, it must be stated clearly that Reeve is demonstrating that some people who are homeless squat as a means of shelter, not that all squatters are homeless people in the sense of squatting through depriva-tion (although it is also true that all squatters are technically of no fixed abode and therefore legally defined as homeless). It must be remembered that there are no viable statistics generally. Indeed, there are not very many statistics about homeless people who squat. As Reeve herself comments:

> Very little is known about squatting as a homeless situation: Despite the relatively high incidence of squatting amongst the homeless population, there is virtually no evidence, awareness, or understanding about the nature and extent of squatting, nor about the situations, profile or experiences of homeless people who squat.
>
> (Reeve and Coward, 2004: 2)

Conclusions

From its beginning as a movement in the late 1960s, political squatting has clearly made an impact on the society from which it emerged, with squatters taking advantage of the huge amount of empty properties in London, Brighton and other cities to house themselves and others. As Bailey commented, 'what we had learned from all our campaigns was that direct action worked where individual complaints failed' (1973: 28).

Once a movement had been established, squatters used their rent-free existence as a springboard for many other projects, with a long tradition of self-organised venues, gardens, cafes and social centres which stretches into the present day. Squatting may well have been a lifestyle, but not in the pejorative sense intended by right-wing politicians. It was more a commitment which involved hard work in repairing buildings, solidarity in supporting other social struggles, and cooperation with other squatters. The English squatters' movement declined both in number and political importance in the 1980s, when many squats were legalised or formed into housing cooperatives, yet the legacy lives on in today's movement, such as it is. The unsuccessful attempts to criminalise squatting which resulted in legislation in 1977 and 1994 serve to indicate the force of the squatters' movement, if only as something significant enough to necessitate attempted regulation by the state. However, the stronger collective memory of squatting heritage in places such as Berlin, Copenhagen and Amsterdam also suggests that there must be reasons for the lack of history in the English context.

Most importantly, the pragmatic and legal right to squat continues to exist in England, despite squatting in residential buildings recently being made a criminal offence. If criminalisation was designed to stop squatting, it will assuredly not succeed, since when there are both empty buildings and enough people willing to occupy them, the lesson of history is that squatting will occur. A report by the homelessness charity Shelter released in December 2012 declares:

> Britain is now at the centre of a perfect storm of housing problems. High and rising rents, the cripplingly high costs of getting on the housing ladder and the lowest peacetime building figures since the 1920s have all combined with a prolonged economic downturn to increase the pressure on families.
> (Carlyon, 2012: 3)

When the Conservative Party is threatening to cut housing benefit for everyone under 25 and *Guardian* journalists suggest that 'Cathy Come Home's lesson will soon be learned again' (Toynbee, 2011), then it seems rather more likely that squatting will return as a major issue to the political stage, despite criminalisation.

Squatting can be represented as the complex intersection of a multiplicity of factors, which include and are not limited to the need for a roof over one's head, anti-capitalist direct action, the desire to live autonomously and a moral attitude concerning use of empty space. Squatters occupy houses to live in, and from there organise in a variety of political and cultural ways. As Reeve comments, 'squatters in the 1960s and 1970s were as much concerned with "material subsistence" as they were with developing alternative lifestyles, and the experiences of many present day squatters reveal the endurance of the "struggle for one's daily bread"' (2005: 215).

The English squatters' movement arose in the 1970s and may well return to its former size again, since all preconditions for this to happen appear to have been met. Criminalisation could then be seen as a calculated attempt to prevent future squatting activity, yet while legal measures may defeat a social movement's cultural aims, they are unlikely to override material need. If people need houses they will take them. Squatters will continue to play a role in shaping English society in the years to come.

Box 3.1 *Criminalisation One Year On*

Needle Collective

Section 144 of the Legal Aid, Sentencing and Punishment of Offenders Act (LASPO) has created the new criminal offence of being inside a residential building as a trespasser while living (or intending to live) there. A few people, including Alex Haigh in London and Michael Minorczyk in Blackburn, have already received prison sentences, but the law appears to be used mainly by police forces throughout England and Wales (squatting was already a criminal offence in Scotland and Northern Ireland) as a way to harass the street homeless, either threatening them with arrest if they do not leave the places where they have found shelter, or arresting people but then not charging them. Thus the police have taken on a new role as guardians of private property. Such conduct had a horrific outcome in Aylesford, Kent, when Daniel Gauntlett froze to death sleeping outside a derelict bungalow. He had been warned by the police that he would be arrested if he entered the property.

Many squatters have simply switched to occupying nonresidential properties (as others already do), and it is difficult to track exactly how many people have been convicted or even arrested under section 144 since police forces do not always record minor arrests. After six months, of the 92 people arrested under the new law in London, 41 were Romanian, which the right-wing press took as an indication that immigration laws should be tightened. In fact, this served only to indicate how much of a political football the criminalisation of squatting had become. It also backs the point made above about the street homeless, namely that the law is being used in the main to attack people who may not have a good grasp on the English language and/or their legal rights.

However, the first court cases in which people have pleaded not guilty to the new law have gone quite well for squatters. In Brighton, three squatters were arrested just days after the law change (as reported in this chapter). When the case eventually came to court, the charges were immediately thrown out against two of the three since there was no evidence that they lived or intended to live in the property. The other squatter, Dirk Duputell, was convicted but promptly appealed, and the conviction was overturned in October 2013, again for lack of evidence. In the same week as the Brighton acquittal, Tristan Dixon was cleared on appeal of squatting in Moelfre, Wales. His argument, upheld on appeal, was that he had never intended to live at the property but wanted to grow trees and vegetables on the land.

It is then perhaps harder than the police imagined to act as property guards. It appears to be very difficult to prove that someone lives or intends to live somewhere without engaging in a major surveillance and forensic operation, which of course would be farcical for such a minor offence. (Such an operation would likely tip off observant squatters in any case.) The appeal judge in the Brighton case refused to engage with the further question of how exactly a residential property is defined in law. These criticisms had already been raised by groups from the squatters' movement such as Squatters Network of Brighton, Squatters Legal Network and SQUASH (Squatters Action for Secure Homes).

Activists hope that squatting in England and Wales will follow the trajectory of squatting in the Netherlands and Spain, since in both these countries criminalisation has done little to stop the occupation of empty property. In the Netherlands there was a period during which the new rules to the game were established, and this appears to be the situation currently in England and Wales.

A recent high-profile occupation in Southwark, London highlighted another line of attack against section 144. Two council-owned residences about to sold off were squatted in protest against stock being disposed of in a borough which has thousands on its housing waiting list. While the houses were clearly residential, the organisers HASL (Housing Action in Southwark and Lambeth) claimed that no one was living there and it was a protest occupation, thus making it a civil matter between owner and squatter. This approach worked, although this was perhaps a consequence of the high level of mainstream media interest in the action, since the houses were sold off for almost £3 million. The squatters were evicted but they had made their point.

Acknowledgement

My thanks for conversations are due to several anonymous squatters, and to Clifford Harper, Miguel Martinez, Tony Greenstein, and members of the Squatting Europe Kollective, Squatters Network of Brighton (and Hove Actually), and Squatters Action for Secure Homes.

Notes

1   He adds, 'this figure is based on known squats and probably severely underestimates the actual number squatting'.

2   Incidentally, the homelessness charity Centrepoint had already been set up in 1969 and was not formed as a response to this action as is sometimes reported.

3   Alara Wholefoods began in a squat in Tolmers Square, as did a law firm, Hodge Jones & Allen.

4   The squatters also collaborated with a film-maker to produce *Tolmers Square – Beginning or End?* which was shown twice on BBC2.

5   Peter Rachman (1919–1962) was a landlord in the Notting Hill area of London in the 1950s and early 1960s, whose name became synonymous with the exploitation of tenants (information from Wikipedia).

6   He was never convicted, although a civil court awarded £6 million damages against him – which he swore he would not pay.

7   In 2012, there were almost 1,000 properties that had been empty for longer than six months, of which 137 were owned by the council.

8   As of December 2012, the shopfronts under the small block of flats built on the site remain empty, possibly because of the Stokes Croft riot of April 2011, in which a new and bitterly opposed Tesco Metro was destroyed after the police raided a squat opposite searching for nonexistent Molotov cocktails.

9   Specifically, section 144 of the Legal Aid, Sentencing and Punishment of Offenders Act (2012).

10   The report states in a footnote: 'In summarising the consultation responses in the following sections, we have taken a qualitative rather than quantitative approach because 1,990 responses (i.e. almost 90 per cent of the total) were received in support of a campaign organised by Squatters' Action for Secure Homes (SQUASH). While we recognise that the statistical weight of responses was therefore against taking any action to deal with squatting, it is important that the views of other individuals and organisations are reflected in the summary of responses – even if in percentage terms, they are minority views' (MoJ, 2011b: 7).

References

Angry Brigade Chronology (1985) (anonymous authors.) London: Elephant Editions.

Aufheben (1995) *Aufheben 4* (self published).

Bailey, R. (1973) *The Squatters*. London: Penguin.

Batty, E. and Reeve, K. (2011) *The Hidden Truth about Homelessness: Experiences of Single Homelessness in England*. London: Crisis.

Blunden, M. and Parsons, R. (2012) 'Ilford: a community besieged by squatters', *Evening Standard*, 12 January. www.standard.co.uk/news/ilford-a-community-besieged-by-squatters-7306974.html (accessed December 2012).

Brighton Photo Biennial (2012) *Another Space: Political Squatting in Brighton 1994–Present*. Brighton: Brighton Photo Biennial

Brighton Source (2011) 'Broken Brighton fixed?' http://brightonsource.co.uk/features/broken-brighton-fixed/ (accessed December 2012).

Brighton Voice (various issues).

Burbridge, B. (2012) 'Political squatting: an arresting art', *Guardian*, 28 September. www.guardian.co.uk/culture-professionals-network/culture-professionals-blog/2012/sep/28/squatting-art-brighton-photo-biennial?newsfeed=true (accessed December 2012).

Campbell, K. (2011) 'Criminalise squatting,' http://yougov.co.uk/news/2011/11/11/criminalise-squatting/ (accessed December 2012).

Carlyon, T. (2012) *Eviction Risk Monitor 2012*. London: Shelter.

Caulfield, M. (2012) 'Diddly squat', *Argus*. www.theargus.co.uk/opinion/letters/8474001.Diddly_squat/ (accessed December 2012).

Dee, E. T. C. (2012) 'Moving towards criminalisation and then what?' in SqEK (eds), *Squatting in Europe: Radical Spaces, Urban Struggles*. Wivenhoe: Minor Compositions.

Elgin Avenue Squatters (nd) *No Evictions!* (self published).

Franklin, A. S. (1984) 'Squatting in England, 1969–79: a case study of social conflict in advanced industrial capitalism.' Working paper, School for Advanced Urban Studies, University of Bristol.

Gardner, B. (2011) 'Brighton new homes site overrun by squatters', *Argus*,

1 December. www.theargus.co.uk/news/9397092.Brighton_new_homes_site_overrun_by_squatters/ (accessed December 2012).

Longstaffe-Gowan, T. (2012) *The London Square: Gardens in the Midst of Town*. New Haven, Conn.: Yale University Press.

Mahony, T. (1969) 'London Squatter Talks in Nusight', *Nusight*, 1 September.

Martínez, M. A. (2012) 'The squatters' movement in Europe: a durable struggle for social autonomy in urban politics', *Antipode* 45(4), 866–87.

Ministry of Justice (2011a) *Consultation Paper: Options for Dealing with Squatting*. London: UK Government.

–– (2012b) *Consultation Report: Options for Dealing with Squatting*. London: UK Government.

Mudu, P. (2004) 'Resisting and challenging neo-liberalism: the development of Italian social centres', *Antipode* 36(5), 917–41.

Needle Collective versus Bash Street Kids (2014) 'Ebb and flow – autonomy and squatting in Brighton', in A. Katzeff, L. Hoogenhuijze and B. Steen (eds), *The City Is Ours: Squatting and Autonomous Movements in Europe from the 1970s to the Present*. Oakland, Calif.: PM Press.

Owens, L. (2009) *Cracking under Pressure: Narrating the Decline of the Amsterdam Squatters' Movement*. Pennsylvania: Penn State University Press.

Parsons, B. (2012) 'Pressure mounting for licensed squats', *Argus*, 10 February. www.theargus.co.uk/opinion/comment/9525676.Pressure_mounting_for_licensed_squats/ (accessed December 2012).

Parsons, R. (2012) 'Squatting victim begs ministers to speed up change in law', *Evening Standard*, 18 January. www.standard.co.uk/news/squatting-victim-begs-ministers-to-speed-up-change-in-law-7309059.html (accessed December 2012).

Platt, S. (1999) 'Home truths: media representations of homelessness', in B. Franklin (ed.), *Social Policy, the Media and Misrepresentation*. London: Routledge.

Pruijt, H. (2004) 'Okupar en Europa' ['Squatting in Europe'] in R. Adell and M. A. Martinez (eds), *¿Donde Esta las Llaves? El Movimiento Okupa: Practicas y Contextos Socials* [*Where are the Keys? The Squatters' Movement: Practices and Social Contexts*]. Madrid: La Catarata. English version available at: www.eur.nl/fsw/staff/homepages/pruijt/publications/sq_eur/ (accessed December 2012).

Reeve, K. (2005) 'Squatting since 1945: the enduring relevance of material needs', in P. Somerville and N. Sprigings (eds), *Housing and Social Policy*. London: Routledge.

–– (2009) 'De Britse kraakbeweging, 1968–1980' ['The UK squatters' movement, 1968–1980'] in *Kritiek – Jaarboek voor Socialistische Discussie en Analyse 2009* [Kritiek – Yearbook of Socialist Discussion and Analysis 2009] (English version kindly supplied by author).

Reeve, K and Coward, S. (2004) *Life on the Margins: The Experiences of Homeless People Living in Squats*. London: Crisis.

SchNews (2011) 'Treacherous Weatherley: EXschCLUSIVE – anti squatting MP for Hove Mike Weatherley exposes himself in SchNews 800.' www.schnews.org.uk/stories/TREACHEROUS--WEATHERLEY/ (accessed December 2012).

SNOB(AHA) Private email correspondence with author, 2011–12.

Squat.net (2011) 'Facing up to Mike Weatherley's fearsome gauntlet' https://brighton.squat.net/?p=167 (accessed December 2012).

—— (2012) 'Squatting and Tory truth – a "chat" with Mad Mike.' https://brighton.squat.net/?p=375 (accessed December 2012).

Toynbee, P. (2011) 'Cathy Come Home's lesson will soon be learned again', *Guardian*, 14 October. www.guardian.co.uk/commentisfree/2011/oct/14/cathy-come-home-lesson-rents-mortgages (accessed December 2012).

Wates, N. (1976) *The Battle for Tolmers Square*. London: Routledge.

—— (1984) *The Tolmers Tale End* (self-published).

Wates, N. and Wolmar, C. (1980) *Squatting: The Real Story*. London: Bay Leaf.

Weatherley, M. (2012) 'Despite recent attack by violent squatters Mike delivers speech to Sussex students.' www.mikeweatherleymp.com/2012/12/07/despite-recent-attack-by-violent-squatters-mike-delivers-speech-to-sussex-students/ (accessed December 2012).

Williams, S. (2012) Police statement on squatting, 20 January 2012. www2.redbridge.gov.uk/cms/council_tax_benefits_housing/housing/strategy_and_development/empty_properties/police_statement_on_squatting.aspx (accessed December 2012).With thanks for conversations with anonymous squatters, Clifford Harper, Miguel Martinez, Tony Greenstein, Squatting Europe Kollective, Squatters Network of Brighton (and Hove Actually), Squatters Action for Secure Homes.

4

The Power of the Magic Key: The Scalability of Squatting in the Netherlands and the United States

Hans Pruijt

When considering alternatives, a classic question is whether they can be scaled up beyond a proof of concept. In the case of squatting, activists have tried to do this, and this chapter taps into this experience. It is based on evidence from the Netherlands, especially Amsterdam, and the United States, especially New York City (NYC). The Netherlands is interesting because squatting grew to be widespread for a relatively long time. In the United States, squatting was possible but it was much less sustained. Also the context is different. In the United States, there is what Esping-Anderson (1990) calls a liberal welfare state regime. The Dutch welfare state regime can be seen as combination of the social democratic and paternalistic types.[1]

The history of squatting is quite complex, especially in the Netherlands, because there was such a large and variegated movement. A book chapter can only cover a small part of it; this chapter focuses on the question of how squatting can grow to encompass more people, become more durable, or entail greater cultural and economic change. It also addresses limitations and mechanisms that can force squatting into a decline.

Below, I examine various episodes in the history of squatting in the Netherlands and the United States. First I discuss some theoretical considerations that relate to movement growth.

A Unique Power

Within the complete stock of real estate, there is a section consisting of buildings that are vacant, but not for sale or offered for rent, although many people would like to use them, or are even desperately in need of them. Squatting is virtually the only practical way for citizens to get access to such properties. As such, it as a unique power. It is also a precarious power. Viable, growing squatting involves dealing with the challenge of (re) discovery, propagation, legitimation, harnessing, maintenance, expansion and preservation of the power of squatting. A further challenge for squatters is to assure the day-to-day viability of their squats, given the uncertainty that squatting entails.

Squatting can lead to further cultural and economic change when beyond being a form of self-help, it constitutes an intervention in urban politics and urban planning. Spatial transformations tend to manifest themselves by the appearance of empty buildings, which take place between the moving out of the first tenant and final razing of the site. By pushing for preservation or a change in plans, squatting can make its mark on the urban fabric, possibly in a way that differs from a profit-driven development.

Squatting can also contribute to a sector in society that can be seen to some extent and in varying degrees as being in opposition to some capitalist principles. However, it needs to be noted that ideologies espoused within the squatters' movement vary, as do interpretations by observers. Squatting is not the implementation of some anti-capitalist programme.

Squatting in the Netherlands

Events in Amsterdam show that without prior organisation or promotion, and without much support, provided that the authorities do not interfere with it, relatively large-scale squatting can start on an urban renewal site. In 1963 dozens of people, including a community of artists, were squatting on Kattenburg, an island in the central district of Amsterdam, where the city was moving all tenants out to prepare for a complete demolition followed by the construction of new housing. Although utility companies refused to connect water or electricity, squatters were able to get water from still-remaining legal neighbours, and electricity sometimes from lamp posts. As their number increased, squatters increasingly got together socially and cooperated. The communist newspaper *De Waarheid* (1963) publicized the opportunity, describing squatted Kattenburg as the

'Montmartre' of Amsterdam, and in 1964 the student weekly *Propria Cures* exhorted students to move to Kattenburg: 'Save a small property'. A problem for the squatters on Kattenburg was the appearance of people who made a mess. Poldervaart (2004) recalled:

> Empty buildings also attract less pleasant people. Thus, around the corner two ether abusers were living who got into a fight almost every night and started to throw stuff. Next door, on the third floor there were American junkies who let their dogs shit on the second floor, which caused an enormous stench.

Such behaviour triggered a media backlash. The newspaper *Telegraaf* wrote about the 'human rats' of Kattenburg. It also brought some of the remaining tenants to the verge of attacking squats; in the end, squatters were able to prevent this by evicting the addicts themselves.

Organising Squatting

Squatting on Kattenburg was spontaneous, but in 1965 the first organised squatting action followed in the Vetterstraat. It focused on housing newly wed couples and garnered a lot of media attention.

In 1966 the Provo Anarchist group took up the theme when they issued a pamphlet on a Witte Huizenplan (White Houses Plan: see Box 4.1). In this pamphlet, a 'working group' announced that they would distribute lists of empty houses and would paint doors and doorjambs of empty homes white.

In 1969 the term '*kraken*' came into use for squatting. The group Woningbureau (Housing Bureau) de Kraker published the first squatting manual (Van Tijen, 2008). This group expanded the scope of squatting by not restricting squatting to married couples, as had been the case in the 1965 actions, and by linking squatting to protest. They protested against the planned demolition of a tenement block to make room for student housing, against a hotel conversion plan and against a lack of affordable housing policy in general. They were allowed to stay temporarily in a bank office that they squatted, were the first group to barricade a squat to make eviction difficult, and the first squatter group to be evicted by police in riot gear.

In 1970, there was a big leap in squatting. Neighbourhood action committees, trying to stop bulldozer urban renewal, started to employ squatting as a tactic (Pruijt, 2004b). A new informal organisation, Aktie

Box 4.1 *Provo*

Alan Smart

Between 1964 and 1967, a neo-anarchist social movement called Provo engaged in a political struggle meant to transform the manner of addressing dominant culture. Its unpredictable success transformed the traditional political culture of the Netherlands (based on a confessional system called the *Verzuiling*) and influenced urban struggles of the time. Its self-dissolution led the first groups of squatters who formed, a few years later, the Dutch Krakers movement.

Publishing was an important part of the movement, and pamphlets, posters and a magazine were produced. Presses were set up in Amsterdam and other cities in the Netherlands. Provo become an easily reproduced franchise which spawned local groups across the Netherlands. Maastricht Provo groups publish the magazine *Ontbijt of Bed* and are involved in 'experimental' 'non-object' art practices.

A series of 'white plans' were produced in which an object was adopted for its symbolic value, painted white and used to stage a 'happening'. The 'white bicycle plan' positioned bicycles as an alternative icon to the private automobile and created a small fleet of white bicycles available for public use. Not intended to be a practical solution, the plan served rather to precipitate a repressive response from the police and force issues of private property and public space into popular discourse. Other white plans addressed issues of gender and family structure, mirroring modernist attitudes towards the collectivisation of childcare except with a communitarian bent.

The 'white housing plan' politicised squatting practices that were already becoming common, and took issue with both the inefficiencies of state housing policy and the vacancy rate caused by speculation in a perversely incentivised real estate market. A system for listing vacant spaces was instituted and an office set up to place people in squatted housing.

'70, made it easier for people to join in actions, by being much more accessible than previous groups which only had a PO box number, and by reaching out to home seekers. Aktie '70 set up a stall outside the municipal office where home-seekers needed to go to register for the waiting list.

A wealthy former advertising executive turned activist supplied Aktie '70 with resources and public relations expertise (Duivenvoorden, 2000).

In 1970, there was a national diffusion of squatting, through among others the Kabouter (Gnome) Movement, founded by former Provos. The Kabouter movement was nationwide, and declared an 'alternative state', Oranje Vrijstaat. The Oranje Vrijstaat's infrastructure consisted of squats, recycled goods shops and organic food stores.

In various cities, there were alternative youth aid agencies that involved their homeless clients in squatting. In contrast with some of the other groups, the youth aid agencies systematically respected eventual eviction orders. Not only did youth aid agencies stimulate squatting, it was also the other way around. Aktie '70 organized a national squatting day, which prompted the creation of Release in Haarlem, a still existing alternative aid agency that started squatting for families in precarious conditions.

At Release's instigation, lawyers began to challenge the legal basis of evictions in court. As a result, the Dutch Supreme Court in 1971 decided that the 'house right', which protects homes from being entered against the will of the occupants, applies to squatters. From that moment, it became illegal for landlords to evict squatters and squatting was no longer considered to be a criminal offence, provided that the building was neither in use nor being worked on. The history of squatting in the Netherlands (Duivenvoorden, 2000) clearly shows the effect of legal protection. The 1971 Supreme Court decision which gave squatters protection meant a turnaround. Prior to that point, the police had evicted squatters swiftly and it proved impossible to establish long-living squats. This situation changed completely. Squatters were now even able to resquat and finally secure some buildings from which they had previously been evicted (Duivenvoorden, 2000: 69).

The Nieuwmarkt Neighbourhood Struggle

In the early 1970s, the Nieuwmarkt neighbourhood in Amsterdam was threatened by an urban motorway built in a corridor cleared for subway construction, and lined by office blocks projected as the site for a new hotel. Activists, determined to fight for preservation of the neighbourhood, set up a group that allocated houses that would be squatted. To be accepted, prospective squatters had to meet criteria such as being prepared to stay to the end (that is, till eviction) and be ready to fight. The activists backed this up by establishing a scheme in which the squatters would collectively pay for necessary repairs, which made squatting houses that were in an exceptionally bad condition a more reasonable proposal, and by running a technical service centre where various construction tools could be borrowed. They also made a commitment to arrange for rehousing after a possible eviction.

The group's informal leaders exercised control in the neighbourhood and sought to remove drug addicts (Bosma et al., 1984). Activists had to manage the conflict of interest between the preservationists and inhabitants who wanted to move out of the neighbourhood anyhow and were planning to benefit from a rehousing scheme when their home was demolished, and the problems caused by the conflicting lifestyles of squatters and longstanding residents. They regularly produced newsletters that gave information about developments in the fight for preservation, and on the work that was done to convert squatted commercial buildings into living space. An old Smithy (de Smederij) was squatted to use as a meeting place for the neighbourhood.

In the end, squatters were able to hang on to their buildings on the Zwanenburgwal and Ververstraat, preserving them from demolition. The struggle against a planned motorway through the Nieuwmarkt neighbourhood (with a subway line underneath and surrounded by office blocks), involved a coalition between elitist conservationists, who were mainly interested in preserving monuments, and anarchist activists who wanted a mixed-use, affordable vibrant neighbourhood in which the human scale could dominate. The subway line was built as planned but the motorway project was stopped after an activist campaign, which caused prospective developers of office buildings to lose interest. Furthermore, the city government made two changes to the plans which were in accordance with the activists' demands, which entailed restoring the original street plan. One decision was to place a new housing block at the south side of the Anthoniesbreestraat in such a way that only a space wide enough for a narrow street remained, precluding an eventual later development as a major traffic artery. This decision was made after a violent confrontation at an attempted demolition in 1974 and following a recommendation by officials to give in to the demands as a way to prevent a further deterioration in relations (Hoekema, 1978). The second decision was to construct new housing on top of the subway tunnel, a considerable extra outlay, which was added to the subway construction budget (Mamadouh, 1992).

In 1975, while the squatters were preparing the defences of the squats on the Rechtboomssloot, which included a hanging bridge across the canal, the city council revoked an earlier decision to create new subway lines after the one that cut though the Nieuwmarkt.

Full Squatting

After the Nieuwmarkt battles, activists across the Amsterdam squatter scene got together to systematically strengthen the squatters' movement. The strategy built on the concept of office hours at which prospective squatters could get information. Long foreshadowing social policy ideals that would become mainstream around 2010, a stated principle was to 'emphasise from the beginning that the squatting action itself, the fixing up and/or conversion, and preventing eviction, are based on the home-seekers' own initiative, and that otherwise it is better to refrain from squatting'. Groups were organised for legal, technical and strategic support, care for evicted squatters and their stuff was coordinated, and vacancy was studied. A bi- or tri-weekly squatters newspaper, the *Kraakkrant*, was started. Its articles informed squatters about what was discussed in meetings, and disseminated experience gained in squatting actions. It also publicised squatting opportunities. In 1979, the *Kraakkrant* introduced the circle and arrow squatters' symbol. In 1979 a squatters' radio station began operation.

In many of Amsterdam's neighbourhoods, squatters' bars were opened that served as meeting places and hangouts for the neighbourhood squatters groups, hosted meetings and operated office hours for prospective squatters. Profits from the sale of beer went into funding for actions. Regular city-wide squatters meetings were organised. Other cities in the Netherlands organised squatting by and large in the same way as Amsterdam (Pruijt, 2013a).

There were also regular national squatters' meetings. A key point on the agenda was counteracting government strategies to outlaw squatting. Squatting had become virtually legal in 1971, basically as a result of legal technicalities, against the preference of the political majority in Parliament. As a result political efforts were initiated to stamp out squatting. Such efforts were met with protest, including national squatting days. In 1978, a proposed anti-squatting bill failed in parliament after lobbying by the Council of Churches. It issued a detailed report about squatting in the Netherlands. Squatters or former squatters were involved in the research. It was the result of a deliberate strategy to build an alliance with progressive people within church organisations.

It took more than a decade before legislation was passed with the aim to curtail squatting. It provided for the protection of only those buildings that were registered in a special file for vacant buildings. It turned that this never materialised; for squatters, the law remained inconsequential.

Thus, squatting could proceed relatively undisturbed by legal measures. In Amsterdam, the city inadvertently helped squatting grow by writing off largely the existing housing stock in the 19th-century central ring, envisioning replacing it with office blocks, other 'city functions' and lower-density housing. Tenants were moved out and apartments partially wrecked to prevent squatting. Nevertheless, these houses were systematically squatted and fixed up, an often relaxed affair because the owners could not do much with their buildings anyway, that is, except criminal owners who wanted to get extortionate rents illegally from desperate home seekers. Organised defence kept such owners at bay. City officials barely reacted to the massive squatting, and utility companies normally connected squats without problems. Especially for people with a relatively short-term perspective on housing, such as students, there was hardly a downside to squatting these types of building.

It was also relatively easy to squat buildings that had lost their function but for which there were no new plans, such as, in Amsterdam, the monumental Haarlemmerpoort (the last remaining city gate), the fire brigade house on the Prinsengracht, the row of lock operators' houses at the Oranjesluizen, schools, military buildings, the warehouses which became unused after the seaport on the east side of the city shut down, or the gigantic shipyards that had gone bankrupt. A further example is the entire village of Ruigoord, which was slated to disappear for an expansion of the Amsterdam harbour.

More ambitious in terms of risk was squatting a building for which the owner had more or less speculative plans. Still, this was feasible, because when an owner could not get an eviction on the basis of trespassing, the only road to eviction was to take the squatters to court in a civil dispute. For years, squatters used to prevent this by keeping their family names secret until a change in law made it possible to sue anonymous occupants. Owners employed spies in some cases.

By and large, it can be said that around 1980, squatting in the Netherlands expanded to such an extent that few opportunities remained unused. Squats housed artists' work spaces, practice facilities for bands, recording studios, women's houses, restaurants, print shops, theatres and movie theatres, tool lending services, alternative schools, daycare centres, party spaces, art galleries, book and info shops, spiritual centres, give-away shops (shops in which everything is free), food shops, saunas, workshops (for example, for bicycle repair or car or boat restoration), environmental or third-world oriented projects, or social projects such as a shelter for people in distress and an advisory service with language training for migrants. Some of these squats were in prominent locations, such as the former NRC newspaper building next door to the Royal Palace in Amsterdam. Ostensibly defying the capitalist spatial logic, it featured among other things a vegetable shop. A few commercial companies grew out of squatting, such as a brewery and specialty beer importer. In Utrecht, there is the Strowis hostel which is part of the social centre ACU, which was bought by the squatters themselves.

An effective tactic for expansion was the practice of combining artistic, cultural or political entrepreneurial squatting projects with housing. Therefore, these squats were, unlike south European-style social centres that do not include housing, not in a zero sum competition for a share of the alternative audience.

Taking with them the notion of applying direct action to troubled spots in society, some squatters branched out into other fields. A few examples are blockading the road leading to the nuclear power plant in Dodewaard and blockade actions against transportation of nuclear waste on its way to be dumped in the sea. Squatters blockaded the entrances to the Shell laboratory complex in Amsterdam as part of anti-apartheid protests. Direct action tactics, pioneered in the squatters' movement, were also transferred to anti-militarist protest. Military command bunkers and one military office were raided, and documents detailing contingency plans in case of a State of National Emergency were stolen, displayed and published. A similar action occurred at a building used by a covert police observation unit. A raid to disrupt an extreme right-wing party meeting in a hotel ended in a devastating fire caused by a smoke bomb, leaving the party leader's girlfriend mutilated. Squatters also played a major role in urban protests, for example against the construction of the new town hall – occupying the site with an 'anti-City circus' – and ruining Amsterdam's campaign to attract the Olympic Games by harassing the International Olympic Committee members assembled in Lausanne.

Many of the protests and direct action that involved squatters had a festival-like atmosphere, helped by, for example, the still-existing marching band Fanfare van de Eerste Liefdesnacht. In general, life in the squat scene meant that was no shortage of parties.

Around 1980, the Netherlands was in the midst of an economic crisis with a high unemployment rate. For unemployed people, squatting and related movement activity provided an opportunity to do something useful and fun. Thus the movement benefited from indirect subsidies.

Consolidation

Many squatters abandoned their buildings when the rightful owners claimed them. In the Netherlands, this especially applied to tenements slated for replacement by new low-income housing. Squatters tended to leave such buildings voluntarily without protest in time for the scheduled demolition and construction work to start. In Amsterdam, in 1981, slightly more than half of all squatters lived in working-class neighbourhoods which were built at the end of the 19th century and the beginning of the 20th century (Van der Raad, 1981: 37). Virtually all squats in these areas were eventually replaced by low-income housing. With very few exceptions, squatters in these areas left voluntarily (Pruijt, 2003). Basically, squatters did not want to get in the way of the construction of affordable housing, something that neighbourhood groups had fought for. The city also rehoused some of the squatters.

It was completely different when squatters did not agree with the owners' or the authorities' plan for the building. One line of approach was to try to change the plan. An opening was that the government had failed to deliver on an earlier promise to create more housing for young people. It seemed, and later proved, to be possible to induce social housing providers to buy squatted buildings for low prices, because of the real estate crisis that erupted in 1978, and to arrange for funding of renovations in cooperation with the squatters.

There was also a second line of approach. Three years after the Nieuwmarkt battles, the tactic to make eviction difficult was revived. A turning point was an eviction in the Kinkerbuurt in 1978. Planning to put the movement on a more militant tack, a group of squatters barricaded a building that was slated to be demolished and replaced by a small park. Squatters who turned up to show their solidarity in a nonviolent blockade, hoping that this would give the pause to the city administration, were severely beaten by police officers in riot gear. This led to debates about the possibilities for effective resistance against evictions. This was never really resolved, but in 1979 a row of five canal houses on the Keizersgracht, the Groote Keijser, were barricaded with welded steel plates and beams in defiance of a court order for eviction. The authorities prepared for eviction involving a force of around 2,000, but the mayor, fearing that people could get killed, called it off. Eventually, the houses were bought and turned into social housing. Early in 1980, a building on the Vondelstraat was resquatted, after an eviction based on a fake rental contract. Squatters chased away riot police and occupied the square. With the help of army tanks the police retook the square, but the squat was not evicted again, but legalised.

Justified concern among the authorities that at the upcoming coronation of Queen Beatrice, a few weeks later, there would be riots, prompted the city to quickly purchase a set of big squats, including the NRC Newspaper building next door to the Royal Palace.

After the Vondelstraat, resistance against eviction had little direct effect. Some squatters felt, however, that causing high eviction costs would induce the city to try to avoid further evictions. When the eviction of luxury apartments on the Prins Hendrikkade was announced, squatters barricaded the building and lined the rooftop with objects like washing machines, making it clear that they would be prepared to actively defend the building. A large police force appeared for the eviction, accompanied by marksmen from the army who installed themselves, with guns, in skips that were hoisted high in the air by mobile cranes. To their surprise, they found one lone squatter waiting for them, with flowers. In the days before, the squatters had made an underground passage into the basement of the neighbouring church. Nevertheless, a riot broke out on the streets.

At the end of 1980, squatters tried to save a large squat, the Grote Wetering, from being demolished and replaced by an office building. They did this by trying to get the building listed, and by attacking the developer and the bank funding him and pulling the strings behind him. When eviction seemed inevitable, the building was barricaded and people mobilised for street actions. The police came with a force of over 1,000 and an armoured car to break through the barricades; plain-clothes police officers molested demonstrators.

The violence put off many people, both outside the movement and within it. It seems that for some people, resisting evictions became somewhat of an end in itself. In 1983, many of the active squatters did not want to participate in an almost paramilitary campaign to resquat and defend the Lucky Luijk squat from which people had been evicted earlier. The city had already made the concession of allocating the site for social housing, thus in the end the dispute was more about control than about housing. In the riot, a tram was destroyed by fire. This event is often noted as the occasion at which the squatters' movement lost all support (Van Noort, 1988). The Lucky Luijk case shows a weakness of the decentralised autonomous movement model: participants can avoid a full debate about the wisdom of a proposed action by either doing what they want to do or voting with their feet. Nevertheless, squatters later got a lot of support in their campaign to prevent criminalisation (Pruijt, 2013b).

A completely different approach was followed in 1984, by the squatters of the immense Weijers buildings. When the court ordered eviction, there were already several collectives living communally in this building, a squatters' bar, a restaurant, an espresso bar and a performance space; the building's full potential had not yet been realised, and new initiatives were being added. It was not barricaded, but instead opened up for anyone who wanted to support the squatters. Finally, inside about a thousand supporters awaited the police.

Over time, the Municipality of Amsterdam bought 200 of the buildings that were occupied by squatters (Duivenvoorden, 2000: 323), thereby legalising them. In the beginning, the justification for this was the contribution to affordable housing for young people. Later the emphasis shifted to the economic value of squats as 'breeding places' providing workspaces and living/working spaces for individual artists and groups of artists and cultural entrepreneurs (Pruijt, 2004a). The strategy of legalisation tended to be relatively successful when real estate prices were low, and in cases where the owners did not have well-defined plans for the building.

Officials turned most of these buildings over to established housing associations, which concluded lease contracts with individual squatters (Draaisma and van Hoogstraten, 1983). Soja (2000: 124) labels this policy as 'slightly repressive tolerance'. This institutionalisation was not the end of squatting in Amsterdam. The heyday of legalisation was in the early 1980s. Three decades later, squatting was still going on. One observer, Van Noort (1988: 180) suggested that concessions even contributed to the radicalisation of the movement.

We might wonder whether legalisation results in the loss of an oppositional edge. An in-depth study on squatted 'free spaces' in Amsterdam describes commonly occurring effects of legalisation as a loss of links to various societal structures, of ties with other free spaces, and a decline of dynamism and political engagement (Breek and de Graad, 2001: 77).

There are projects where the oppositional identity did not wither away, but rather died abruptly with legalisation, such as the Groote Keijser, the already mentioned canal houses on Keizersgracht 242–252. In other legalised squats it eroded gradually, for instance in the NRC complex and Tetterode in Amsterdam. Sometimes a role in alternative culture has remained, as in the case of the Poortgebouw in Rotterdam, which has remained a venue for music. An important factor is the level of control that occupants can retain after legalisation. Often legalisation involves a housing nonprofit organisation taking control of the building and turning the squatters into individual tenants. In other cases, the ex-squatters remain in control as a collective (Breek and de Graad, 2001: 50).

Legalised squats, far from being monuments for co-optation, are still low-revenue-generating functions on expensive land, so they are potential focal points for future conflicts. A precursor of this is the conflict recently won by the anarchist volunteer-run bookshop Fort van Sjakoo in Amsterdam, established in a squat in 1977, legalised in the 1980s and almost strangled by a 900 per cent rent increase in 2003.

Consolidation of squats was important because opportunities for opening new squats declined. The city started to handle urban renewal more cautiously, and to avoid causing massive vacancy. Real estate prices soared, making it easier for developers to push their plans through. In 1984 squatting buildings that had been empty for less than one year became illegal, and in 2010 squatting any building became illegal (Pruijt, 2013b). A very important development in terms of curtailing squatting was the success of the 'anti-squat' companies which offer to protect empty buildings by placing people in them who are not tenants but basically tightly controlled guardians, and who have hardly any rights but have to pay for the privilege. In 1980, the first anti-squat company, de Zwerfkei, started. The sector expanded to such an extent that the number of anti-squat guardians is estimated as at least ten times the number of squatters. Cites and social housing providers routinely use anti-squat services, as do the owners of the millions of square metres of office space that is empty and remains listed on the investors' books at unrealistic values. By putting only a handful of students in an office building, anti-squat companies can make them impossible or hard to squat because their inhabitants effectively act as security guards.

Nevertheless, there are still places that only seem to be accessible through squatting. An example is the former animal shelter near the Muiderpoort railway station. It was squatted in 2010 and is now the de Valreep social centre (www.valreep.org). It is a solitary listed building which remained after surrounding buildings were demolished as part of a redevelopment scheme. When polluted soil was cleared, all connecting piping and wiring was stripped from the area, leaving a kind of sandy desert. There was no anti-squat company involved, which seems likely to be because of the complete lack of connections for water, sewer, power and gas on the site. A rented Portaloo and wood stoves assisted squatters in making de Valreep a successful social centre and living space.

Squatting in the United States, Especially in New York City

Like in the Netherlands, 1970 was a peak year for squatting in the United States, at least in NYC. This is probably not a complete coincidence. The peak in squatting was part of the late 1960s protest wave which the author-ities could not handle. A dramatic example was the killing of unarmed students at an anti-war protest at Kent State University in 1970.

Squatting on an Urban Renewal Site on the Upper West Side of Manhattan

In 1970, the Upper West Side of Manhattan, then a working-class area, was in the throes of urban renewal and planned displacement of poor, predominantly immigrant families, to make room for more market-rate housing. There were scores of both empty and still (partly) occupied buildings in the neighbourhood that were slated for demolition, while some families doubled or tripled up because they could not find an affordable apartment. These circumstances made a squatting wave possible, which started from a housing movement encompassing various social movement organisations trying to stop and reverse the displacement of low-income families, destruction of usable housing, and lack of maintenance and warehousing of empty apartments. The city gave an extra impetus to the mobilisation because it promised that displaced tenants could return to the neighbourhood, but then failed to deliver. Squatting actions followed an incident in which a boy died from carbon monoxide poisoning due to a boiler that the city had refused to fix, despite repeated pleas by the boy's mother.

Activists mobilised families, including the family that had suffered the tragedy, to squat in 30 vacant apartments that were in better shape than the ones which the families were living in. Muzio (2009: 121) describes the action as 'more spontaneous than part of a deliberately planned strategy of an organized movement'. It was the start of the organisation Operation Move-In (OMI), which focused on squatting city-owned buildings, and set up an office in a squatted storefront.

The squatters' movement attracted people from a wide variety of locations. This was against the preference of a group of Puerto Ricans, named El Comité, operating from a squatted storefront, who got involved in OMI with the goal to restrict squatting in the area to residents, or former residents, from the neighbourhood (Muzio, 2009: 124). One of the organisers explained:

> We decided we wanted to control the housing situation in a more organized fashion. … We started planning which building should be taken over, which families should go here or there. We became more organized, rather than spontaneous.
>
> (Muzio, 2009: 124)

Also, activists involved in the fight against gentrification on the Upper West Side started to use squatting as a tactic to pressure urban planners to allocate a higher proportion of low-income housing on redevelopment sites (Muzio, 2009). Schwartz (1986: 12) states that they 'tried to use the squatters as bargaining leverage'; in the end some squatters were evicted, and others legalised.

Squatting Church-Related Property on Morningside Heights

In neighbouring Morningside Heights, organised squatting occurred in buildings that were standing virtually empty because the owner, a nonprofit organisation, was planning to build a facility for the elderly. A small team of five or six young men who lived and studied or worked in the area were interested in housing issues, and according to Brotherton (1978: 196), were looking for a 'summer project'. The activists recruited families from OMI's waiting list. They organised meetings, the actual squatting, legal assistance, and facilitated contacts with the media and supportive organisations. In this case repression was not an urgent problem, since the developer was church-related and therefore sensitive to normative pressure to avoid police action against poor families. This suggests that a subtle difference in the opportunity structure can affect a development in either the autonomous or institutional direction.

The organisers planned to transfer leadership to the squatters, who continued to hang on to their buildings as a loosely self-organising group, their main collective project being 'Plaza Caribe', a park which they constructed themselves in a vacant lot (Brotherton, 1978). In her ethnographic study, Brotherton (1978: 53) notes that 'I soon discovered ... that in spite of the squatting being done on Morningside Heights, there was no squatter organization there comparable to Operation Move-In in the urban renewal area. The Morningside Squatters were their own organization.' Compared with OMI, this was a bold experiment because it entailed privately owned buildings. Squatters wanted to consolidate their project and work out a plan to buy the buildings, which was not successful. However, in a 1979 court ruling, the Morningside squatters won the title to their buildings. A spillover effect was the creation of the UHAB (Urban Homesteading Assistance Board) sponsored by the Episcopal Cathedral of St John the Divine to assist squatters. UHAB supports the self-management of buildings saved from abandonment. The organisers found that the media were interested, but mainly in the human side, making it difficult to propagate squatting.

Hippies

A further category of people active in the movement were 'hippies' (Muzio, 2009). A collective of activists opened the Local Storefront, a 'free, squatter store'. According to their mission statement, they aimed for a 'collective life'. They chose to bring people together by means of events such as film screenings and a food co-op, and to inform neighbourhood residents by publishing a newspaper, the *Broadway Local*, which covered squatting in the area, and helped mobilise supporters. It also, for example, brought news about squatting in Italy, and information about birth control. Three decades earlier than similar initiatives in Europe, the Local Storefront also served as a give-away shop.

The Disappearance of Squatting in New York

It is apt to see the squatting in NYC covered above as a wave. Most of it happened in the year 1970, and it declined rapidly. In contrast, squatting in the Netherlands was not a wave-like phenomenon. An explanation for the difference is that in the United States, squatting as an end in itself did not develop, partly as an effect of the dependence on organisers who saw squatting as a tool. In the Netherlands, activists constructed a movement that was more focused on squatting as an end in itself.

The Abandonment Crisis and Urban Homesteading

In the United States, squatting resurfaced in the late 1970s. The backdrop was a crisis situation in which several cities faced an accumulation of thousands of abandoned buildings that had become city property because the owners had not paid their taxes.

A widely promoted federal solution was urban homesteading: self-help housing in abandoned buildings and 'sweat equity', the substitution of labour for money. Following experiments in several cities, a national framework for urban homesteading programmes was enacted in 1974, in Section 810 of the Housing and Community Development Act (Borgos, 1986). This act specified the conditions under which a public agency or a 'qualified community organisation' could be funded to act as a 'local urban homesteading agency'. It required local homesteading agencies to select potential homesteaders who were relatively poor but simultaneously able to repair properties. The act also mandated the conclusion of 'homesteader agreements' (e-CFR, 2012). Borgos (1986: 432) describes official homesteading programmes as a route to 'tame' squatting.

However, it seems that official homesteading helped to legitimise squatting. In 1978 a group named Banana Kelly in the South Bronx squatted in three buildings as a strategy to speed up an official homesteading project. A contact within the city administration suggested to the group that they might start clearing rubble from the buildings before the official permission came through (Brandes Gratz, 1989). Some officials were weary of bureaucratic delays while suitable buildings were deteriorating. Jonnes (1980) quotes Philip St George, an official at the city's Department of Housing Preservation and Development, as saying:

> I've been an advocate of a squatters' zone in a place like the South Bronx. Typically, people see squatters as evil, but they have a tremendous creative energy that would be good to harness in places like the South Bronx. Using their own labor and materials, they would be creating something for nothing. I can already hear the buildings code people howling, but when you have a situation like the South Bronx these may be the only people who could pioneer it again.

The launch of the urban homesteading model, and the disappointment that followed when the bureaucracy blocked its widespread implementation, opened up opportunities to fill the gap caused by the decline in squatting. An organisation that played a large role in this was the Association of Community Organizations for Reform Now (ACORN), a formal organisation with 75,000 members and branches in 27 US states. In 1979, ACORN's Philadelphia office lambasted the city council member who was in charge of homesteading for diverting buildings to speculators, and started a squatting campaign. ACORN's rules mimicked the rules that were laid down in the Housing and Community Development Act: ACORN required prospective squatters to sign a 'squatters contract' (Borgos, 1986).

In 1985 the ACORN groups in New York organised squatting actions in 25 buildings in Brooklyn, even enticing a state senator to participate in the action. The city had originally planned to auction the buildings off, but after the squatting action the city changed its policy and turned 58 buildings over to ACORN/Mutual Housing Association of New York, which incorporated the squatters. Furthermore, the city provided funds for rehabilitation.

It is worth noting, however, that the cooperative attitude of state actors was far from uniform. In several cities, ACORN's squatting actions met with repression (Borgos, 1986).

The legitimacy created by the urban homesteading concept affected the field of urban squatting in New York as a whole. The urban homesteading frame appealed to a wide range of home seekers, which is understandable because it does not focus on deprivation but on renovation of abandoned buildings. This made it interesting for people such as artists, who had a low income but did not identify themselves as deprived. However, some of them found themselves excluded from the institutional movement. Lower East Side artist and squatter Rolando Politi explained:

> 'You were either 'good' or 'bad.' 'Good' if you had connections with the Lower East Side network of Catholic churches who had the leverage to deal with the city for turning over the properties to them and fit them in the official 'Homesteading Program,' and also 'good' if you had access to local politicians who would somehow legalize you into the system under any obscure program they could come up with.
>
> (email communication)

A further aspect of exclusion attached to official homesteading was that the city did not allow homesteaders to move into their buildings before all the work was finished, which could take years. This reduced risk because abandoned buildings often had no floors or stairs left, and a roof that was leaking or partially missing. One squatter was killed in a fall, and others were injured. An effect of this policy was that it excluded people who had nowhere else to live. Finally, the volume of institutionalised homesteading opportunities was minute compared with both the number of people who needed cheap housing and the number of abandoned buildings.

On the Lower East Side of Manhattan, people who did not fit into an institutional movement or who were excluded by institutional groups squatted anyway, thereby starting an autonomous squatters' movement. This movement was organised in the sense that there was cooperation and mutual help, and an arrangement in which squatters worked together to help prevent evictions, but there was not an organisation behind it. Residents moved from one squat to the next, and there was a general squatters scene in the neighbourhood (Ferguson, 2007). There was no alignment with political or other organisations. Frank Morales, a long-time New York and Lower East Side activist explained:

> As far as the left goes, we would often interact with various sectors of the left. Whether it's the housing movement or the political left, whoever that might be, from *The Nation* to various sectarian parties to the various leftist groups, and none of them wanted to deal with us, probably because we were autonomous.
>
> (quoted in Jaffe 2007: 202)

Squatting was the core of the movement's identity; it was end and means at the same time. This helped making squatting continuous. New squats were opened on the Lower East Side of Manhattan from 1983, when six buildings were squatted in 13th Street, until 1992 (713 East Ninth Street) (Ferguson, 2007). A total of 25 buildings were squatted. In 2002, a legalisation processes started for 11 buildings; in 2012 some buildings were legalised and renovated, while other buildings were still at the first stage of legalisation.

While exclusion drove some squatters towards building an autonomous movement, it left them slightly marooned in terms of their social identity. International diffusion solved this. The squatters' movement has to some extent become transnational. Self-labelling of squatters involves the use of the international squatters' sign, first seen in the Kraakkrant in Amsterdam. Europeans, acting as movement brokers (McAdam, Tarrow and Tilly, 2001) linked the New York and European squatters scenes. An Italian artist who left the anarchist scene in Berlin to move to New York organised the squatting of vacant apartments in three buildings on the Lower East Side in 1981. A British woman introduced the New York scene to political ideas that were common among squatters in Europe. In 1988, a Dutch woman took the initiative to open up a large building in New York. She had previously squatted in the Netherlands, and tried, with partial success, to introduce the cooperative features that were common in the Netherlands, such as a squatters' bar, regular consultation and mutual support between buildings, a tool exchange, facilities for artists and a theatre. In turn, American squatters made visits to European squatters' movements.

The institutional homesteading frame entailed dissonance for home seekers who were attracted by it but simultaneously excluded because of their social circumstances (see Walder, 2009). This dissonance made a favourable reception of the European squatting frame possible. A Lower East Side squatter recalled:

> We were still arguing about the use of the word squatting, and whether we should be squatters or homesteaders. Most people wanted to call it home-steading. ... But we weren't homesteaders. We didn't qualify for any of the [homesteading] programs, and most of those programs wouldn't want us anyway, even if we did [laughs]. Then English Steve and Cathy came and started using the term squatting left and right, and we kind of went with it from there.
>
> (quoted in Ferguson, 2007: 151)

Michael Shenker noted in an interview, 'We found a lot of reinforcement and encouragement through hearing what was going on in Europe. It helped to validate our analysis that this thing is possible, that it is real.'

Another activist reminisced, 'I took to preaching the reformed gospel of the European Squatters with the irritating zeal of some television preacher' (Tolia, 2007: 479).

A significant difference between New York and Amsterdam is that technical obstacles to squatting were more severe in New York. This can be seen by comparing squatters' manuals. The New York manual explains to would-be squatters how to assess whether a building is in danger of collapsing. It prepares them to deal with roofs with big holes in them, rotten timber and floors, absent water pipes, staircases with missing steps and the need to provide a front door and doorframe. As far as the manual is concerned, the squatters should not expect to be able to install flushing toilets. Elsewhere in the New York squatting literature, we see a particular squat described as having flushing toilets as a special feature. By contrast, the 1996/97 edition of the Amsterdam squatting manual does not mention any construction-related hurdles. The earlier edition from the 1980s contained some construction advice, without suggesting that extensive damage was the most likely condition that squatters would encounter. A New York activist noted about Amsterdam, 'Dutch squats had flush toilets, restaurants, radio stations but all this luxury just made squatters cynical' (Tobocman, 1999: 238).

Consolidation

However, consolidation of about half of the buildings proved to be possible. Legalisation through the mediation of UHAB started in 2002. What helped here was that typically, the opponents of squatters on the Lower East Side were not-for-profit organisations planning to develop low-income housing on the sites. In contrast with Amsterdam, where non-profit developers in urban renewal areas could be counted on to be reliable and predictable, to charge affordable rents and comply with neighbourhood committees' wishes, in New York it tended to be uncertain whether building plans would go through, and commitments to charge affordable rents were time-limited. This made the not-for-profit developers vulnerable, and the squatters could argue that they had already successfully created low-income housing (Pruijt, 2003).

A spectacular case of consolidation is the arts/community centre ABC No Rio in New York. Organically, the city had made the building available to a group of artists as part of a deal to make them give up another building that had been occupied to house an art show. Subsequently, city officials tried for nearly 20 years to get rid of ABC No Rio, for example by cutting the water supply. Finally they offered ABC No Rio the opportunity to buy the building for $1. ABC No Rio is now in the process of raising funds for the construction of an all-new building on the site. [Chapter 6 has further information on the organisation of ABC No Rio and its operational details, in particular the bicycle workshop and the practice of spreading across its community the cultures of the bicycle and of sharing.]

Diffusion or Lack Thereof

In 1987 Matthew Lee, after gaining experience as an official homesteader and as a squatter in the autonomous movement on the Lower East Side, moved to the Bronx where he started a neighbourhood newspaper in which he promoted squatting. He then organised a group named ICP (Inner City Press)/Community on the Move which squatted in 20 buildings. The European style, autonomous squatting of the Lower East Side did not diffuse. Several buildings were lost because of fires and evictions.

As an outgrowth of the autonomous squatters' movement on the Lower East Side, in 2012 the Museum of Reclaimed Urban Space was created in a legalised squat. In 2011 and 2012, activists with a background in the autonomous movement on the Lower East Side played an important role in the collective Organize for Occupation and the organisation Picture the Homeless, with the aim of facilitating the squatting of empty buildings by people from the homeless shelter system (Picture the Homeless, 2011).

Concluding Notes

A society, a city or a neighbourhood in which squatting takes place is different from one in which there is none. This depends on how ambitious the squatting is in terms of the constraints it puts on the owner, by violating their property rights, or on a third party. We can picture this as a ladder:

1 The squatting of empty buildings that the owner does not care about at all. Citizens are empowered to take action when they are faced with immediate needs for space that can be met by squatting at no cost to anyone. Authorities are under some pressure not to intervene or to facilitate this. Both in the United States and in the Netherlands, this was possible.

2 The squatting of empty buildings that the owners are prepared to try to take back, but where the owner, or any third party, does not have a legitimate interest that is being hurt by squatting. In Amsterdam,

squatters often put up effective organised resistance against criminal owners.

3 Squatting actions that hurt the legitimate interests of the owner or a third party, such an organisation planning new construction on the site, but where the owner or the third party is subject to a moral obligation to take the interests of the needy into account. Examples are church and state-related organisations. A nice example is the occupation on Morningside Heights in New York that caused a church-related developer to change its plans.

4 Squatting actions that hurt the legitimate interests of the owner or a third party, such an organisation planning new construction on the site, but where the owner or third party is purely profit-driven. Citizens are empowered to take action in a way that pushes use value over exchange value; speculators and those that support and finance them are held accountable. Of the two countries, this only occurred in the Netherlands.

Finally, when consolidation succeeds, this leads to the existence of functions generating a small amount of revenue on expensive land. Even when this is small scale, it creates symbols that alert us to the possibility of alternative development.

Box 4.2 *My Personal Experience as a NYC Neighbour*

Frank Morales

Back in 1980 I was living in the South Bronx, the home of hip hop, rap and graffiti. Sadly, it was also the ground zero of urban poverty in America.

Shaken by the insurrectionary possibilities of the late 1960s (128 cities had 'riots' in 1967), the US corporate/police state initiated a massive ten-year counter-insurgency in the form of class struggle from above against the poor, with its primary agenda being the forcible displacement of the Black and Latino populations from the urban centres by any means necessary, which included turning a blind eye to rampant CIA-sponsored drug-running.

At the time, groups like the Puerto Rican Young Lords and the Black Panthers were organising and squatting in neighbourhoods like Harlem, which lost a third of its population between 1970 and 1980.

In fact, throughout the entire country, in city after city, the same thing was happening. We squatters called the process 'spatial deconcentration', the forced removal of the poor from the urban centres of America.

By the time we started squatting on the Lower East Side (LES) in 1985 we were consequently of the understanding that this displacement was not always caused by economic factors alone, but rooted in motives of social control that explain homelessness and the vast stretches of vacant buildings in a shattered urban terrain.

It was in that context that our squatters' movement erupted spontaneously with some 1,000 people squatting roughly 30 vacant buildings, many with open roofs and in derelict shape. Each of our buildings was autonomous, with two basic agendas: open up more buildings and defend each other through our Eviction Watch, doing whatever we had to do, within a non-violent framework, to prevent the cops from evicting us.

But our lives were also about building solidarity with our neighbours, our first line of defence, throwing parties, organising and participating in collective work days, creating communal kitchens and tool collectives. As I said, our politics was centred around the political attack on the poor, an understanding of homelessness as state repression and the need for squatting as a means of self and community defence. In 1988 the authorities came to shut the Tompkins Square Park, and under the banner of 'Gentrification is Genocide' the neighbourhood ran the riot police out of the place, proving that effective nonviolent resistance need not be passive!

We are today 11 buildings that still exist in a neighbourhood that has meanwhile undergone hyper-gentrification. We have been decriminalised, most with a debt to pay for renovations. Some of us call it the 'World Bank model'. My building voted against signing on for overpriced renovation, demanding that any work paid for by officialdom would be accomplished by us as subcontractors. We have yet to work out a viable plan with them.

It is apparent that in 2013 the idea of squatting is coming back around, like in the 1980s. In the United States, the thousands of home foreclosures have opened up a new discourse on the subject of squatting. And that is why we formed O4O or Organizing for Occupation, actually some months before Occupy Wall Street. Across the United States, there are nearly 20 million vacant homes, 4 million homeless people, with many cities shrinking. All over the world, in the last 50 years, about 370 global cities with more than 100,000 residents have suffered population losses of more than 10 per cent. More than 25 per cent of those depopulating cities are in the United States: Buffalo and Rochester, N.Y.; Cleveland and Youngstown, Ohio; Detroit and Flint, Mich.; Newark, N.J.; Pittsburgh, Pa.; and St Louis, Mo. have lost 37–59 per cent of their people since 1950.

The situation calls for a massive squatter uprising based on need, desire, mandates of survival, and the necessity to construct resisting communities; but more importantly, our homes and social centres must become bases of resistance, fostering a revolution of values, overcoming the decadent and archaic capitalism that is anti-life.

Notes

1   [The issue of scalability, discussed in the Paris SqEK meeting and over the email list, is central to this book, and part of the conclusion is dedicated to this debate. In particular, the experience of Amsterdam is likely to represent the best example in the history of the squatters' movement of how it managed to reach a considerable dimension and become an autonomous organisation which could influence institutional politics. Scalability is also considered in Chapter 5, with the experience of the movements for housing rights which have started in Rome and are now spreading widely over Italy. The nature of these two movements, although very different and stemming from very different social needs, can also be representative of how squatting in European contexts has been evolving and related to the institutional and economic contexts of a particular time.]

References

Borgos, S. (1986) 'Low-income home ownership and the ACORN squatters campaign', in R. Bratt, C. Hartman and A. Meyerson (eds), *Critical Perspectives on Housing*. Philadelphia, Penn.: Temple University Press.

Bosma, J. H., Bijnen, S., Davidson, J., Eissens, K,. van Harn, K. and Nijenhuis, T. (1984) *De beste aktiegroep ter wereld. 40 dorpsverhalen uit de Nieuwmarkt [The Best Action Group in the World: 40 Village Stories from the Nieuwmarkt]*. Amsterdam: Stichting Uitgeverij de Oude Stad.

Brandes Gratz, R. (1989) *The Living City: How America's Cities Are Being Revitalized by Thinking Small in a Big Way*. New York: Simon & Schuster.

Breek, P. and de Graad, F. (2001) *Laat duizend vrijplaatsen bloeien. onderzoek naar vrijplaatsen in Amsterdam* [*Let a Thousand Freed Spaces Flourish: A Survey of Freed Spaces in Amsterdam*]. Amsterdam: De Vrije Ruimte.

Brotherton, M. A. (1978) *Conflict of Interest, Law Enforcement, and Social Change: A Case Study of Squatters on Morningside Heights*. Ann Arbor, Mich.: University Microfilms International.

Draaisma, J. and van Hoogstraten, P. (1983) 'The squatter movement in Amsterdam', *International Journal of Urban and Regional Research* 7(3), 405–16.

Duivenvoorden, E. (2000). *Een voet tussen de deur. Geschiedenis van de kraakbeweging 1964–1999* [*A Foot in the Door: The History of the Squatters' Movement 1964–1999*]. Amsterdam: Arbeiderspers.

e-CFR (2012) 'Title 24: Housing and Urban Development, Part 590: Urban Homesteading.' http://ecfr.gpoaccess.gov (accessed 5 July 2012).

Esping-Andersen, G. (1990) *The Three Worlds of Welfare Capitalism*. Cambridge: Polity Press.

Ferguson, S. (2007) 'The struggle for space: 10 years of turf battling on the Lower East Side', in C. Patterson, J. Flood and A. Moore (eds), *Resistance: A Radical Political History of the Lower East Side*. New York: Seven Stories Press.

Hoekema, A. J. (1978) *De uitgespeelde gemeenteraad. Beschrijving van de invloedsverdeling bij een rooilijnbesluit in een grote gemeente* [*The City Council Outplayed. Description of the Impact Distribution of a Building-Line Decision in a Large Municipality*]. Deventer, Netherlands: Kluwer.

Jaffe, A. (2007) 'Frank Morales', in C. Patterson, J. Flood and A. Moore (eds), *Resistance: A Radical Political History of the Lower East Side*. New York: Seven Stories Press..

Jonnes, J. (1980) 'For squatters, rent-free life is the solution to high costs', *New York Times*, 23 March, R1.

McAdam, D., Tarrow, S. and Tilly, C. (2001) *Dynamics of Contention*. Cambridge: Cambridge University Press.

Mamadouh, V. (1992) *De stad in eigen hand. Provo's, kabouters en krakers als stedelijke sociale beweging* [*The City in One's Own Hand: Provos, Kabouters and Squatters as Urban Social Movement*]. Amsterdam: SUA.

Muzio, R. (2009) 'The struggle against 'urban renewal' in Manhattan's Upper West Side and the emergence of El Comité', *Centro Journal* 21(2), 109–41. www.redalyc.org/articulo.oa?id=37720842006 (accessed 29 January 2014).

Picture The Homeless (2011) *Banking on Vacancy. Homelessness and Real Estate Speculation*. New York: Picture The Homeless.

Poldervaart, S. (2004) 'Vrijplaatsen door de eeuwen heen' ['Freed spaces throughout the ages '] in F. de Graad, H van der Horst, F. Kallenberg, F. and I. van Liempt (eds), *easyCity: Interventies in een verscheurde stad* [*EasyCity: Interventions in a Divided City*]. Amsterdam: De Vrije Ruimte.

Pruijt, H. (2003) 'Is the institutionalization of urban movements inevitable? A comparison of the opportunities for sustained squatting in New York City and Amsterdam', *International Journal of Urban and Regional Research* 27(1), 133–57.

–– (2004a) 'Squatters in the Creative City: rejoinder to Justus Uitermark', *International Journal of Urban and Regional Research* 28(1), 699–705.

–– (2004b) 'The impact of citizens' protest on city planning in Amsterdam', in L.

Deben, W. Salet and M. T. van Thoor (eds), *Cultural Heritage and the Future of the Historic Inner City of Amsterdam*. Amsterdam: Aksant.

–– (2013a) 'The logic of urban squatting', *International Journal of Urban and Regional Research* 37(1), 19–45.

–– (2013b) 'Culture wars, revanchism, moral panics and the creative city. a reconstruction of a decline of tolerant public policy: the case of Dutch anti-squatting legislation', *Urban Studies* 50(6), 1114–29.

Schwartz, J. (1986) 'Tenant power in the liberal city, 1943–1971', in R. Lawson and M. Naison (eds), *The Tenant Movement in New York City, 1904–1984*. New Brunswick, N.J.: Rutgers University Press.

Soja, E. (2000) 'The stimulus of a little confusion: a contemporary comparison of Amsterdam and Los Angeles', in L. Deben, W. Heinemeijer and D. van der Vaart (eds), *Understanding Amsterdam. Essays on Economic Vitality, City Life and Urban Form*. Amsterdam: Het Spinhuis.

Tobocman, S. (1999) *War in the Neighborhood*. New York: Autonomedia.

Tolia, K. (2007) 'Activism by an activist', in C. Patterson, J. Flood and A. Moore (eds), *Resistance: A Radical Political History of the Lower East Side*. New York: Seven Stories Press.

Van der Raad, J. W. (1981) *Kraken in Amsterdam [Squatting in Amsterdam]*. Amsterdam: Roelof Kellerstichting.

Van Noort, W. (1988) *Bevlogen bewegingen. Een vergelijking van de anti-kernenergie, kraak- en milieubeweging* [   ]. Amsterdam: SUA.

Van Tijen, T. (2008) 'Zwartmakers en een pleidooi voor een "Witboek Kraken"' ['Black Makers and a plea for a "White Paper Crunch"']. http://imaginarymuseum.org/LimpingMessenger/WitboekKraken2008.html (accessed 29 January 2914).

Walder, A. G. (2009) 'Political sociology and social movements', *Annual Review of Sociology* 35(1), 393–412.

5

Ogni Sfratto Sarà Una Barricata: *Squatting for Housing and Social Conflict in Rome*

Pierpaolo Mudu

Introduction

All over the world, especially in large metropolitan areas, shanty towns and homelessness go together with various forms of resistance. In neoliberal capitalism, lack of housing is a well-known mechanism which separates people with housing needs from the available buildings. In Italy, the case of Rome is particularly interesting for the well-articulated forms of resistance and for the high number of people involved, among the highest in European cities. But as in other cities, housing policies in Rome provide a powerful mechanism which operates to perform class selection and social exclusion within the population through explicit spatial patterns. Resistance to such a mechanism is a relatively new phenomenon which has occurred during the last 60 years. It has gone through at least four phases. The first phase, between the 1950s and the 1970s, was principally led by the Italian Communist Party (PCI). In the 1970s the emergence of organisations from the extraparliamentary left changed the characteristics of resistance trajectories, and the PCI was no longer the sole main actor (Balestrini and Moroni, 1997). From the beginning of the 1980s a third phase developed, lasting around 20 years, where the action of organisations from the radical left was not directly linked to any political party, and groups experimented with new ways of action. The first decade of the 21st century represents a fourth phase in the struggles for housing, because both the level of mobilisation and networking have increased significantly.

This chapter focuses on the last decade, when there was a strong downturn in the supply of social housing, resulting in mass exclusion from the right to the city. Various waves of social conflict have contested such institutional apathy towards the lack of housing, behind which certainly lay violent class politics. This chapter is divided into four main sections. In the first there is a brief historical description of the development of housing policies and the resistance to them in Rome from the 1950s to the end of the last century. In the second there is a description of current housing conditions from the perspective of the movements engaged in occupations. A third section contains some relevant examples of occupations for housing in Rome. The fourth and final section discusses the social dimensions of squatting for housing and its contribution to the reconfiguration of housing as a field of conflict that is not only related to the simple goal of obtaining a roof for people.

A Brief Summary of Housing Policies and Struggles for Housing in Italy and Rome since the 1950s[1]

A note on terminology: the term 'squat' is probably inadequate to describe the Italian situation. In Italian, the word 'squat' is used more rarely than the word *occupazione* (occupation). Occupation refers to a very broad range of political and social actions, and implies a larger range of meanings than squatting, such as the illegal occupation of workplaces, squares, apartments, buildings or land, so that it is a more appropriate term to describe such a broad social phenomenon. Nevertheless, the term 'squatting', which is used in Italian as an English neologism, will be used through this text, mainly to denote the action of illegal occupation of empty buildings and land for housing (so that a social centre is understood as an *occupazione* but not as a 'squat'). In the following text I describe the evolution of housing policies and protests, with squatting as the fundamental tool employed in the struggle for the right to housing (and beyond). The practice of occupation of apartments, buildings or land lies at the intersection of two definitions. First, an occupation is an action that interrupts phases of homelessness, or of living under degraded housing conditions. Second, it is an action that allows people to build a material and symbolic lifestyle alternative to the trends of mainstream capitalism.

Changes in the forms of protest matched some structural changes in the urban development of Rome. After the Second World War, the fascist dictatorship, which had never opposed speculation in land and buildings, left a heritage of *borgate* (poor-quality public housing outside the city) and shanty towns built by immigrants and people displaced from the city centre (Insolera, 2011). Between 1947 and 1976, the ruling Christian Democrats (DC) led the development of the city in an open agreement with speculators (Insolera, 2011). In the 1950s and 1960s, the struggle for decent housing was organised by the PCI, which denounced a situation of extreme poverty and bad housing conditions for around 100,000 people, as reported by a commission set up by the national Parliament in 1952 (Berlinguer and Della Seta, 1976). Massive housing plans were implemented in the 1950s. These were mostly linked to speculation and illegal building practices, and only a few involved affordable housing projects (Clementi and Perego, 1981). At the beginning of 1961, after a long struggle, Law 1092 of 6 July 1939 against urbanisation was abolished. This fascist law had denied registration in the municipal civil registry to thousands of unemployed immigrants, who in many cases had been resident in Rome for more than ten years. They were then denied the right to vote and the opportunity to receive health care and social security (Berlinguer and Della Seta, 1976).

The struggle for housing rights in the 1950s and 1960s was different from that of the following decades. In the 1950s and 1960s people in *borgate* suffered very bad housing conditions, with no running water or toilets. Between the 1950s and the advent in 1976 of the PCI municipal government, movements for housing rights also used public demonstrations against the political authorities to demand access to basic services such as electricity, sewage, public transport and parks.

Squatting, as a collective form of protest, emerged for the first time in the 1960s (Tozzetti, 1989). The actions and involvement of the PCI in these housing struggles continued until the party won the municipal elections of 1976. The PCI controlled the municipality for nine years, and oriented much of its political action towards housing problems, rehabilitating once and for all the old *borgate* and providing as many apartments as possible. In the 1970s, the occupation of empty apartments was in many cases also linked to a more general struggle against the *carovita* (meaning intolerable inflationary pressure hampering the life of working-class people; Daolio, 1974).

After the 1973 oil crisis, the policies that addressed the economic crisis showed how far capital was willing to push its attack against the living conditions of the working class, and 'a wave of struggles dictated by the working class's need to protect their wage gains, and to ensure adequate access to essential goods and services such as food, housing, utilities and transportation' took place (Ramirez, 1975). Organizations close to the PCI (such as the *Unione Nazionale Inquilini Assegnatari*, UNIA or National Alliance of Tenants) promoted squatting, but only of public housing, as a means to negotiate with public institutions. In the 1970s, the left extraparliamentary organisations targeted private housing instead, claiming that rents should take up no more than 10 per cent of wages. The practice of *autoriduzione* (self-reduction) – the refusal to comply with price increases in essential services – was the answer which emerged from these struggles (Balestrini and Moroni, 1997).

In Italy between 1969 and 1975, 20,000 apartments were squatted. In the mid-1970s in Rome there were 4,000 squatted apartments (Comitati autonomi operai di Roma, 1976). These struggles cannot be isolated from the climate of police and social violence which was enforced in Italy. The most dramatic episode occurred in Rome in San Basilio, a working-class neighbourhood designed during the fascist period in the north-eastern suburbs. In September 1974 Fabrizio Ceruso, a militant from Autonomia, was killed during a clash between police and squatters (Lotringer and Marazzi, 2007). In 1978, after this long cycle of struggles, the rental market was regulated at a national level, by the Equo Canone law (Law No. 392/1978) which capped rents in cities at affordable prices for low to medium-income tenants, with automatic renewals of contracts, but few property owners complied with this law, producing an effective boycott of it.

In the 1980s the PCI gradually lost its political capacity to mobilise classes living in suburban areas (Coppola, 2008), mainly because of a general incapacity to understand the newly rising social trends of migration and poverty, coupled with the developing reactionary policies against poverty, the working class and migrants. Influence-peddling within the administration of social affairs as it was run by the DC, and the PCI's inability to propose a new social project for the city after the rehabilitation of its *borgate* and *periferia*, led to a crisis phase just as neoliberal urban policies were coming into fashion among governing elites. In the last 20 years, Rome has adopted all the policies familiar from other cities governed by neoliberals (Brenner and Theodore, 2002). The shift to these neoliberal policies happened during the 1990s and 2000s.

Their main features included a new master plan, the defunding of many municipal housing assets, the privatisation of municipal services and the promotion of major events (such as the Football World Cup) to justify huge construction and development plans.[2] Neoliberal policies could ensure better profits, privileges and more efficient social control by the wealthiest than the previous (and itself corrupt) welfare system. As neoliberal policies were implemented, they adopted local features and connected them to national and global patterns. In fact, several changes affected people's housing conditions: national and local policies, the institution of a 'free' market in formerly public housing, and the processes of construction. These in turn affected the composition and struggles of the movements for the right to housing.

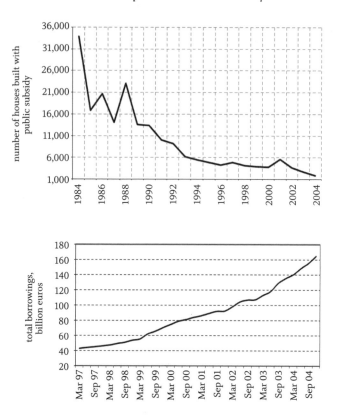

Figure 5.1 Houses built with public subsidy, 1984 –2004 (a) and debt for purchasing houses, 1997–2004 (b)

Source: ANCI-CRESME (2005).

In the 1980s, the first suggestion to public institutions from promoters of a free market was for families to leave public housing and to buy their own apartments (see Figure 5.1). In a few years the majority of Italian people were convinced to change to ownership of their apartments. In 1971, 47 per cent of families rented the apartment where they were living. By 2001 that figure was 20 per cent. This shift from renting to owning generated long-term revenue for banks offering mortgages. The borrowers typically took decades to repay their mortgage loans. In 20 years, beginning in the 1980s the amounts due to be reimbursed to the banks rose to more than €160 billion (ANCI-CRESME, 2005). It was necessary for the market to change in significant ways for this shift to be successful. Rental prices increased to a level higher than mortgage rates, and unregistered rent contracts were tolerated, putting tenants in difficult positions. This made the rental market marginal and subordinate to the sales market. However, this perverse mechanism could not last forever. Currently in Italy, people with a yearly income below €14,000 spend between 63 per cent and 94 per cent of their income on housing, which is disproportionate when a 'fair' percentage is estimated to be around 30 per cent (CNEL, 2010). The average rent under new contracts in Rome is estimated by CNEL as between €740 and €1,100 per month, while the average monthly income of lower-income tenants is less than €1,200 (CNEL, 2010).

The case of national policies on rent regulation and deregulation is emblematic. In 1992 a new law favouring owners was passed; in 1998 the rent market was completely deregulated (by Law 431/1998), abolishing the Equo Canone law. In the same year the fund for affordable housing, at both the national and local levels, was abolished (by Law 112/1998). At a national scale neoliberal dogmas were adopted by the Democratic Party (the successor to the PCI) which were discontinuous with past social welfare proposals and the governance experiences of the PCI. This swift reconfiguration of the public housing sector pulled the rug of basic subsistence out from under a great many members of the Roman working class.

At a national level, during the last Berlusconi government (2008–11), there were two *Piano Casa* (housing plans) aimed at 'solving' the housing problem (Law 112/2008 and Law 106/2011). In reality both of these constituted further steps in deregulation, and they were passed as a favour to builders and speculators. The measures of the *Piano Casa* were based on incentives to builders who committed to offer a percentage of their newly built apartments at low rent for social housing. This new model of social housing meant that its provision was delegated to private for-profit companies, and taken away from the public sector. In the past the public sector was heavily involved in providing social housing, although it was poorly managed and corruption was common. The average rent for social housing under the new schemes was calculated to be no less than €500–600, well above the threshold of social sustainability (CNEL, 2010).

In Rome, the centre-left coalition that ruled the city between 1993 and 2008 supported the implementation of neoliberal policies, but it was confronted with increasing resistance. Discussion about local policies for housing and their implementation have both been very difficult. In 1999 there was the first ratification of the 'Protocol on the housing emergency' (*Protocollo sull'emergenza abitativa*). But the protocol was implemented slowly, and the pressure of the movements for the right to housing forced the municipality to pass a new resolution on the housing emergency (resolution 110/05: *Deliberazione programmatica sulle politiche*

abitative e sull'emergenza abitativa nell'area comunale romana). This resolution was not applied, and in 2008 a change of administration from the
centre-left coalition to a right-wing grouping meant an exacerbation of
influence-peddling, indifference to housing problems and support for
building speculators.

Challenging Housing Policies in Neoliberal Rome: Contested Numbers

Rome's master plans for housing have represented a huge favour to
landlords and building speculators (Insolera, 2011). The new master plan
was based on the mechanism of 'transfer of development rights' (*compen-
sazione*), by which the rights of speculators to build in the city were
protected. The planning process for the new master plan started in 1994.
It was adopted in 2003 and finally approved in 2008, almost 50 years after
the previous one (Berdini, 2008). The previous master plan of 1962 was
intended to develop a Rome of up to 5 million inhabitants. The new master
plan provides for new construction of 70 million cubic metres to create
a city that can house more than 3 million inhabitants. This is equivalent
to an average of nearly 10 square metres of new construction per inhabitant. The population of Rome has not increased in the last 40 years. In
fact it has decreased slightly, and was approximately 2,600,000 in 2012. In
2012, claiming to be 'unsatisfied' with the gigantic provisions of the master
plan, the municipality of Rome proposed 64 resolutions adding plans for
129,000 new hectares to be developed, almost 20,000 new cubic metres of
concrete, and 66,000 apartments to be built (and likely to be left empty).
There is no relation between these proposals for building construction and
people's needs. Housing, it seems, is not planned rationally any more, it is
only mentioned for electoral purposes.

In 2001 (the last census for which we have data), the size of the housing
stock in Rome was approximately 1,000,000, with 11 per cent vacant (this
figure is probably an underestimate). The incidence of vacancy in Rome is
considerably higher than that found in other major Italian cities, where the
percentage of vacant houses is around 6 per cent of the total housing stock.
It is clear that housing needs are not simple quantifiable objects. In 2008,
during the last campaign to elect a mayor of the city, post-fascist candidate
Gianni Alemanno promised to see 30,000 new affordable apartments
built if elected. After the election he did not act to fulfil his promises (see
Figure 5.2).

If we adopt the perspective of the people in need, the numbers are
different. Current statistics produced by Movimenti per il diritto all'abitare

Figure 5.2 Poster for a public meeting to denounce Mayor Alemanno's promises as 'flimflam' (*pacco*)

(Movements for the Right to Inhabit), the largest network for squatting houses, count 50,000 people in need of affordable housing (Franchetto and Action, 2004) (see Figure 5.3). This number is derived from the number of people under threat of eviction (*sfrattati*) and the number of applications for affordable accommodation presented to the administration office. The Ministry of Interior counted 7,206 eviction requests in 2011 and 8,015 in 2010, mostly because of inability to pay rent (70 per cent of cases). The number of requests for public housing was 42,000 in 2009 (and very few apartments were available). New applications were not accepted for three

Figure 5.3 Activists holding a banner, 'Get off the cloud, 50,000 affordable apartments are needed' at a demonstration on housing[3]

years after 2009. To fill out this picture, there are those who have given up looking for affordable housing because they are resigned to cohabiting with family or friends, or living in bad conditions, who are usually not counted. The municipality manages approximately 80,000 apartments, and every year it has about 1,500 available for new tenants. Clearly, in the absence of a supply of subsidised houses, people will try to find other solutions.

From the perspective of people in the movements for the right to housing, it is clear how to interpret the statistics and how to deal with such numbers (see Figure 5.4). The decrease in available apartments at an affordable rent correlates with an increase in squatting.

Social housing in Rome has been built under conditions of social emergency through a series of measures tailored to specific interests. The hegemonic idea of public institutions has been and still is to privatise existing public housing, with the objective of eventually providing new apartments in the outskirts for those in need. The real objective was to put an end to the practice of providing accommodation to the poor through public housing: that is, apartments owned by the municipality and assigned to low-income families and particular social groups at rents below the open market level.

In the last 20 years, foreign immigrants have emerged as particularly relevant actors in patterns of housing segregation (Mudu, 2006a, 2006b). They tend to be strongly segregated for housing purposes, and this is often related to their lack of documents permitting legal residence, or refugee status. Between 8,000 and 15,000 immigrants are estimated to have been

Figure 5.4 The decline in social housing from 2004–2008, a graph/poster produced by a group of housing rights associations

surviving in unfit housing, in shanty towns, or are homeless in Rome (Mudu, 2006a).

We can see a change over the years in the population involved in squatting. During the 1950s, many immigrants from the south of Italy occupied small pieces of land to build houses. Until the 1970s squatting was carried out by people who had been living in shanty towns (*baraccati*) and the homeless, while during the 1980s evicted tenants started to mobilise to squat big public housing units. Foreign immigrants became progressively more involved. Beginning in the 1980s, and accelerating throughout the decade, Italy and Rome began to receive foreign immigrants. Occupations soon occurred, as in the case of Polish immigrants who squatted in San Basilio in 1988 (Il Tempo, 1988), but housing activists at first did not consider these occupations as a new political possibility of intersection between migrant issues and housing needs. In a few years the situation evolved toward an increased use of squatting by immigrants.

The sociopolitical use of squatting by immigrants emerged clearly in 1990 when the former pasta factory of the Pantanella, close to Porta Maggiore in the centre of the city, was occupied by an increasing number of people, mainly migrants from Bangladesh. The number of squatters in the Pantanella reached 2,000 in 1991 shortly before they were evicted. In Corviale, a massive popular housing project in the south-west of the city, 340 immigrants, mostly from South America and undocumented, lived in a squatted building owned by the social housing institute IACP (ASPE, 1993). Also at the beginning of the 1990s, 100 immigrants mostly from India and Pakistan lived in a former seaside hostel in Ostia (ASPE, 1993).

In September 1993 during Mayor Rutelli's centre-left administration (1993–2001), the Coordinamento cittadino lotta per la casa occupied the FederImmobiliare building in Ostia, consisting of three large apartment blocks which had been left empty for over ten years. This represented one of the first large-scale occupations in which there was a strong presence of migrants (out of 220 participants approximately 40 per cent of the squatters were not Italian, with 19 different nationalities represented). This period marks the development of a social intercultural movement in a context where the right to housing for migrants had not been recognised.

Migration policies in the last ten years have shifted from being a social question to a criminal issue. In 1998, Law 40 ordered the construction of special temporary detention centres (*Centri di Detenzione Temporanea*) for undocumented immigrants preparatory to their expulsion. In 2008 and 2009 migrant issues were inserted into a set of security laws, the so-called *pacchetto sicurezza* (Law 125/2008 and Law 94/2009). It is evident that the purpose of these measures was to create obstacles to migration for reasons of family reunification. Before these laws foreign immigrants claiming the right to family reunification simply had to prove that an apartment complying with the minimum requirements set by regional laws for public housing was available to them. After these laws came into force, foreigners instead had to demonstrate that the available apartment also complied 'with the hygiene and health requirements established by the competent municipal authorities' (Law 94/2009). This subtle change has shifted decision making away from the clearly set criteria defined by regional regulations, to often arbitrary judgements by municipal authorities. Tracking the most extreme forms of poverty suffered by immigrants provides a useful viewpoint for recognising how segregation processes have spatially and socially expanded, while other patterns are now cyclical. Unlike the 1950s, marginal housing conditions are now spread all over the territory; they have penetrated into the whole metropolitan area, so that Rome is also the 'capital of homeless people'.

During Mayor Veltroni's administration (2001–08) 1,700 apartments were assigned to families, but since 2008 under Mayor Alemanno's administration only 300 have been assigned. The municipality of Rome spends €32 million yearly to support 1,300 families living in 19 residential blocks that are badly managed and degraded (Lombardi-Diop, 2009). This amounts to almost €25,000 per family.

The second half of the 1990s saw new developments highlighting the increasingly restricted access to housing for many people – the use of debt to govern people's lives and a range of responses to the worsening situation, which included not only squatting but electoral participation by squatters' candidates, proposals for self-renovation (*autorecupero*) that involve the municipality paying for major structural renovations, and cooperatives formed by squatters to pay for interior renovations, as well as many public meetings and demonstrations (altremappe, 2004).

The Present: The Struggle Is Rescaled

The end of the century also marked a change in the composition of the squatters. In addition to evicted tenants, they currently include a variegated group of precarious workers, unemployed, students and a large proportion of foreign migrants. Currently the largest number of people involved in collective occupations for housing are organised by three organizations: Coordinamento cittadino lotta per la casa (Citizens Platform for the Housing Struggle), Action, and Blocchi Precari Metropolitani (Metropolitan Precarious Blocks) (see Table 5.1).[4] Coordinamento cittadino lotta per la casa is the oldest, and was already active in 1988, when 350 apartments were squatted in San Basilio. It demonstrated a creative and practical capacity, in contrast to municipal institutions. For example, in 2008 after the occupation of the abandoned Volturno theatre, close to the main railroad station, a municipal department for social housing (Assessorato popolare alla casa) was created by the Coordinamento. In 2002 Action was formed, and networked with former post-Autonomist Disobbedienti. It immediately organised large squatting campaigns (Franchetto and Action, 2004). Action managed to have one of its members elected as a councillor in the municipality of Rome in the 1997, 2001 and 2008 elections. Action is a structured organisation, also supported by some social centres (for example Corto Circuito), and manages occupations which openly constitute a political confrontation and challenge to mainstream policies [to this extent, the Jeudi Noir organisation in Paris – see Box 5.1 – has similar institutional tactics]. One occupation – Lucia y Siesta – also engages with gender politics, as it is run solely by women.

The Blocchi Precari Metropolitani, supported also by people from Action, was born in November 2007 from a general strike organised by grassroots trade unions. It runs ten occupied spaces which also programme social and cultural activities, and migrants are strongly involved.

These three organisations have clearly different histories, organisational methods and relationships with public institutions. Action is often associated with a more Leninist type of activism which also negotiates and participates in institutional decision-making processes. Coordinamento

Table 5.1 Main movements for the right to housing in Rome

Name (and English translation)	Year	Origins	Example of occupations
Coordinamento cittadino lotta per la casa (Citizen Coordination for the Housing Struggle)	1988	Squatting of 350 apartments in the San Basilio neighbourhood. Represents the development of struggles carried out by Autonomists in the previous years.	Porto Fluviale: 130 families live in a former military barracks complex in a semi-central position
Action	2002	Occupation in the San Lorenzo neighbourhood. Originated from the Tute Bianche and Diritto alla Casa groups operating at the end of the 1990s.	Sans Papiers: 50 families live in a building owned by the Italian central bank in a central position
Blocchi Precari Metropolitani (Precarious Metropolitan Blocks)	2007	Mobilisation for a general strike of the grassroots trade unions in November 2007.	Metropoliz: 40 families live in a former salami factory in the suburban area

lotta per la casa and Blocchi Precari Metropolitani have a more pragmatic approach focused on renovation of buildings and requesting funds for renovating squatted properties. All the organisations network with small cooperatives that carry out renovation work, and experiment with new techniques of sustainable architecture.

The increasing coordination among the three main groups that organise occupations for housing only emerged in the last few years. On 6 December 2012, Movimenti per il diritto all'abitare (a joint venture of the three above-named groups) organised a spectacular event, a series of occupations in the city of Rome.[5] Around 2,000 people took eight buildings to lay claim to the allocation of funds for public housing, to contest the privatisation of public housing, and to promote self-renovation projects. The *autorecupero* proposals by the Coordinamento went along with the formation of a cooperative with 100 members to support such a practice (Agostini, 2011). In the 1990s 12 projects of *autorecupero* of squatted houses were implemented, although so far this practice has been used more by Italians than by immigrants (Agostini, 2011).

[The case of Rome is a good example of what could be considered the beginning of a counter-hegemonic strategy, of the type presented in Chapter 1, against neoliberal housing. In fact, as we can see from Table 5.1, Figures 5.4 and 5.6 and the text that follows, the evolution of occupations for the right of housing into active social centres, such as Porto Fluviale, Sans Papiers and Metropoliz, is a sign of a coalition between common people and more radical squatters. The very idea of *autorecupero*, a widespread do-it-yourself (DIY) strategy for home renovation, is based on the self-organisation of the network and on its autonomy from public institutions, just like the practices that squatters all over Europe and North America have traditionally employed in their activism.]

The tensions caused by certain famous actions of Action did not prevent the municipality from recognising its importance. Mayor Veltroni (who headed a centre-left coalition) asked Action to collaborate with the municipality. In 2005, representatives of the movements for the right to housing were received by a UN delegation, which reported that in recent years it was only through their struggles and occupying actions that a basic right – recognised by international treaties, but violated by individual governments – could be made effective (*Corriere della Sera*, 2005).

In a 2010 report, the Security Commission of the Rome municipality listed the squats in the city (Comune di Roma, 2010). The report, based on information from citizens and the municipal police, is poorly organised and underestimates the number of squats in the city, but nevertheless it was cited widely in the press. Movements for the right to housing are tolerated by left parties and opposed by centre-right parties, property speculators and the mass media. In fact, building developer companies control the local Roman newspapers: for example Caltagirone owns *Il Messaggero* and Bonifaci owns *Il Tempo*. From time to time newspapers launch criminalisation campaigns against squatters and are obsessed with producing maps of the occupations present in each neighbourhood of Rome as an attempt to control them. In these articles all squatters are compared with terrorists whom the police should arrest (Desario, 2009a, 2009b; Panarella, 2013; Rossi, 2009). Moderate parties accuse people occupying apartments of compromising public housing policies by not respecting the assignations to accommodation that are regulated by objective lists.

Squatting for Housing Movements: Between Autorecupero and Legalisation

The Movimenti per il diritto all'abitare has been able to extend the territorial reach of its practices and resistance, which now covers the city's metropolitan area. A debate with similar movements in other Italian cities is now going on, which proves the movement's capacity to rescale its actions. Some squatted houses remain local experiences where much effort is devoted to renovating the squatted place, while others have started to engage the surrounding neighbourhoods and/or even to open a dialogue at an international level. The use of the internet has increased the visibility and capacity of the last wave of squatting. In contrast with past experiences of squatting for housing, leisure facilities are made available to the whole neighbourhood once an occupation is in progress. Spaces are distributed according to the number of family members, and parties are organised to show off the space (Careri and Mazzitelli, 2012).

This kind of multi-scale action has built up the strength of squatters and weakened the repressive network of the authorities. Evictions of large numbers of people are one of the most dramatic events that squatters can suffer (Smart, 2012). In some cases people are just thrown onto the streets; in other cases people are divided and dispersed into improvised housing solutions; in other cases still, people are sheltered by other squatters. Not only is housing taken away, social relations are discontinued, such as school attendance or job relationships that have been built up in the area around the squatted place. The movements for the right to housing have to post several pickets per day to prevent evictions (Schawrz, 2012).

The movements for the right to housing seem to have learned from the past experience of struggles in the 1970s that the fight for housing should not be a struggle that is extinguished when people get a roof and occupations are legalised. When this happens, the painfully acquired political conscience vanishes into the individual right to an apartment. The capacity to maintain forms of mobilisation after occupations have been legalised is an important asset for the movements (see Figure 5.5).

Collective occupations for housing have become a powerful device compared with individual squatting. This type of squatting still exists: many individuals take an apartment just because they need it, without any support from organisations. If possible they pay some money to people who are leaving an apartment, or they know an apartment is going to become available and squat it. Deprivation-based squatting exists because it is legitimate (Pruijt, 2013), but this process involves marginalised people in severe poverty with limited networking capacities (De Angelis, 2010).

Figure 5.5 A leaflet from a successful *autorecupero* project

Movimenti per il diritto all'abitare maintains lists of people to accommodate, updates lists of abandoned buildings, and organises meetings to prepare the occupation of entire buildings, not just single apartments. Discussions on the difficulty of squatting and the need to support other squatters are open, and held with all the people involved for many months before the day when the squatters move in.

Squatting is not only a collective form of protest useful for negotiating a possible legalisation or a process of *autorecupero* with the authorities. It has become an alternative form of urban living. The squats produce real spaces of proximity, and the squatters devise alternative urban forms to capitalism:

> We don't want to open all the gates and make the new square become a place of passage and circulation like all the other squares around the city: this would simply replicate the current experience of the city, whose public spaces are meant for capitalistic consumption. The new square sets aside any capitalistic logic and wants to be the place to experiment with new activities and ways of exchanging and paying back the services that the community will offer.
>
> (Talocci, 2012)

Blocchi Precari Metropolitani states:

> In the spaces we occupy there are now supportive communities networking with the surrounding territory, in an attempt to practise a way of living

which stands in open conflict with the current model of development, based on the capitalist valorisation of our lives and of the places we inhabit.

(Urbanrise, 2013)

The cases of Metropoliz and Sans Papiers show an increased capacity of networking, and attempt to fill the gap between occupations for social centres and squatting for housing which has historically separated the radical left in Rome (see Figure 5.6). In fact, the house squat Sans Papiers has adopted the acronym CSOA (Centro Sociale Occupato Autogestito) to define a space open to the rest of the city (Figure5.6).

Over time there has been an evolution in the type of properties targeted for squatting. For example, in the 1990s the focus, particularly for Movimento lotta per la casa, was on abandoned public buildings such as schools. In the past the source of information for these organisations was a census of abandoned properties. Now the city is constantly emptying buildings, so the task of spotting and listing potential targets is much easier.

Metropoliz, a former salami factory, was squatted by the Blocchi Precari Metropolitani in 2009. At the beginning, there were only Italians and a few refugees. After six months Romas expelled from via Casilina arrived, followed by other migrants (Bagnoli, 2011). In 2011, 90 immigrant families got a residence permit which would have been impossible to obtain had they been homeless. Most of Metropoliz's inhabitants come from north and central Africa (including Morocco, Tunisia, Eritrea and Sudan), Central and South America (Peru, Santo Domingo), Eastern Europe (Poland, Ukraine, Romania) and interestingly 100 are Roma people. This is one of the few examples in Italy where a group of Roma have joined a radical local movement. This occupation involved not only self-renovation but also the construction of new small apartments. When it began, the Roma preferred to live in tents. Then they collected enough money (approximately €400) to build small basic apartments. Using the existing structure of the abandoned warehouses they would lay a brick wall and put in a couple of windows in order to close off an apartment (Bagnoli, 2011). The distribution of facilities such as toilets also followed a different pattern in Metropoliz. While the main block where Italians and South Americans reside has private toilets, the Roma have set up communal toilets and washing basins. To get Metropoliz 'citizenship' people must comply with a short set of rules (which are written down and affixed to a wall). Cleaning and respect for common spaces is required, alcohol cannot be abused, and women and children must be respected. Those who do not comply with these rules are forced to leave.

Figure 5.6 Posters for public meetings at the Metropoliz, Porto Fluviale and Sans Papiers squats, 2010

The people currently squatting are very different from the actors within the radical left who squatted in the past. People now who decide to join a collective squat do so because they are in desperate need of housing, and despite the facts that they have a very limited political background, and are unaware of Italian and radical left history and practices. Nevertheless, the people who promote and organise squatting are all from the radical left. In the first phase of the organisation of collective squatting, there is a distinction between activists and squatters. During the preparatory meetings, this is made progressively indistinct. The Movimenti per il diritto all'abitare can put together a very heterogeneous mix of people. The global financial crisis enlarged the number of people who, while previously able to pay rent, have now unexpectedly become homeless. For many, squatting for housing is a stage along the way to a permanent residence. The mass squatting actions for housing in Rome reveal an extended network of people which is able to resolve basic needs outside the official market and circuits of social assistance. In so doing the Movimenti per il diritto all'abitare has politicised a large number of people, familiarising them with the practice of self-organisation and self-management which is the reverse of what mainstream policies are pushing. Politicisation and continuous activism is usually a positive path for squatters, although it takes a lot of effort to continuously mobilise people with precarious jobs (Agostini, 2011). However, continuous mobilisation is not optional for squatters, since the need to have a roof is more important than job insecurity.

Self-management means organising rounds of pickets, providing water, cleaning common spaces and collecting money for common expenses. The squatted places have also been reconfigured, with internal squares, working areas, meeting points, children's corners and common spaces. This reconfiguration embodies an explicit criticism of the neoliberal city, commoning space in a direction different from the previous private/public dichotomy. The configuration of these squatted spaces is part of a process that also negotiates difficulties in understanding one another, comprehending different time activity patterns, and reshaping spaces designed for purposes totally different from housing. In several cases the condition of the abandoned buildings is very poor, or the building was built for purposes other than housing. This means that at the early stages of an occupation squatters need to share toilets and kitchens. This difficult stage has a positive role, strengthening the collaboration among the squatters, circulation of information on the job market, and solving everyday problems, like support for single working mothers (Agostini, 2011). A common space for children to play together was created in the Porto Fluviale, as well as self-managed schools to learn Italian (Careri and Mazzitelli, 2012).

For the first time since the 1970s, the work of the Movimenti per il diritto all'abitare in the last few years has attempted to supersede the opposition between squatting as a way of meeting a housing need and squatting as a way of satisfying the need for countercultural and/or political expression that holds in most European countries (Pruijt, 2013). This division persists in organisations that address deprivation-based squatting (Pruijt, 2013). In Rome it is difficult to distinguish between squatting because of deprivation and squatting as an alternative housing strategy. Movimenti per il diritto all'abitare, in different ways, has invested much effort into producing alternative forms of housing, while in recent years social centres have been mainly active with a different profile than in the past. In the case of Rome the current paths reflect a shift in the relationship between the mobilisations of social centres and of house squats. In fact networking is now much stronger than 15 years ago; while in the 1990s the two movements were pretty unconnected, and squats for housing never organised social activities in their premises, now several squats are open to the public and a few of them are very similar to social centres.

Over time networking between house squats and social centres has increased, and there is little correlation between the trends and cycles of occupations of social centres and those of squatting for housing.

If we analyse the patterns of squatting for housing in Rome we find a complex picture. In general terms the Movimenti per il diritto all'abitare in Rome is composed of individuals and variously formed collectives of different sizes which pursue various objectives. The most common one is obtaining a house; the second political objective is the redistribution of economic resources in more egalitarian ways. Two more objectives are also pursued: challenging the environmental burden of housing policies and their unsustainable consumption of land, and addressing housing policies that fail to integrate immigrants and Roma people.

Squatting involves a range of different people excluded from the housing market, including extremely marginalised people, the evicted, immigrants, students and activists. Although the labels 'evicted', 'immigrant' and 'student' are quite general and represent a multitude of persons, they all share the same low housing possibilities. Nevertheless, they do not share the same paths. From official statistics we know that in 70 per cent of cases eviction is requested because people cannot pay their rent, and the evicted are mostly elderly people living on state pensions, people who lose their jobs, and precarious workers (with children). Extremely marginalised people include a set of 'outcasts', for example former prisoners and families with mentally disabled members, who have no chance of affording *any* rent. In a system that has encouraged people to buy their own homes, the common trait of the evicted is that they lack the bank guarantees necessary to purchase their home (which is often sold by a public institution), or to pay rent. Official statistics ignore immigrants. 'Home-seeking' immigrants are mainly from a few countries in North Africa, Central and South America, and Asia (for instance, Bangladesh), and tend to have precarious and low-paid jobs.

In some cases immigrants and asylum seekers have been the only actors organising the squatting of a building. Two examples can be quoted. First, the Hotel Africa was squatted between 1999 and 2004 by approximately 500 Sudanese, Eritreans and Ethiopians, who self-managed an abandoned building owned by a railway company (after the eviction some of them organised the Naznnet squat with Action). Second, the Salaam Pace was squatted in 2006 at the former Faculty of Letters of the second University (Tor Vergata). Many squatting actions by immigrants are carried out with no public visibility, and in some cases the squatters have ended up in conditions no better than those of shanty towns (Mudu, 2006a).

Finally, students are squatting. In Italy 20 per cent of students are enrolled in a university out of their region of residence (320,000 students), and in Rome a bedroom in an apartment shared with others costs approximately €500 per month (ANCI-CRESMEU, 2005). For these reasons the number of students involved in squatting has increased, resulting in the occupation of student residences (*studentati occupati*). In this way, student struggles related to the education system intersect with housing problems. These squatters are by no means a part of the Italian mainstream middle class. Most of the actors involved are commonly labelled lower class, but more accurately they form a fluid antagonistic class in between the lower class and the middle class. Many people of limited means attend or have attended courses at the university level, or have higher education degrees, in particular immigrants.

The life trajectories of people squatting are diverse, and collective squatting is a point of intersection. Three important conditions construct collective squatting:

• Squatters widely acknowledge that direct action works when legal means fail.
• Segregation and racist attitudes exacerbate the inaccessibility of legal channels to those seeking housing.
• There is an organised body of activists that can manipulate power relationships through intimidation and exposure (Corr, 1999).

There is some squatting by a group of people linked to the anarchist movement, but they constitute a tiny number. The financial crisis also is producing small groups that squat outside of the organised squatters' movements.

Conclusions

In Europe neoliberal cities have largely abrogated a social housing policy. Housing has been transformed into a commodity to be produced and regulated by the 'free' market. The term 'social housing' has lost any meaning, and needs to be reconsidered and redefined. The term 'housing' also needs to be reconsidered, since it represents not only having a roof and a shelter but also the possibility of redefining citizenship norms and of challenging policies regarding surveillance and security. There is no longer any need for large building projects to create social housing, since the number of dwellings greatly exceeds the number of people in need of accommodation.

If the city is a common property, the way to manage it differently is not to look to some invented past of a commons for all, but to look at new ways to manage the commons based on real existing practices. Rome has experienced a shift from using a large affordable housing stock, both legal and illegal, as a device of social control and political consensus, to new forms of social control based on building a market which delivers a lack of housing. Even though approximately 40,000 newly built apartments remain unsold, plans for more constructions are incessantly being advanced by speculators (Agostini, 2011).

The resistance strategies developed by different people in order to have access to housing are interesting for various reasons. For poor people housing has always been a crisis; for the poor, the housing crisis is business as usual. The Movimenti per il diritto all'abitare adopted a name which reflects not only the struggle for housing but also the struggle for alternative living conditions. The squatters from housing organisations do not constitute a political lobby, nor do they beg for help from politicians. They reclaim the city, assert the right to housing, and take it. Recently fashionable participatory processes, such as Agenda21, do not resolve structural issues, but direct practices of appropriation lead to results.

In general terms, the Movimenti per il diritto all'abitare has been successful because:

- it has a long-term strategy based on direct action, organising collective attempts to evade the seemingly inevitable correlation between poverty and housing segregation in large social housing blocks in the periphery and shanty towns
- it is able to mobilise large numbers of heterogeneous people
- it is able to carry out self-organised renovation work
- it is able to mediate with authorities when necessary
- it is able to network and organise public demonstrations, and organise solidarity and support in cases of eviction
- it furthers discussion about new forms of sustainable housing, which is absent from mainstream politics

- it address the issue of the social integration of migrants and Roma people.

The new wave of squatting favours the emergence of new forms of citizenship, showing to what a large extent the social integration of immigrants has been left to initiatives from among the most deprived classes.

Squatting in Rome organized by the Movimenti per il diritto all'abitare has provided an effective form of welfare from below. Between 2000 and 2005 in Rome 1,700 units of social housing were assigned to tenants. In the same period all the movements for the right to housing provided accommodation to more than 2,000 families at no public cost, which is in sharp contrast with the high costs for public housing incurred by a bureaucratic administration. Self-management, self-organisation and the practices of *autorecupero* represent viable alternatives to the centralised capitalistic system, particularly at a time of acute economic crisis.

Currently the number of buildings squatted for housing is around 50. They host around 2,500 families comprising approximately 6,000 people, 70 per cent of whom are foreign immigrants. In practice, Movimenti per il diritto all'abitare has rescaled its actions to such an extent that it is providing not just 'welfare from below' but an alternative way of inhabiting the city. This rescaling has also entailed a reconstruction of the common squatted places, which makes explicit through architectural form ongoing discourses and practices on alternative economics. The group itself addresses spaces of reproduction of the population, critiques of job market oppression, and the system of production, circulation and consumption of goods. To what extent this practice can be extended further in the way that happened in the last decade depends on various factors. The local Italian direct action struggles seem successful, while at the national level the project has not been articulated. As Mayer rightly pointed out, current struggles over urban policies:

> are much more about resistance to and scandalizing of issues of poverty and exclusion and the concomitant infringements of rights and the urban integration machinery has been fine tuned for roll-out neoliberalism, making broad resistance more and more difficult.
>
> (Mayer, 2007: 110)

The success and continuity of the squatters and housing movements, or the lack of them, are related to the power relationships that this broad movement is able to generate within society and its institutions. All opportunities arise through changing power relations. It is inspiring to see the squatters' movement's practice of assigning a secondary role to politicians and official parties, in order not to subordinate real needs and demands to others and their priorities. The Movimenti per il diritto all'abitare goes beyond the claim of housing rights; it claims the right to inhabit the city, a more radical proposal that bypasses legal rights by using practices of self-appropriation of buildings and land from which people have been dispossessed. In Rome in recent years, the famous slogan *ogni sfratto sarà una barricata* (every eviction will be a barricade) has really been operationalised, offering the possibility to reconquer and rebuild spaces which can provide a different economy, not only for income but also for the production of resources and the development of alternative social relations.

Box 5.1 *The French Housing Movement: Squatting as a Mode of Action Among Other Tools*

Thomas Aguilera

When SqEK members came to visit Paris and to meet squatters (March 2013), they were very surprised about two issues. The first was how and why some squatters (mainly artists) make a deal with local officials to get a contract, to be legalised and sometimes to leave buildings before police evictions without any resistance. Second, two groups of squatters were seen as striking examples of a so-called 'French model'. They came from two housing movement groups: Droit Au Logement (DAL/Housing Right Association) and Jeudi Noir (JN/ Black Thursday).*

These two collectives have three common features. They both use squatting as one mode of action among others (demonstrations, sit-ins, real squats, symbolic squats, hunger strikes, office occupations, illegal accommodation and concerts) to temporarily host precarious people. They struggle for new and more efficient housing policies, for the real application of the right to housing and for the requisition of vacant buildings to build social housing. They use the media as a tool to put pressure on representatives and officials in order to change national housing policies and to relocate squatters immediately in social housing. Both DAL and JN manage databases of vacant buildings.

DAL began to squat in 1993, and squatted again in 1994. These first two squats received much attention from the media, and the association achieved three main results. First, the squatters were relocated by the state. Then, the Requisition Law of 1945 (an expropriation-requisition law) was applied. Finally, the right to housing was declared as 'a constitutional goal'. We can confirm that DAL is 'efficient' in the sense that the squatters (Western African migrant families) are usually relocated into social housing or temporary housing by municipal authorities (around 1,000 people in 20 years). DAL also influences national housing policies by putting pressure on decision makers. Squatting is a strategy to build a balance of power with officials to have a short-term (relocation) and long-term impact on housing policy.

JN was born as a collective in 2006 in order to denounce the high and increasing prices of housing in France. The activists (mainly young students) began to squat in 2007 with DAL, from which they got squatting skills and experience. Over five years, they opened about 20 squats where they have hosted precarious workers, students and families. The goal of the collective is to attract attention from the media and the politicians to the bad housing conditions in France, and above all in Paris. Their strategy is to make visible the problem through squatting actions that oblige deputies, ministers and housing sector representatives to react. JN activists have been recognised as experts, and are nowadays consulted for policy proposals. The collective is a 'public agenda stimulator', and the opening of a squat is the occasion to invite officials to propose or to implement new policies. JN has friendly relationships with left-wing parties, whose representatives always support their actions.

However, these two groups are strongly criticised by other squatters, since they are accused of being too close to the political sphere, and hence not struggling for alternative ways of occupying the city. They are blamed for not positioning themselves against owners and for using the families they help to build members' own political careers, which is seen as a deception of the essence of squatting. [In the conclusions, which include the results of a debate we had on the scaling up of squatting as an alternative to capitalism, we address these issues. The debate was prompted during our meeting in Paris, continued over the email list and was inspired also by the clear-cut division we could witness in the Paris squatters' movement.]

---

* The name Black Thursday was chosen by the activists as a reference to the 1929 financial crisis and because Thursday is the day when private owners publish their rental adverts in the special newspaper *PAP* (*Particuliers à Particuliers*).

Notes

1 [In offering the case of Italy and Rome this chapter complements the historical section on the 'invention of the squat' in Chapter 2, and in particular, the presentation of the housing question in Spain discussed in Chapter 1.]

2 155,000 dwellings owned by the former IACP were sold by the city administration to private corporations between 1993 and 2006, realising a total of €3,665 billion, an average of less than €23,700 per apartment (Pozzo, 2009).

3 This demonstration was held in the EUR neighbourhood in front of the building site of the 'Cloud', a congress hall building designed by the famous Italian architect Massimiliano Fuksas.

4 There are also other organisations such as Comitato inquilini del centro storico, Comitato popolare di lotta per la casa, Comitato obiettivo casa and Unione inquilini.

5 The event was repeated on 6 April 2013, and ten buildings were squatted on the same day.

References

Agostini, F. (2011) *Inventare l'abitare* [*Inventing Housing*]. Rome. www.coordinamento.info/home/materiali/135-pubblicazioni/881-inventare-labitare.html (no longer available).

ANCI-CRESMEU (2005) 'Le politiche abitative in Italia. Analisi e valutazioni – Maggio 2005' ['Housing policies in Italy. Analysis and evaluation – May 2005']. Rome. http://62.77.53.204/repository/ContentManagement/information/P256039977/Indagine%20Anci-Creme%20%28maggio per cent202005%29. pdf (accessed July 2013).

ASPE (1993) 'Degrado abitativo e interventi di emergenza: la situazione casa a Roma' ['Housing deprivation and emergency interventions: the housing issue in Rome"], *ASPE 32*(4), 8–15.

Bagnoli, L. (2011) *La città meticcia* [*The Mixed City*]. Rome: Terre di mezzo.

Balestrini, N. and, Moroni P. (1997) *L'orda d'oro* [*The Golden Wave*]. Milan, Italy: Feltrinelli.

Berdini, P. (2008) *La città in vendita* [*The City for Sale*]. Rome: Donzelli.

Berlinguer, G. and Della Seta, P. (1976) *Borgate di Roma* [*Rome's Borgate*]. Rome: Editori Riuniti.

Brenner, N. and Theodore, N. (2002) 'Cities and the geographies of "actually existing neoliberalism"', *Antipode 34*(3), 349–79.

Careri, F. and Mazzitelli, A. G. (2012) 'Metropoliz, de la Torre de Babel a la Pidgin City' ['Metropoliz: from the Tower of Babe to Pidgin City']. *Anuario de Antropología Social y Cultural en Uruguay* 10, 81–93.

Clementi, A. and Perego, F. (1983) *La metropoli 'spontanea': Il caso di Roma* [*The Spontaneous Metropolis: The Case of Rome*]. Bari, Italy: Dedalo.

CNEL (2010) 'La crisi degli affitti e il piano di edilizia abitativa. Osservazioni e proposte' ['Rent crisis and housing plans. Observations and proposals']. Rome. www.cnel.it/53?shadow_documenti=18326] (accessed July 2013).

Comitati autonomi operai di Roma (ed.) (1976) *Autonomia Operaia [Workers' Autonomy]*. Milan, Italy: Savelli.

Comune di Roma (2010) *Mappatura degli stabili di proprietà pubblica e private occupati abusivamente [A Map of Illegally Occupied Public and Private Properties]*. Rome: Ufficio dell'Assemblea Capitolina Commissione consiliare speciale per la Sicurezza Urbana.

Coppola, A. (2008) 'Le borgate romane tra '45 e '89: esclusione sociale, movimenti urbani e poteri locali' ['Rome's borgate between '45 and '89: social exclusion, urban movements and local powers'], in M. Cremaschi (ed.), *Tracce di quartieri [Neighbourhood Tracks]*. Milan, Italy: Franco Angeli.

Corr, A. (1999) *No Trespassing*. Cambridge, Mass.: South End Press.

Corriere della Sera (2005) 'Sfratti, il Comune chiede aiuto all'Onu' ['Expulsions: the municipality calls the UN for help'] , 31 January.

Daolio, A. (1974) *Le lotte per la casa in Italia [Housing struggles in Italy]*. Milan, Italy: Feltrinelli).

De Angelis, R. (2010) 'Roma: Gente di torri, ponti e serpentoni' ['Rome: people of towers, bridges and queues'], in G. B. Sgritta (ed.), *Dentro la crisi [In the Crisis]*. Milan, Italy: Franco Angeli.

Desario, D. (2009a) 'Occupazioni, 80 situazioni sotto stretta sorveglianza' ['Occupations: 80 contexts under surveillance']. *Il Messaggero*, 2 September.

–– (2009b) 'Racket delle occupazioni, 5 arresti' ['Squatting racket: 5 arrests']. *Il Messaggero*, 15 September.

Franchetto, I. and Action (2004) *Action: diritti in movimento [Action: Rights on the Move]*. Naples, Italy: Edizioni Intra Moenia.

Insolera, I. (2011) *Roma moderna [Modern Rome]*. Turin, Italy: Einaudi.

Leitner, H., Peck, J. and Sheppard, E. (eds) (2007) *Contesting Neoliberalism: Urban Frontiers*. New York: Guilford Press.

Lombardi-Diop, C. (2009) 'Roma Residence' ['Apartment complex Rome']. *Interventions* 11(3), 400–19.

Lotringer, S. and Marazzi, C. (2007) *Autonomia*. New York: Semiotext(e).

Marcelloni, M. (1974) 'Roma: momenti di lotta per la casa' ['Rome: moments of housing struggle'], in A. Daolio (ed.), *Le lotte per la casa in Italia [Housing Struggles in Italy]*. Milan, Italy: Feltrinelli.

Marchini, R. (2008) 'La piovra palazzinara: mattoni, banche e giornali' ['The octropus of real-estate speculators: bricks, banks and newspapers']. *Carta settimanale*, 19 June.

Mayer, M. (2007) 'Contesting the neoliberalization of urban governance', in H. Leitner, J. Peck and E. Sheppard (eds), *Contesting Neoliberalism: Urban Frontiers*. New York: Guilford Press.

Membretti, A. (2007) 'Centro Sociale Leoncavallo: building citizenship as an innovative service', *European Urban and Regional Studies* 14(3), 252–63.

Mudu, P. (2006a) 'La circonferenza apparente: la periferia romana tra luoghi comuni e non comuni' ['The apparent circumference: Rome's periphery between common and non-common situations']. *Parolechiave* 36: 117–42.

–– (2006b) 'Patterns of segregation in contemporary Rome', *Urban Geography* 27(5), 422–40.

–– (forthcoming) 'Housing and homelessness in contemporary Rome', in I. Clough-Marinaro and B. Thomassen (eds), *Global Rome: Changing Faces of the Eternal City*. Bloomington and Indianapolis, Ind.: Indiana University Press.

Panarella, E. (2013) 'Caserme, scuole e palazzine: ecco la mappa delle occupazioni' ['Barracks, schools and condominums: here is the map of occupations'], *Il Messaggero*, 10 January.

Piazza, G. (ed.) (2012) *Il movimento delle occupazioni di squat e centri sociali in Europa* [*The Squatters and Social Centres Movement in Europe*]. Milan, Italy: Franco Angeli.

Pozzo, A. M. (2009) *Finanziamenti per la casa e opportunità per l'edilizia pubblica* [*Housing Financing and Opportunities for Public Housing*]. Rome: Federcasa. www.slideserve.com/deidra/finanziamenti-per-la-casa-e-opportunita-per-l-edilizia-pubblica] (accessed July 2013).

Pruijt, H. (2013) 'The logic of urban squatting', *International Journal of Urban and Regional Research* 37, 19–45.

Ramírez, B. (1975) 'The working class struggle against the crisis: self-reduction of prices in Italy', *Radical America* 10(4).

Rossi, F. (2009) 'La casa è un diritto, occuparla un reato' ['Housing is a right, but occupying it a crime']. *Il Messaggero*, 15 September.

Schawrz, G. (2012) 'A Roma dieci sfratti al giorno e gli alloggi popolari sono bloccati' ['Rome: ten expulsions per day and social housing is blocked'], *La Repubblica*, 22 October.

Smart, A. (2012) 'Squatter settlement clearance', in S. J. Smith (ed.), *International Encyclopedia of Housing and Home*, Vol. 7. Oxford: Elsevier.

Talocci, G. (2012) 'Occupying and new monuments: DPU summerLab at Porto Fluviale, Rome'. http://blogs.ucl.ac.uk/dpublog/2012/09/24/occupying-and-the-new-monuments-dpu-summerlab-at-porto-fluviale-rome/ (accessed July 2013).

Il Tempo (1988) 'Occupano le case Iacp per paura di abusivi polacchi' ['Social housing homes are occupied for fear of Polish immigrants'], 27 April.

Tozzetti, A. (1989) *La casa e non solo: lotte popolari a Roma e in Italia dal dopoguerra a oggi* [*Housing and Not Only It: People's Struggles in Rome and in Italy from 1945 Till Today*]. Rome: Editori Riuniti.

Transform! (2004). *La riva sinistra del Tevere. Mappe e conflitti nel territorio metropolitano di Roma* [*Tevere's Left Bank, Maps and Conflicts in the Rome Metropolitan Area*]. Rome: Carta.

Urbanrise (2013) 'Crisis regimes and emerging social movements: Blocchi Precari Metropolitani/ Precarious Metropolitan Blocks.' http://urbanrise.net/2013/01/15/bpm/ (accessed July 2013).

Part II

Specific Issues

6

Squats in Urban Ecosystems: Overcoming the Social and Ecological Catastrophes of the Capitalist City

Salvatore Engel-Di Mauro and Claudio Cattaneo

Cities as Social and Environmental Centres of Devastation

Large, industrialised capitalist cities, especially those in imperial states (such as the United States and NATO countries), have been built by radically altering if not obliterating pre-existing societies and ecosystems. They rely upon vast quantities of resources from the surrounding countryside and from most of the rest of the world, often at the expense of people whose subsistence is predicated on those resources. It has been estimated that such cities require more than 100 times their land resource capacities.[1] Hence they have been, or tend to be, social and environmental disasters and/or to be causally linked to social upheaval and environmental degradation elsewhere.

Possessing elevated pollutant concentration in water, air, and whatever is left of soils and vegetation (Alberti and Marzluff, 2004; Detwyler and Marcus, 1972; Pickett et al., 2011), these cities are a health hazard. Soils are often eroded, paved over (reducing soil surface area and contributing to higher-intensity floods), replaced or covered by debris, or highly and permanently contaminated (Meuser, 2010). Vegetation is usually eradicated or replaced with sparse monocultures of trees, shrubs and/or grasses. Biodiversity within large industrialised urbanised areas is often drastically reduced through habitat loss and concentrations of toxic substances, among other impacts, which also lead to lower biodiversity in areas affected by resource extraction and infrastructure (such as roads, large-scale dams, bridges, railways and nuclear power plants) that has been created to build, maintain and expand such cities (Botkin and Beveridge, 1997; Goudie, 1990). Greenhouse gas emissions tend to be higher in these cities, where average temperatures are often higher than in surrounding areas. This 'heat island effect' can ironically (in combination with greater earthworm activity) raise the decomposition rates of organic material (which improves nutrient cycling), as for example in New York City (NYC) (McDonnell et al., 1997), but it also induces even greater energy use, contributing to higher demand for mostly fossil-fuel energy and thereby increasing greenhouse gas emissions and mining for such fuels.

They are sites of vast consumption and waste not only of nonrenewable energy, but also of water, leading at times to the reduction of surface and subsurface waters, if not the drying up of rivers and lakes, impacts that devastate other communities that need those water supplies to survive. When hydroelectricity is involved, such consumption levels are directly linked to the destruction of people's livelihoods and valley ecosystems through inundation and starving people and ecosystems downstream of sediment and water. The immense quantities of construction materials consumed imply large-scale deforestation and mining, often at the expense of entire communities living in the source areas, and the diffusion of polluting industries, among other destructive activities in many places at once. The generation of waste is notoriously monumental, much of it highly toxic and impossible to biodegrade, and its disposal and even (mostly partial) recycling has been to the detriment of poorer communities or people under colonial dictatorship (Boone and Modarres, 2006; Bullard, 2005; Frumkin, 2005; Geddicks, 2001).

These processes, when viewed in relation to urban sprawl, resemble the carcinogenic development of skin melanomas. This is what Madrid-based economist J. M. Naredo (2004), inspired by the rapid sprawling of his city into the desert, claims with a series of parallelisms: like the profit motive of neoliberal capitalism in urban environments, skin melanomas are characterised by a fast and uncontrolled growth; while metastasis appears in different places of the human body, the carcinogenic sprawl of conurbations appears across different spatial scales beyond the central city (with the construction of residential neighbourhoods and of infrastructures necessary to maintain the connection with the inner city). Further, in the human metabolism carcinogenic cells later become undifferentiated from the rest, just as in the social metabolism, a universal urban lifestyle unifies typologies of building and of city structure (car culture, shopping malls, central business district and periurban residential areas, and so on). Finally, while adjacent tissues are invaded and destroyed, urban sprawl and universal lifestyles do the same with pre-existing settlements and buildings. The result: the (peri)urban meets and devastates the rural.

The evidence is clear: for the most part these kinds of city are socially and ecologically disastrous. But what occurs in cities and how they interconnect to the rest of the world is the product of highly uneven power relations both within and beyond cities themselves (Cronon, 1991; Heynen, Kaika and Swyngedouw, 2006; Lefebvre, 1968; Smith, 1984). Cities, especially large industrialised ones, are highly diverse in social composition and replete with political contestation and repression relative to how a city is structured, spatially organised, and physically built and maintained, among other aspects of urban life. In such situations of highly concentrated power and powerlessness and resource over- and under-consumption, squatters' movements exemplify an important current that works against this system of social and environmental plunder.

Cities, the Environment and Squats

The connections between squatters and environment have typically been considered in the light of urban poverty (especially with the concepts of 'squatter settlements' or 'slums'), or with respect to refugee camps, in regions of the world defined as 'developing' or 'underdeveloped'. Usually, the issues highlighted are ones of environmental degradation, both caused and suffered by people living in such conditions (Davis, 2004; Pugh, 2000; Satterthwaite, 2003). Very little has been written about the environment and squatters' movements, understood as anticapitalist, political movements (Martínez, 2012; Pruijt, 2012) in highly industrialised contexts. Yet occupying and living in urban space means at the same time being affected by and contributing to biophysical environmental processes.

One reason for the paucity of thinking about the relationship between anti-capitalist squatters' movements and the environment is that cities are not usually thought about as ecosystems. Only in the past few decades have there been attempts to overcome this view, albeit largely caged within a technocratic approach (Botkin and Beveridge, 1997; Cook and Swyngedouw, 2012; Newman, 2006; Swyngedouw, 1996). The still predominant misconception of cities as devoid of 'nature' is related to the culture–nature dualism typical of capitalist ideology, with separations of rural from urban, agricultural from industrial, wild from civilised, female from male, and so on (Merchant, 1980). It is urgent that an ecological worldview of cities be brought to bear in the struggle to overcome capitalism. Such a view can enable the recognition of things that are otherwise unnoticed or downplayed and that, except in the delusional world of capitalism, cannot be priced or owned, like rock strata, soils, air movement, cloud formation, biodiversity, groundwater flow, cycling of trace elements, and the potential for agricultural and wild foods. Such an ecological approach also points to an understanding that cities are not isolated and that they have a far-reaching environmental impact, as well as being subject to environmental problems such as droughts, extreme weather and earthquakes. Cities are both ecosystems and a part of wider biophysical processes. Still, an ecological worldview does not necessarily favour more democratic access to and control over city space. In fact, it can be quite the opposite. Those who would like to add an environmentalist concern might find it sobering that organic gardens also exist in prisons (ABC News, 2012; Berger, 2012). In other words, ecological thinking does not automatically beget social justice. In this case, it serves to reinforce the prison ideology.

Squatters' movements are not immune to the ecological reality of the city and to the contradictions of capitalist practices and ideologies. Even though squatters' movements have, in fact, developed alternatives that are sensitive to these issues, there has not yet emerged a general understanding of anti-capitalist autonomy or self-management which is founded not only on alternative social relations or politics, but also on independent and ecologically sustainable resource provisioning and production (water, crops, fuels, construction materials, fibre for clothing, and other such means of subsistence). Several squatter communities in Barcelona point the way forward in this respect, but existing practices in cities like NYC also show that a push towards a material severance from the capitalist city is at least inchoate in squatters' movements. In other words, the urban squatting experience offers a way to combine anti-capitalist (social justice) and ecological concerns. The ideology of squatters' movements and the lifestyles built around them form the possibility of environments beyond the city that are simultaneously social and biophysical, where anti-capitalist ethics are embedded within local ecosystems. As squatting practice evolves into more autonomous ways of living, it becomes more independent from the specifically capitalist city, both ideologically and materially. We shall focus on squatters' alternative transport initiatives, community gardens, and rural-urban (rurban) development as salient examples of such post-capitalist development of city space.

Squatters' Movements as Socio-Ecological Alternatives to the Capitalist City

There are many ways in which the squatters' movement provides a lived, practical alternative to the capitalist city. We touch on just a few here to exemplify how squatters' movements not only subvert existing urban infrastructure by using it to egalitarian ends, but also develop practices challenging the reigning political despotism of the capitalist city, with its largely plutocratically elected officials, technocratic planners, and virtually unaccountable business class, including developers and land speculators ('the market').

The Bicycle as an Alternative Transportation System

One way of subverting and challenging capitalist modes is through promoting and developing infrastructure for alternative means of transport. For instance, since 1992, the use of bicycles to call into question the marriage of urban planning to cars and oil has been the focus of what has come to be known as Critical Mass, which, in Spain and elsewhere, has been linked to squatters' movements as part of efforts to demonstrate the practical potential of much less environmentally impacting modes of transport (Lorenzi, 2010). Large cities like Rome, and then Madrid, have promoted even more large Critical Mass events than the ones organised on a monthly/weekly basis. The Massa Critica Interplanetaria, or Ciemmona ('big CM' in Italian), developed in Rome in 2004, spread to Madrid between 2009 and 2010 and Bilbao in 2011 (renamed Criticona, in Spanish, and KritiKona in Basque), and to Paris in 2010 and Marseilles in 2013 (as Vélorution Universelle in French). It attracts thousands of cyclists from all over the country and abroad. The events last a few days and give visibility to the bicycle subculture. They are enlivened by bicycle workshops hosted in squats, such as ex-Snia and Forte Prenestino in Rome, Patio Maravillas in Madrid, Kukutza in Bilbao, and Biciosxs in Barcelona.

In Barcelona, Biciosxs is comprised of a collective that since 2006 has squatted abandoned or empty property in Nou Barris, a working-class neighbourhood in the north of the city. Beginning with a plot from a demolished small house, the bicycle workshop has been evicted twice and has moved to the 15O building, an emblematic example of an unfinished block of flats left abandoned after the blowout of the Spanish real-estate crisis. Beyond the workshop, the collective has promoted a bicycle culture among youngsters in the neighbourhood, who suffer from a lack of public infrastructure and social services. Local Critical Mass events have also been promoted on special occasions, such as to celebrate the workshop's anniversary and to welcome the visit to Barcelona of bike collectives from other cities. A strong relationship has also been built with other cultural groups in Nou Barris, manifested in Biciosxs' participation in neighbourhood celebrations and open-air cultural events. There is a strong bond between the squatters and neighbourhood civic and cultural associations, which themselves originate from squatted infrastructure. This is characteristic of many other squats and neighbourhoods of Barcelona, and it builds on the noninstitutional legitimacy of such relationships.

At NYC's ABC NoRio,[2] a squat established in 1980, a collective bicycle repair and knowledge-sharing space has been established for a number of years in collaboration with Time's Up! (http://times-up.org), a group dedicated to making city life ecologically sustainable. The project involves hundreds of people, within and beyond the squat itself (Bill DiPaola, personal communication) and inserts itself within increasingly successful grassroots and institutional scientific pressures to reconstitute road networks and re-envision urban mobility, at least through the lens of human health (e.g. Chen et al., 2012). The interconnections between squatting, the environment and health have therefore been made more explicit through collaboration between ABC NoRio and Time's Up! By joining existing popular concerns, and engaging in rides where they are not officially permitted (squatting the streets), there is also the possibility of raising consciousness about squatting among social groups that may not be sympathetic to the squatters' movement. In addition, such actions encourage the development not only of distribution of democratic resources (such as bicycle parts and technical understanding), but also of skills necessary to overcome dependence on a thoroughly polluting technological complex based on fossil fuel combustion, with an increasingly intense and expansionistic landscape impact (Martin, 1999).

Such squatters' day-to-day activity promotes the use of the bicycle by offering free tools and by providing spare parts that are recycled or donated. Self-help with repairs and learning by doing are the norm, and occur through mutual help among participants. The process 'you see, you do it, you teach' insures that there will always be continuity in the transmission of information about 'how to' and that the method proceeds in a self-organised and self-replicating manner. Moreover, in some workshops, this is not limited to the promotion of bicycle use. It extends to any pedal-powered machines (with some at times being invented on the premises) that follow the 'no fuel' approach. The squatting collectives take differing approaches to workshop activities, varying from bicycle mechanics and maintenance work to more artistic expressions such as the building of tall bikes (when two or more bicycle frames are welded on top of each other, wheels are assembled on the lower frame and handlebar and sit on the upper frame) or of any creative visual product, including the production of screen-printed T-shirts, and of patches, banners and other materials for street events. The combination of these elements, mixed with the active participation of many people, contributes to the creation of a bicycle riders' urban subculture closely related to squats and offering a powerful alternative to capitalism, evident in the money-free activities of the collectives. Carlsson (2008) and Carlsson and Manning (2010) refer to such activities as a form of strategic exodus from paid work – hence from the working class and capitalism in general.

Urban Food Production

Another contribution of squatters has been through urban gardens. Urban gardens are not necessarily tied to the right to housing or anti-capitalism, so the purposive combination of food production with squatting presents a direct response to capitalist social and environmental degradation all at once. The promotion of urban gardening is hardly new. Government incentives for such activity have been introduced during times of economic crises, especially in industrialised countries, such as the War (Victory) Gardens promoted during the Second World War through aggressive advertising campaigns by the Roosevelt administration in the United States. In most of the world, however, food production in urban areas has been commonplace.

Arguably, the periodic resurgence of urban gardening typifies societies characterised by a rural–urban split (McClintock, 2010). What is broadly novel is that urban gardening is occurring in a context of rapid global urban area and population expansion, burgeoning and cumulative environmental problems extending to formerly non industrialised countries, greater public awareness of environmental degradation problems, and a rising frequency in the incidence of urban food insecurity. In industrialised countries, urban gardening has taken on characteristics which contrast with those of previous periods, when it served as a temporary instrument to attenuate widespread economic hardship. There is instead now much greater initiative and planning from below, explicitly community-oriented aims, much environmental sensibility behind establishing urban gardens, and increasing official recognition of urban gardening as a positive development (rather than a setback or throwback) and even as a form of agriculture. Barthel and Isendahl (2013) show that urban farming is a pertinent feature of urban support systems over the long-term and global scales, which contributes to the resilience of cities particularly in times of energy scarcity. And of course it should be noted that many urban gardens, for example in cities like NYC, began by way of occupation without the owner's permission – that is, the squatting of vacant lots.

Built between the Mediterranean sea and the hills of the Collserola Natural Park and with one of the highest population densities in Europe, Barcelona is a metropolis which suffers from a serious lack of green space. Moreover, the possibility of interaction between people and the urban (green) environment goes beyond the production of public parks, where the rights of use and management of the open environment are very limited. Urban gardens contribute to an understanding of interactive cities in which their inhabitants can make active use of outdoor space. In Barcelona, these types of garden flourish wherever possible, and most of them are on squatted land. They are often cultivated by retired people, in many cases migrants from impoverished rural areas of Spain. These gardens are often visible at motorway intersections, or near railway tracks, on the slope of the hills right after the last block of a neighbourhood, and wherever a source of water is available. Despite the fact that green urban spaces and often organic produce contribute to greening the city in general, mainstream urban policies often discriminate against these areas (Domene and Sauri, 2007), given that the type of green policies they seek are those that promote bourgeois nature conservation (such as pristine natural parks where human use is severely restricted). Institutional promotion of public green space, such as urban parks, has little relative use for food security, and contrasts with the vision of a post-capitalist interactive city.

In spite of the risk of eviction, many gardeners continue to spread an environmentalist message across the city which takes a community perspective based on collective grassroots organisation. The Can Masdeu community gardens, established in 2002, are an example of this, promoting participants' self-organisation – usually retirement-age gardeners, sometimes involving younger members. There are monthly assemblies and working committees to carry out communal tasks, such as water management (from mountain sources and a 70 metre deep well, with water stored in common ponds), redistribution of compost and manure, organisation of social events (such as common lunches and participation in the neighbourhood's carnival parade), and management of communal allotments. There are also some individual or family allotments. In contrast, at Can Piella, another rurban squat situated in La Llagosta, a village 15 km from Barcelona and evicted in May 2013 after three years of autonomous life, the community garden project was shared by all participants.

Barcelona is peppered with squatted community gardens and squats with their own gardens. The food produced is largely symbolic, particularly given the poor soil quality, such as in the case of Hort del Chino, in the city-centre neighbourhood of Raval, which grew out of what remained of the Ruina Amalia squat, whose buildings had been demolished immediately following its eviction. Establishing urban gardens on the vacant lots of demolished buildings represents an opportunity to green the city and promotes agro-ecological culture. Perhaps, given the poor soil quality and the often limited access to sunlight, particularly evident in compact cities with high buildings surrounding the gardens, the value of these experiments of 'squatting under the sun' does not depend on the amount of food produced. As long as cheap fossil fuels keep supplying abundant energy-intensive inputs to the agro-industrial process, most experiments in urban agriculture are not worth the effort in terms of produce. Much of the real value of these experiences rests on the promotion of agricultural alternatives, such as low-input, do-it-yourself, noncommercial food production. Because of their urban location, these examples offer greater visibility to food production, a process that the capitalist model of agriculture has largely severed from most people's lives. This deeply distorts people's ideas about food provenance, illustrated by some urban children's belief that food comes from supermarkets.

The visibility of urban gardens is an opportunity for agroecological and environmental education. In the Can Masdeu example, one of the 30 garden allotments is dedicated to hands-on school group visits. A side effect of open-air squatting of no mean importance is the visibility that these gardening experiments receive. While what goes on inside a squatted building can only be witnessed by those participating in squat events, urban community gardens – particularly those that are not hidden behind walls or high fences – offer anyone passing by the possibility of seeing without having to physically enter the space. This helps counter the negative images of squatting inculcated by the mass media, among others. It also subverts the rigid identity separation in this imaginary about what constitutes a squatter (for example, to what extent is a random user of a community garden a squatter?).

NYC is similarly dotted by hundreds of community gardens involving thousands of residents. Many of the community gardens have been established since the 1960s. Their scope is not restricted to producing food, they are important for developing community ties and creating open space and zones of solitude in a busy urban environment. For some it is a way of securing land tenure (Saldivar-Tanaka and Krasny, 2004). In the 1990s, much grassroots organising helped to at least partly resist the Giuliani administration's attempt to annihilate urban farm space through the privatisation of municipal lots (Schmelzkopf, 2002; Smith and Kurtz, 2003). Some of these gardening spaces involved the squatters' movement of the Lower East Side (in south-eastern Manhattan, which was simultaneously fighting for its very existence since the late 1980s), with campaigns organised by groups like Earth Celebrations and the Sixth Street Community Centre.

Along with the survival of 11 of the squats, there are spaces where gardens have been introduced or were in existence previously. These tend to be small (usually no larger than 10–20 square metres) and largely provide vegetables. The soil has been imported, with liners separating it from the presumably contaminated indigenous soil below, and it is uncertain how well protected the crops are from contaminants derived from vehicular traffic (Bill DiPaola, personal communication 2012; Moynihan, 2012). Even if they are limited in extent and scope, squatters' food-producing spaces are a way in which the squatters' movements contribute a crucially anti-capitalist edge to the development of urban farming, which is generally absent in community gardens and food movements (e.g. Freudenberg, McDonough and Tsui, 2011). Furthermore, squatters' movements can contribute to undermining private property regimes and show how issues of shelter are inseparable from those of food. In this manner, the right to the city is a matter of overhauling everyday notions and practices towards both ecologically sustainable and substantively democratic ends. There can be no egalitarian food production and distribution without egalitarian provision of housing.

Beyond the City: Rurban Communes, Their
Material Autonomy and Social Impact

Arguably the examples of squatting that fundamentally rupture the entire edifice of the capitalist city are those that overcome the urban–rural divide by going beyond it. The case of Barcelona is particularly instructive in that there seem to be few parallels in terms of explicitly anti-capitalist squatting being combined with both urban and rural elements. This also counters not just recent trends in the destructive urbanisation of farmland ('sprawl') and any legislative attempts to preserve periurban farmland, but also less conventional initiatives led by farming groups vying to preserve their livelihoods and hence farmland (Paül and McKenzie, 2013). Squatters' movements in this sense create and preserve farmland simultaneously by integrating the rural and urban in their everyday social practices and overall objectives.

Three remarkable social spaces in Barcelona are Kan Pasqual, Can Masdeu and Can Piella.[3] [They constitute interesting examples of radical communes where the squatted place not only serves – among other social centre functions – as a roof for its inhabitants, but within it egalitarian and cooperative relationships are developed in a similar way to the examples offered in Chapter 2 of the Geneva squats and the Berlin house projects.] The first two are located on the Collserola hills, a recently created natural park whose zone reaches the city limits, and which constitutes a unique example of a large green area in the middle of the Barcelona metropolitan area. The remains of an agricultural past are often visible in the city. One of its peripheral district neighbourhoods, for example, is called Horta (orchard, in Catalan) after the many farmhouses found there (Diez i Quijano, 2003).

High up in the Collserola hills, isolated from public transport, is Kan Pasqual, squatted in late 1996. Its commune – consisting of about 12–15 people – has set up an integrated management project that covers geographical, social and natural aspects characterising the local territory. The objectives are to rehabilitate and maintain the building by using, as far as possible, uncontaminated materials derived from renewable sources and not based on social exploitation. The new infrastructure built by the squatters highlights sustainability by implementing permaculture designs. The area is accordingly divided into different resource use zones. Renewable energy sources are preferred, and there are photovoltaic panels, solar ovens, hot water solar panels, self-assembled wind turbines and the like. Waste management aims at closing the material cycling loop, where the organic fraction is composted and the use of nonrenewable or nonrecyclable goods is highly reduced. Waste water treatment passes through the biological processing of local riparian species and the water is then reused. Social activities are oriented to popular education over the environmental crisis. Finally, a library has been established that specialises in social and economic issues and serves as a point of counter-information with respect to socially and environmentally unsustainable behaviours and practices.

The direct action tactics of the Kan Pasqual collective are famous. Right after the initial occupation, they cut the electricity connection to the main grid and in its place they lit candles, which were slowly replaced by second-hand and later new solar photovoltaic panels. Subsequently, the solar panels were integrated with a windmill the collective made and mounted on an 18 metre high steel pole. The windmill construction was turned into public workshops sometimes attended by more than 40 people.

Can Masdeu features a slightly different social-ecological strategy, but it is still oriented towards strengthening the rural–urban connection and striving for a drastically reduced dependence on waged employment. Its commune has since the beginning focused on the opening of a social centre dedicated to community gardens and environmental education. The location is closer to public transport and the immigrant neighbourhood of Nou Barris, where a highly frequented social centre was not too difficult to establish. It promotes Sunday activities and workshops also related to environmental issues and local environmental management.

Can Piella, on the other hand, was set in a more rural and less hilly landscape, where primary activities such as cereal growth and sheep farming are still performed by some of its neighbours. The commune consisted of a stable group of around 12 people that did not change throughout the duration of the Can Piella experience. The house was part of a large property where land is still cultivated, but it required much restoration work. Proximity to the city made it possible to recycle and access construction material as well as attract people to come and help or participate in the many events that the Can Piella social centre offered, activities that included practical self-organisation and training towards the achievement of material autonomy. Beer brewing and, to a minor extent, fruits from the orchards provided the main sources of the collective's income.

In all three cases there is a strong identification of the house group with the promoters of the social centre. In this sense, we can understand these three groups as political collectives that undertake an important lifestyle choice, that of living and working together towards self-reliant production, and that share a social interest in the public promotion of this way of life, offering basic training and stimulating network creation. It has been shown (Cattaneo and Gavaldá, 2010) that the effectiveness of rurban squats offers a remarkable example of how we can move towards energetic sustainability (and to a post peak-oil, post-capitalist society). However, it must be stressed that ecological sustainability is only one aspect of a multidimensional alternative to capitalism offered by these intentional communities. They are lifestyle alternatives that demonstrate the possibility of living with much less dependence on money (which implies less reliance on capitalist markets). The capitalist logic is undermined by abstaining from selling labour-power and by practising egalitarian organising and communal economies.

The people who squatted at Can Piella had imagined the possibility of pooling their personal savings, aiming for a total communal economy. The group's main collective financial project was brewing beer, which later shifted to the safer (at that time) premises of Can Masdeu. This is an interesting example of mutual aid between squats. Can Masdeu has the lowest level of communal economy of the three rurban communes discussed here, but it still provides members with basic food, shelter, internet access, construction materials, tools and basic training in exchange for money (€45 per month) and labour time. Members must contribute to the two collective working mornings per week, and do two kitchen shifts per month, three two-day working shifts per year for the opening of the Sunday bar/restaurant of the social centre, plus the work necessary to manage the house and various projects (such as the garden, collective work-day organisation, finances, food purchases, events and environmental education). Each person has their own income, on average €300 per month, of which €45 goes to the house project and the rest is for extra personal costs.

This is a powerful example of how a material alternative to capitalism can be reached in a squat that is empowered by food production, with many workshops and tools, and collective self-management. The squatting practice is both a necessary and sufficient condition for delinking from the capitalist economy. The amount of money saved by not paying rent and the collective running of a house enable a completely different relation to the labour market. This in turn frees up time that, if collectively organised, can be dedicated to household production of goods and services that contribute to the direct satisfaction of most needs. Moreover, when tools and space are available (in the form of rooms for setting up workshops and for storing materials, or land for direct cultivation), a higher degree of autonomy is reached. The space can be used for growing fresh vegetables or to raise chickens that supply fresh eggs and some meat. It can be used for workshops and the storage of materials, among many other uses, such as the social kitchen for the Sunday bar/restaurant in Can Masdeu, and the bakery and brewery of Kan Pasqual and Can Piella.

In contrast with the idea of a basic social income, which is largely intended as wealth redistribution through monetary flow, the rurban communes of Barcelona highlight the importance of material autonomy, which comes from access to physical resources. So, rather than asking for access to money, social justice is reclaimed here in the form of accessing open land and nonresidential spaces which in turn contribute to personal and collective wealth. To this extent, the rurban experience is a step between the money autonomy of many urban squatters – who rely on recycling capitalist waste flows (including buildings) but have no access to land – and the more isolated rural squats (and communities) that, set at higher distance from the capitalist city and in closer relationship with agro-ecosystems, achieve higher degrees of autonomy. Finally, there are possibilities for individual self-fulfilment and monetary income, by for example selling vegetables or baked goods to consumer cooperatives, as is done in Can Piella and Can Masdeu respectively. In Kan Pasqual initiatives for personal income are not favoured, but commercial uses of collective resources nevertheless enable personal income flow. The squats evince a variety of degrees of social integration between the individual and the collective, with greater pooling occurring in the more isolated rural situations, and in this way they exemplify existing alternatives to capitalism (Cattaneo, 2011).

But to consider only the potential of these nonmonetary collective *oikonomies*[4] is too limited a view. The value of their social practice is that it can be scaled up. The potential of rurban squats, like their rural counterparts, is that they achieve some degree of material autonomy from the capitalist mode of production. At the same time, like urban squats, they contribute to urban struggles with their periurban location. In particular, the focus of their urban struggles goes towards greening the city and stopping sprawl. To this extent, while it would be difficult to scale up their strategies within the limits of the capitalist city, their reconceptualisation of the city–environment relationship can be useful in greening the city from the bottom through self-organised neighbourhood actions (rather than the self-organisation of capitalist market actors or top-down government policies).

For example, Can Masdeu has been influential in spreading the idea of freeing land with neighbours in need of cultivation space, thereby extended the notion of squatting to what is beyond the walls of a building and beyond the imagination of young counter-cultural activists. The social dimension of 'squatting under the sun' and its reach to hundreds of monthly visitors since its establishment in 2002 have contributed to shaping public understanding of the city. In their public campaigns, the rurban communes and the social movements related to Collserola have joined forces in protecting the Park of Collserola – and the (neo)rural practices present there – from urban sprawl (http://www.collserola.org/manifest_Solana.html). The Can Masdeu collective and its team of architects have recently succeeded, aided by the financial and building sector crisis, in convincing the municipality to improve the connectivity between Barcelona and its natural park through establishing green corridors and encouraging urban agriculture (http://w1.bcn.cat/portesdecollserola/). Even the local government recognises that the squat, though illegal, contributes cutting-edge ideas and practices to a reformulation of the relationship between the city and its natural environment.

[A hypothesis that the passing of time might prove is that the Can Masdeu social centre and the principles of greening the city generally promoted by these rurban experiences are effectively shaping institutional policies and, to a certain extent, changing city plans to develop and urbanise its Natural Park. If this was true – and not only the result of a temporary halt in development plans after the severe economic crisis that hit Spain and Catalonia – then we could take it as an example, similar to the historical one presented in Chapter 4, that reinforces the case for squatting as capable of generating medium-scale alternatives to capitalism.]

Social and ecological challenges to the squatters' movement

These practices of infrastructural subversion and political democratisation are not without problems. Capitalism does not merely consist of a set of methods or technologies; it is a system of social relations. In fact, if squatting is reduced to a political technique to deal with urban housing stress, then it can conceivably be subsumed under capitalist relations (e.g. Kearns, 1979). The same applies to alternative technologies and techniques. For instance, the introduction of low-fee bicycle rentals or bicycle-sharing systems in cities like Toronto, Paris and Copenhagen does not raise awareness of any urban social injustice. The development of transport alternatives centred on mass mobilisation of cyclists or bicycle infrastructure can be emptied of politically inconvenient content and used instead to promote 'green' capitalism (see also Pearsall, 2012, for the case of NYC). It also contributes little towards fighting against the social and environmental devastation associated with, for instance, the mining, processing and refining of raw materials (including heavy metals and rubber) to manufacture and maintain bicycles.

Similarly, the diffusion of farming in cities is already being co-opted for ulterior objectives by many national and international institutions, which see in urban gardens prospects for improved nutrition and fresh food access without altering power relations. It is therefore unsurprising to see such institutions focusing on the new employment opportunities and market niches forged through urban community gardens (FAO, 2010; Mougeot, 2005: 11–13; Schmelzkopf, 2002: 332–3). Some of the same institutions also look to urban farming as a way of greening cities with the implication of absolving capitalists from paying for the long-term pollution problems they have caused. Urban food production helps reduce greenhouse gas emissions (for example, because of the lower food transport distance), resource consumption and municipal organic waste. It raises biodiversity and attenuates urban heat island effects. It can alleviate soil degradation problems, by conserving, restoring and even generating soils, which can also function as sinks for contaminants and greenhouse gases (Ajmone-Marsan and Biasioli, 2010; Lichtfouse, 2010). In other words, urban gardening can effectively socialise the cost of urban pollution if it is put in place without any effort to redress social inequalities, including exposure to contaminants.

In this connection there are contaminants that will not disappear, regardless of the relative success of any squatters' movement. Heavy metals in particular constitute a major urban environmental problem associated with numerous deleterious health consequences, including cancer. Unlike most other contaminants, they present a long-term, cumulative toxic hazard through soil-particle ingestion or inhalation, or through assimilation by eating food produced on contaminated soils (Centeno et al., 2005; Kabata-Pendias and Pendias, 2001; Säumel et al., 2012). Not all such contamination is caused by industrial impact, so a thorough grasp of environmental processes is essential to understand the problems that must be confronted in urban farming and the political ramifications of responsibility for such contamination (Engel-Di Mauro, 2012). In fact, this aspect already shows that social critique is necessary but insufficient in the struggle for an egalitarian city. Biophysical processes must also be understood to achieve this (Bryant and Callewaert, 2003).

There are additional problems that are the outcome of wider social and environmental processes, some of which are the result of global-scale capitalist impacts. Squatters' movements can no more ignore the physical and ecological contexts of a place than they can the social injustices against which they struggle. And each urban ecosystem has its particular characteristics, so there are no straightforward solutions that can be offered. The study of ecological processes acquires fundamental importance in the struggle for an egalitarian and ecologically sustainable city.

For example, Barcelona lies in a region that is not too far from the Sahara, a source of dust, and that is prone to earthquakes (Cid, 1998). Dust storms can have detrimental consequences on health, but this is coupled with high amounts of fine dust (PM 2.5) from vehicular traffic, shipping (especially sulphates) and construction. These sources of particulate matter have been linked to cardiovascular failure and other related causes of mortality (Ostro et al., 2011). These human and nonhuman sources of dust have not been addressed at all by the squatters' movement, but they do contribute to the overall pollution problems to be faced. Barcelona's location in a seismically active region means, at a minimum, that buildings should be reinforced and rendered sufficiently flexible to withstand vigorous vibration. Any squatting efforts therefore need to consider not only capitalist marginalisation and speculation pressures, but also the uneven distribution in the potential for seismic events.

Heavy metals and other contaminants (especially chromium and copper) have been detected in local water supplies and soils, which is of significance especially for those resorting to direct groundwater use, crop production, or to untreated wastewater to irrigate gardens (Bech et al., 2008; Cabeza et al., 2012). In any case, a Barcelona that would be freed of capitalism would still be subject to the long-term consequences of water contamination. Local inhabitants have also been exposed to persistent organic pollutants, such as dichlorodiphenyltrichloroethane (DDT) and polychlorinated biphenyls (PCBs), which threaten long-term health impairment if not premature death, especially for women (Porta et al., 2012). This links to other gender issues: women in particular face a struggle not only for housing, but for access to medical care and the maintenance of healthcare infrastructure, which is currently being undermined through state-sanctioned financial austerity favouring the ruling classes.

The case of NYC is not too different with respect to long-term water, soil, and bodily contamination by heavy metals, persistent organic pollutants, and other elements and compounds at toxic or near-toxic levels. But there are salient differences between the problems squatters have to confront in NYC and Barcelona. The southern part of Manhattan, where the squats discussed above are located, is marked by coastal flooding and extreme weather events (such as hurricanes), which are increasing in frequency and magnitude as a result of global warming (Colle, Rojowsky and Buonaito, 2010; Salmun et al., 2009). People in this area are also affected by higher incidence of respiratory diseases because of exposure to, among other pollutants, fine particulate matter near streets and subway trains (Querol et al., 2012; Wang and Gao, 2011). Those fighting for a transport system that is less health-threatening cannot rely solely on the spread of bicycle use, especially if trains contribute to the problem. In southern Manhattan, the problem is worsened by the additional massive amounts of toxic compounds and dust created when buildings collapsed in the attacks of 11 September 2001 (Maslow et al., 2012). In this case, a long-term health hazard, which affects local squatters among many others, cannot be tackled by local struggles alone. It involves, among other things, fighting against state violence, which includes US imperialism.

The Role of the Squatters' Movement in
Anti-Capitalist Socio-Ecological Struggles

It could be argued that such problems severely constrain the potential that squatting offers for overcoming capitalist relations in ecologically sustainable ways, especially when it comes to dealing with environmental degradation on the world scale. But it is precisely because of these problems that the squatters' movement can lead to a social and ecological antidote to the current depoliticisation of the urban ecosystem (Swyngedouw, 2009). The bicycle, the community garden, and the collapse of the rural–urban divide are not just elements of alternative techniques of living. They are also means by which to forge communal relations which cannot allow for social exclusion or for the imposition of health hazards. Bicycles are a much less environmentally destructive mode of transport than motorised vehicles, and their reuse and collective maintenance extends their lifespan and reduces the demand for new models, with the environmental impact that implies including mining of raw materials. When there are problems of long-term soil contamination, social relations of the kinds established by squatters enable a community to confront the environmental problems or hazards in democratic ways, instead of expediently dumping them on the least empowered. The development of rurban living contributes to bridging the city – and its rampant individualism – with the rural environment, which provides the material basis necessary for sustaining life. Not surprisingly, eco-social experiments flourish by combining the communalism typical of rural life with the greater political visibility of nearby cities. These projects contribute to shaping the way a city relates to its natural environment, and if we accept the underlying hypothesis of a natural resource-based crisis of capitalism, the basis is set for building up greener post-capitalist experiences, as Carlsson (2008) also highlights.

The core questions are how to avoid people being detrimentally affected and how to devise ecologically sustainable ways to overcome the problem. By insisting on the collective reappropriation of urban space and on the development of ecologically alternative and autonomous ways of life, the squatters' movement connects what are usually disparate issues, such as shelter, transport and food, and offers practical ways of overcoming, if not replacing, the capitalist city with a form of human settlement that is both socially and ecologically constructive. Destructive processes such as warfare, large-scale mining and global warming cannot be addressed directly by localised urban struggles alone, but they can be curbed by undermining authoritarian structures, liberating urban spaces and putting alternative ways of living into practice.

Many of the decision-making processes that induce world-scale devastation and reinforce global authoritarian mechanisms are centralised in institutions located in large industrialised cities. The squatters' movement has a crucial role to play here in displacing if not replacing these decision-making institutions. Democratising the city is one important step towards democratising the world and ending the social and ecological devastation brought about by the capitalist mode of production. Squats, as a form of anti-capitalist political organisation, are much more than efforts at securing housing and much wider than struggles for democratising cities. They are ways to develop radical forms of autonomy, with self-management in the reproduction of life as the primary exit strategy from the capitalist mode of production.

Notes

1   This has been done by measuring the ecological footprint, which is 'the total area of productive land and water required to produce on a continuous basis all the resources consumed and to assimilate all the wastes produced by' a population (Rees, 1997: 66). [This observation relates the capitalist (neoliberal) city to the environmental crisis; Chapter 1 relates the housing crisis to neoliberal capitalism and Box 1.1 relates the capitalist crisis also to the environmental dimension. A complex relationship emerges between the capitalist city, crisis and the environmental dimension. This chapter provides examples of the role squats in the city play in going against its capitalist logic, and that can be beneficial for tackling the environmental crisis.]

2   It is worth noting that the land on which the squatted block of flats was built was the site not only of settler colonial conquest by the Dutch, but also of the eviction in the 1650s of a freed African farmer. In New York, as in probably any capitalist city, the struggle over space is as old as the city's inception.

3   There are similar cases in the Netherlands, with a squatted farm near Amsterdam and several rural squat linked through the Anders Wonen Anders Leven network, like the Ecotribe Teuge: www.omslag.nl/aanloopdag-ecotribe-ecodorp-okt-2013.html

4   By *oikonomy*, we mean the Aristotelian understanding of 'the rules that govern the house/community' which can be done without any use of money. It is critically different from chrematistics, the notion of making money out of money, prevalent in contemporary capitalist society, but condemned as immoral by many Greek philosophers in antiquity.

References

ABC News (2012) 'Inmate Carlos Rosado develops garden, earns college degree behind bars: inmates at N.Y.'s Woodbourne Correctional Facility developed a garden', http://abcnews.go.com/US/slideshow/garden-growingat-wood bourne-correctional-facility-10630693 (accessed 29 January 2014).

Ajmone-Marsan, F. and Biasioli, M. (2010) 'Trace elements in soils of urban areas', *Water Air and Soil Pollution* 213, 121–43.

Alberti, M. and Marzluff, J. M. (2004) 'Ecological resilience in urban ecosystems: linking urban patterns to human and ecological functions', *Urban Ecosystems* 7(3), 241–65.

Barthel, S. and Isendahl, C. (2013) 'Urban gardens, agriculture, and water management: sources of resilience for long-term food security in cities', *Ecological Economics* 86, 224–34.

Bech, J. Tume, P., Sokolovska, M., Reverter, F., Sanchez, P., Longan, L., Puente, A. and Oliver, T. (2008) 'Pedogeochemical mapping of Cr, Ni, and Cu in soils of the Barcelona Province (Catalonia, Spain): relationships with soil physico-chemical characteristics', *Journal of Geochemical Exploration* 96, 106–16.

Berger, M. W. (2012) 'Prison bloom: gardening behind bars offers prisoners fresh chances', *Audubon* 10. www.audubonmagazine.org/articles/nature/inmates-take-organic-gardening (accessed 29 January 2014).

Boone, C. G. and Modarres, A. (2006) *City and Environment.* Philadelphia, Penn.: Temple University Press.

Botkin, D. B. and Beveridge, C. E. (1997) 'Cities as environments', *Urban Ecosystems* 1, 3–19.

Bryant, B. and Callewaert, J. (2003) 'Why is understanding urban ecosystems important to people concerned about environmental justice?' in A. R. Berkowitz, C. H. Nilon and K. S. Hollweg (eds), *Understanding Urban Ecosystems.* New York: Springer.

Bullard, R. D. (ed.) (2005) *The Quest for Environmental Justice: Human Rights and the Politics of Pollution.* San Francisco, Calif.: Sierra Club.

Cabeza, Y., Candela, L., Ronen, D. and Teijon. G. (2012) 'Monitoring the occurrence of emerging contaminants in treated wastewater and groundwater between 2008 and 2010: the Baix Llobregat (Barcelona, Spain).' *Journal of Hazardous Materials* 239–40, 32–9.

Carlsson, C. (2008) *Nowtopia How Pirate Programmers, Outlaw Bicyclists, and Vacant-Lot Gardeners Are Inventing the Future Today!* Oakland, Calif.: AK Press.

Carlsson, C. and Manning, F. (2010) 'Nowtopia: strategic exodus?' *Antipode* 42(4), 924–53.

Cattaneo, C. (2011) 'The money-free autonomy of Spanish squatters', in A. Nelson and F. Timmerman (eds), *Life without Money: Building Fair and Sustainable Economies.* London: Pluto Press.

Cattaneo, C. and Gavaldà, M. (2010) 'The experience of rurban squats in Collserola, Barcelona: what kind of degrowth?' *Journal of Cleaner Production* 18(6), 581–9.

Centeno, J. A., Mullick, F. G., Ishak, K. G., Franks, T. J., Burke, M. N., Koss, A. P., Perl, D. P., Tchounwou, P. B. and Pestaner, J. P. (2005) 'Environmental pathology', in O. Selenius, B. Alloway, J. A. Centeno, R. B. Finkelman, R. Fuge, U. Lindh and P. Smedley (eds), *Essentials of Medical Geology: Impacts of the Natural Environment on Public Health*. Amsterdam: Elsevier.

Chen, L., Chen, C., Srinivasan, R., McKnight, C. E., Ewing, R. and Roe, M. (2012) 'Evaluating the safety effects of bicycle lanes in New York City', *American Journal of Public Health* 102(6),1120–7.

Cid, J. (1998) 'Zonificación sísmica de la ciudad de Barcelona basada en métodos de simulación numérica de efectos locales' ['Seismc zoning of Barcleona city based on methods of numerical simulation of local effect']. PhD thesis, Universidad Politécnica de Cataluña, Barcelona.

Colle, B. R., Rojowsky, K. and Buonaito, F. (2010) 'New York City storm surges: climatology and an analysis of the wind and cyclone evolution', *Journal of the American Meteorological Society* 49, 85–100.

Cook, I. and Swyngedouw, E. (2012) 'Cities, social cohesion and the environment: towards a future research agenda', *Urban Studies* 49(9), 1959–79.

Cronon, W. (1991) *Nature's Metropolis: Chicago and the Great West.* New York: Norton.

Davis, M. (2004) 'Planet of slums: urban involution and the informal proletariat', *New Left Review* 26, 5–34.

Detwyler, T. R. and Marcus, M. G. (1972) *Urbanization and Environment.* Belmont, Calif.: Duxbury Press.

Diez i Quijano, D. (2003) *Les masies de Horta.* Barcelona, Spain: El tinter.

Domene, E. and Sauri, D. (2007) 'Urbanization and class-produced natures: vegetable gardens in the Barcelona Metropolitan Region', *Geoforum* 38(2), 287–98.

Engel-Di Mauro, S. (2012) 'Urban farming: the right to what sort of city?' *Capitalism Nature Socialism* 23(4), 1–9.

FAO (Food and Agriculture Organization of the United Nations). (2010) *Growing Greener Cities.* Rome: FAO.

Freudenberg, N., McDonough, J. and Tsui. E. (2011) 'Can a food justice movement improve nutrition and health? A case study of the emerging food movement in New York City', *Journal of Urban Health* 88(4), 623–36.

Frumkin, H (2005) 'Health, equity, and the built environment', *Environmental Health Perspectives* 113(5), A290–A291

Geddicks, A. (2001) *Resource Rebels: Native Challenges to Mining and Oil Corporations.* Boston, Mass.: South End Press.

Goudie, A. (1990) *The Human Impact on the Natural Environment.* Cambridge, Mass.: MIT Press.

Heynen, N., Kaika, M. and Swyngedouw, E. (2006) *In the Nature of Cities: Urban Political Ecology and the Politics of Urban Metabolism.* London: Routledge.

Kabata-Pendias, A. and Pendias, H. (2001) *Trace Elements in Soils and Plants*, 3rd edn. Boca Raton,, Fla.: CRC Press.

Kearns, K. (1979) 'Intraurban squatting in London', *Annals of the Association of American Geographers* 69(4), 589–98.

Lefebvre, H. (1968 [2009]) *Le droit à la ville.* [*The Right to the City*]. Paris: Economica.

Lichtfouse, E. 2010. Society issues, painkiller solutions, dependence and sustainable agriculture. In E. Lichfouse (ed.), *Sociology, Organic Farming, Climate Change and Soil Science.* Dordrecht, Netherlands: Springer, pp. 1–18.

Lorenzi, E. (2010) Centro social en movimiento. Los talleres de autoreparación de bicicletas en espacios autogestionados' ['Social centre on the move. Self-repair bicycle workshops in self-managed spaces'], in M. Domínguez, M. A. Martínez and E. Lorenzi (eds), *Okupaciones en movimiento: Derivas, estrategias y prácticas* [*Squats on the Move: Drifts, Strategies and Practices*]. Madrid: Tierradenadies Ediciones.

Martin, G. (1999). 'Hyperautomobility and its sociomaterial impacts.' University of Surrey: Centre for Environmental Strategy. www.surrey.ac.uk/ces/files/pdf/0299_WP_Hyperautomobility.pdf (accessed 29 January 2014)

Martínez, M. A. (2012) 'The squatters' movement in Europe: a durable struggle for social autonomy in urban politics.' *Antipode* 45(4), 866–87.

Maslow, C. P., Friedman, S. M., Pillai, P. S., Reibman, J., Berger, K. I., Goldring, R., Stellman, S. D. and Farfel, M. (2012) 'Chronic and acute exposures to the World Trade Center disaster and lower respiratory symptoms: area residents and workers', *American Journal of Public Health* 102(6), 1186–94.

McClintock, N. (2010) 'Why farm the city? Theorizing urban agriculture through a lens of metabolic rift', *Cambridge Journal of Regions, Economy and Society* 3(2), 191–207.

McDonnell, M. J., Pickett, S. T. A., Groffman, P., Bohlen, P., Pouyat, R. V., Zipperer, W. C., Parmelee, R. W., Carreriro, M. M. and Medley. K. (1997) 'Ecosystem processes along an urban-to-rural gradient', *Urban Ecosystems* 1, 21–36.

Merchant, C. (1980) *The Death of Nature*. New York: Harper Collins.

Meuser, S. (2010) *Contaminated Urban Soils*. Dordrecht, Netherlands: Springer.

Mougeot, L. J. A. (2005) 'Introduction' in L. J. A. Mougeot (ed.), *Agropolis: The Social, Political and Environmental Dimensions of Urban Agriculture*. London: Earthscan.

Moynihan, C. (2012) 'Sharing a part of activist history in the East Village', *New York Times*, 4 March, www.nytimes.com/2012/03/05/nyregion/east-village-museum-shares-a-piece-of-activist-history.html?_r=0 (accessed 29 January 2014).

Naredo, J. M. (2004) 'Diagnostico sobre la sotenibilidad: la especie humana como patología terrestre', ['A sustainability check: the human species as an Earth pathology'], *Archipiélago* 62, 13–24.

Newman, P. (2006) 'The environmental impact of cities', *Urbanization and Environment* 18(2), 275–95.

Ostro, B., Tobias, A., Querol, X., Alastuey, A. Amato, F., Pey, J., Pérez, N. and Sunyer J. (2011) 'The effects of particulate matter sources on daily mortality: a case-crossover study of Barcelona, Spain', *Environmental Health Perspectives* 119(12), 1781–7.

Querol, X., Moreno, T., Karanasiou, A., Reche, C., Alastuey, A., Viana, M., Font, O., Gil, J., de Miguel, E. and Capdevila, M. (2012) 'Variability of levels and composition of PM10 and PM2.5 in the Barcelona metro system', *Atmospheric Chemistry and Physics* 12, 5055–76.

Paül, V. and McKenzie, F. H. (2013) 'Peri-urban farmland conservation and development of alternative food networks: insights from a case-study area in metropolitan Barcelona (Catalonia, Spain)', *Land Use Policy* 30, 94–105.

Pearsall. H. (2012) 'Moving out or moving in? Resilience to environmental gentrification in New York City', *Local Environment* 17(9), 1013–26.

Pickett, S. T. A., Band, L. E., Belt, K.E ., Boone, C. G., Cadenasso, M. L., Groffman, P. M., Grove, J. M., Nilon, C. H., Irwin, E., Kaushal, S., Marshall, V., McGrath, B. P., Pouyat, R. V., Szlavecz, K., Troy, A. and Warren, P. S. (2011) 'Urban ecological systems: scientific foundations and a decade of progress', *Journal of Environmental Management* 92, 331–62.

Porta, M., López, T., Gasull, M., Rodríguez-Sanz, M., Garí, M., Pumarega, J., Borrel, C. and Grimalt, J. O. (2012) 'Distribution of blood concentrations of persistent organic pollutants in a representative sample of the population of Barcelona in 2006, and comparison with levels in 2002', *Science of the Total Environment* 423, 151–61.

Pruijt, H. (2012) ' Logic of urban squatting', *International Journal of Urban and Regional Research*, http://dx.doi.org/10.1111/j.1468-2427.2012.01116.x

Pugh, C. (2000) 'Sustainability in squatter settlements', in C. Pugh (ed.), *Sustainable Cities in Developing Countries: Theory and Practice at the Millennium*. London: Earthscan.

Rees, W. E. (1997) 'Urban ecosystems: the human dimension', *Urban Ecosystems* 1, 63–75.

Saldivar-Tanaka, L. and Krasny, M. E. (2004) 'Culturing community development, neighborhood open space, and civic agriculture: the case of Latino community gardens in New York City', *Agriculture and Human Values* 21, 399–412.

Salmun, H., Molod, A., Buonaiuto, F. S., Wisniewska, K. and Clarke, K. C. (2009) 'East Coast cool-weather storms in the New York Metropolitan Region', *Journal of Applied Meteorology and Climatology* 48, 2320–30.

Satterthwaite, D. (2003) 'The links between poverty and environment in urban areas of Africa, Asia, and Latin America', *Annals of the American Academy of Political and Social Science* 590(1), 73–92.

Säumel, I., Kotsyuk, I., Hölscher, M., Lenkereit, C., Weber, F., and Kowarik, I. (2012) 'How healthy is urban horticulture in high traffic areas? Trace metal concentrations in vegetable crops from plantings within inner city neighbour-hoods in Berlin, Germany', *Environmental Pollution* 165, 124–32.

Schmelzkopf, K. (2002) 'Incommensurability, land use, and the right to space: community gardens in New York City', *Urban Geography* 23(4), 323–43.

Smith, C. and Kurtz, H. (2003) 'Community gardens and politics of scale in New York City', *Geographical Review* 93(2), 193–212.

Smith, N. (1984) *Uneven Development: Nature, Capital, and the Production of Space*. Oxford: Blackwell.

Swyngedouw, E. (1996) 'The city as a hybrid: on nature, society and cyborg urbanization', *Capitalism Nature Socialism* 7, 65–80.

Swyngedouw, E. (2009) 'The antinomies of the post-political city: in search of a democratic politics of environmental production', *International Journal of Urban and Regional Research* 33, 601–20.

Wang, X. and Gao, H. O. (2011) 'Exposure to fine particle mass and number concentrations in urban transportation environments of New York City', *Transportation Research* D 16, 381–91.

7

Squatting and Diversity: Gender and Patriarchy in Berlin, Madrid and Barcelona

Azozomox

Squatting as a political movement has been constituted against gentrification, property speculation, vacancy of buildings, shortage of flats, and redevelopments for the wealthy. In its essence, squatting can be seen as a fundamental critique of capitalism and the structure of private ownership which is protected and supported by the state. Among other goals squatting tries to create alternatives in the way of living together and developing self-organised autonomous free spaces of solidarity, mutual help, and also resistance against the overall presence of capitalist reality.

The composition of the squatters' movement varies, and expresses a broad diversity within the frame of anti-authoritarian, emancipatory ideas and politics, as well as reflecting the influence of and interrelation with other social, cultural and political movements.

In a short overview of the squatters we find people with different class backgrounds and political tendencies (anarchists, anti-authoritarians, anti-imperialists, autonomous, anti-fascists, environmentalists) as well as people of colour, migrants, internationalists and transnationalists, refugees, creative artists, workers and more, but also autonomist wimmin[1] and dykes, radical queer and trans people, gays and drag queens/kings.

The wimmin, lesbian and gay movement that began in 1968 and spread worldwide had a great impact on the emerging squatting movements in (West) Germany from the beginning of the 1970s as well as in Spain or in Catalonia from the second half of the 1980s. It initiated important debates over gender, sexism, transphobia and homophobia, heteronormativity, intersexuality and anti-patriarchal struggles.

Alongside the slogan 'the personal is political', which emerged from the 1968 movement, wimmin/lesbians have pointed out patriarchal power structures in society – related to the structure of families, sexuality and the 'given roles' of men and women. The oppression of women is analysed and defined: violence against women, control of their ability to give birth, commercialisation of the female body in adverts and media, (heterosexist and male-dominated) pornography, gene and reproductive technologies, and exploitation of women's paid and unpaid labour such as unpaid domestic work and lower wages. But it has also to be mentioned that the slogan 'the personal is political' has been criticised by women of colour (and not only by them) as a white universal feminist perspective which does not take into consideration the privileges and benefits contributing to the reproduction of power structures in contrast to the realities of migrant women and women of colour.

The 'private' living spaces of mixed squats became some of the various new (battle)fields and scenes of the renegotiation of gender relations. In particular the fields of reproductive work, the understanding of roles (and behaviours) and everyday sexism in all of its many facets, loving sexual relationships as well as sexualised violence, and the right and the power of definition came to determine and frame debates and conflicts within squats.

But the diverse feminist/gay/lesbian movements led also to the development of an independent, autonomous organisation of wimmin, lesbian, gay and queer/trans people within the squatters' environment and other social movements. Apart from mixed structures and places, they squatted their own houses, created their own social centres, book stores, publishers, newspapers, radio channels, video groups and so on, and organised spaces for wimmin and lesbian, queer and trans people only. The reasons for this development have grown out from different aspects of a patriarchal reality, which are discussed in this chapter. The origin of these feminist struggles and their history go back more than 40 years.

While one of the first autonomous wimmin's living space in Berlin[2] was established in the commune of Cosimaplatz in 1970, the first known female/lesbian occupation of a flat in West Germany took place in 1973 at Freiherr-vom-Stein-Straße 18 in Frankfurt am Main. From the first big squatting wave in 1980/81, in which more than 200 houses in total were occupied, until 2013, around 20 houses in West Berlin and (united) Berlin have been squatted by female/lesbian/gay/queer/trans people. Among others, the Houses of Witches in Liegnitzerstraße 5 was occupied on 5 January 1981, and provided a feminist women's health centre. It was followed by the Marianne Devils in Mariannenstraße 97, Naunynstraße 58, a Womencafe in Jagowstraße 12, Kottbusserstraße 8 – the only occupation by migrant women (seven Turkish and one German woman, and five children) – Winterfeldstraße 37, Danckelmannstraße 15 (which housed FFBIZ: a women's investigation, information and education centre), a sex workers' squat (with the self-organised group Hydra) in Potsdamerstraße 139 and the women's centre Chocolate Factory in Mariannenstraße 6.

More squats followed in the 1980s (the first squatted caravan site only for women, next to Georg-von-Rauch-Haus in 1984) and during the second wave of squatting in 1989/90, especially in East Berlin. Some groups were evicted after a short time, including at Mariannenstraße 9–10 (after one day in 1989), Erkel (1990), Dieffenbachstraße 33 (1990), the women's house at Mainzerstraße 3 and the Tuntenhaus (drag queens' house) at Mainzerstraße 4, but some places still existed at the time of writing this in 2013. They include a wimmin-lesbian-trans-house at Brunnenstraße 7, a queer-anarcho-feminist house project at Liebigstraße 34, a women's 'backyard house' at Grünbergerstraße 73 and a queer caravan site at Schwarzer Kanal. In December 2012 another such house existed: the women-only space in the occupied Refugee Strike House in Ohlauerstraße 5.

In Madrid there is still La Eskalera Karakola, occupied in 1996, evicted in 2005 and afterwards legalised at a nearby location in the Lavapiés neighbourhood. Anarchist and pro-Zapatista women opened their own squat in 2009, La Enredadera, after a split with men in a previous squat, La Juli. Both projects were located in the same neighbourhood of Tetuán. La Eskalera was exclusively a social centre, while La Enredadera combined a social centre and housing. Another brief experience of a building occupied almost exclusively by women was La Lunática, in the neighbourhood of Latina, which lasted over three months in 2013. Most of the women squatters of La Lunática were involved in social centres such as Casablanca and Raíces where gender issues were often debated. The squats of Koala (2011–12) and Caldo Vegano (2010–12)[3] also had a feminist and anti-patriarchal agenda.

In the metropolitan area of Barcelona we have experienced the very active squatting group Les Tenses (since 1997), and various women's squats: La Morada (from November 1997 to February 1998), La Fresca (1998), La Mambo (2006–07), Casa de M and I (2008), El sexto sentido y El quinto coño in Hospitalet (2008), Casa y la trini (2008), La Tremenda in Manresa (2005–06), and La Gorda in St Andreu (2005–08), plus the Okupa Queer in Montgat (2004–05). Margarida Tafanera[4] (2011–12) was also a clearly anti-sexist and feminist squat, La Llamborda (since 2012) has predominantly been occupied by women, and since April 2012 the Kuarentena group has squatted at La otra Carboneria, providing a space for *infectadxs* (infected people), *bollos* (dykes), transfeminists, *kuir, maricas* (faggots) and intersex people (www.kuarentena.net).

One of the important reasons for the development of these gender-related experiences has been the critique of male-dominated behaviour and patterns in mixed living spaces, squats or political groups, where often men ignored and rejected the need for independent women's spaces. The women's collective Ligadura which emerged in 1986 in Madrid and participated in the Asamblea de Okupas (Assembly of Squatters) describes its experiences:

> We had been a group of women occupying property and joining the Assembly of Squatters. After a while we noticed that very clear gender roles had been established .... During this time we saw that we were repeating the same roles and stereotypes: the women were cleaning and cutting hair; meanwhile the men were at the barricades, cutting wood ... we wanted to meet among women ... but before this idea finally has been realised, time passed. The drop of water that changed everything had to do with a trip, organised by the Assembly of Squatters, to a squatters meeting in Hamburg, (West) Germany in 1987. In (West) Germany we saw women marching separately on demonstrations, women's self-defence groups, and when we came back we said, 'That's what we want.' A group of women who stand together, that is self-organised, can defend themselves, and from that moment we started to meet.
>
> (Gil, 2011: 79)

A report by the working group 'Women and Squatting' during a nationwide mixed squatting meeting in Münster (West Germany) six years earlier in 1981 had pointed in a similar direction:

> Structural patriarchal violence has many faces and comes along in various manners and shapes, sometimes more subtle, sometimes more massive.
>
> (Frauencafe Moabit, 1982: 38–9)

At that meeting women reported on and explained their treatment by men, noting that they were not taken seriously, that there was a lack of respect towards autonomous women's spaces, that they were confronted with mistrust, a lack of understanding, rejection, insults, that they were sworn at and called names ('men haters', 'uptight/tense feminists' and so on). Such verbal attacks led to a crossing of boundaries, sexualised violence and even rape against women.

One female squatter wrote in 1981 about her bad, 'lousy' experiences with male squatters (Frauencafe Moabit, 1982: 40–2), noting that women were 'sick of the euphoric indulgence of self-adulation of the squatters and the movement'. These women spoke about 'a new chauvinism' and criticised 'macho and aggressive behaviour inside the squats that in some cases leads to beatings as well as typical male sex roles and the monopoly of knowledge'. The rough climate is well documented in another example from the Berlin-BesetzerInnenrat (Squatting Council) in 1981:

> 'Shut your mouth, you old cunt' shouted one squatter to another, and '300 people listened to his outburst of fury without criticizing him'. Later someone wrote in the newspaper *taz*, 'that the forced discussion about the new sensibility by the women movement of the 1970s seemed to be submerged under the stones of the squatting movement'.
>
> (amantine, 2011: 119)

For these and other reasons it seemed, not surprisingly, that the women of the House of the Witches in Liegnitzerstraße 5 did not want to live with men: 'nobody wanted to do that voluntarily, that would have been at least one step backwards', explained one of the witches (*taz*, 26 February 1981).

Sexism and sexualised violence against woman is an ongoing phenomenon on different levels in (mixed) squatted spaces in Berlin and other cities, although it has to be mentioned that issues of domination and sexism have come to be regarded by many squatters as (theoretically) important to work on. Some incidents were horrific. One of the most terrifying cases took place in the well-known squats at the Hafenstraße in Hamburg in 1984. One woman was humiliated, tortured and raped by three occupiers (one man and two women) for 12 hours in the basement of the house. The woman was undressed, gagged, bound and hung up in chains; cigarettes were put out on her body and safety pins pierced through her nipples and genitals (amantine, 2011: 128).

The autonomous women's collective Ligadura, which emerged in the 1980s in Madrid, participating in the Occupied Social Centre Minuesa, also criticised the power structures in mixed political groups as well as the sexism that was evident in both language and behaviour in squatted spaces. To fight patriarchal power structures became for Ligadura as important and necessary as abolishing capitalism and all types of economic, social, political and cultural authoritarian institutions (Sánchez, 2004: 219).

Years later in 1998, the group Les Tenses from Barcelona published a pamphlet 'Por que hablamos de sexismo en los espacios liberados' ('Why do we talk about sexism in the liberated spaces?'), which questioned the male-dominant role (Gil, 2011: 93):

> Because we do live in a capitalist and patriarchal society, and because we

want to construct an alternative to this system, as a first step we must change ourselves. Towards our conceptions of life, relations, sexuality .... The difficulty is not to theorise about the way to do it, but to carry it out in practice. And that's what is not that easy, because we do not want to liberate only spaces but also minds and attitudes.

(Les Tenses, 1998)

In Madrid Las Anacondas Subversivas relied on the formula *Ninguna Agresion Sexista Sin Respuesta!* (No sexist aggression without response) to denounce sexual aggression in occupied places and make them public. The intervention of Las Anacondas Subversivas at the end of a concert from the band Tarzan, in which they spilled paint and Cola over the head of the bassist, who had raped a woman a year before, handed out leaflets and put up a banner, caused fierce debates within the movement, a war of communications, and finally contributed to the dissolution of the group. Members of Tarzan first expressed unconditional support for their bassist, which showed the male solidarity among them, then later expelled him, but nevertheless attacked the Anacondas for their vigilante justice (*Mujeres Preokupando*, 1998).

In El Laboratorio I (squatted from 1997 to 1998) one woman living there was sexually assaulted and in another incident, during a party held by the Ruido collective, another woman was brutally raped in the bath.

The environment of the incident, the failure to take care and the lack of a collective response at that party, which was neither stopped nor closed after the rape, was criticised in the statement *Espacios Okupados, Espacios con Cuidado* (*Occupied spaces, spaces in which to take care/to watch out*) by one woman from the collective Eskalera Karakola, an ex-member of El Labaratorio (*Mujeres Preokupando*, 1998). In the meantime there were some debates in the squat about the sexual assault of the woman who was living there. But the reactions and comments about this attack were so extremely macho and sexist that the woman's group Indias Metropolitanas, which had been giving self-defence classes in the social centre up till then, decided to move to a different location (Devi, 2012: 9–34).

These sexualised assaults cannot be seen as isolated, but rather reflect the reality of a patriarchal society. One woman giving self-defence courses in different squats in Madrid remembers that 'at least 30% of woman, attending their classes, had suffered numerous instances of sexual aggressions' (Devi, 2012: 32).

During the same period, in 1997 a nationwide meeting of squatters was held in Barcelona where a panel discussion about 'Women and Squatting' took place. One woman from the group Dones Esmussades (Valencia) stated very clearly that 'The situation of men and woman in the movement is not the same and when we say this, we talk about power' (Gil, 2011: 94).

The experiences women on that panel exchanged about sexism and the role of women in the occupied spaces led to the idea of producing a newspaper written by women, *Mujeres Preokupando*, to which many groups and collectives from various areas like Barcelona, Madrid, Zaragoza, Valencia, Euskadi and the Canary Islands could contribute. The newspaper was designed 'as a call, for occupying women, with space for all women who can be anyone, to find out what ever might be important for her, to think together how to shatter the world' (*Mujeres Peokupando*, 1998). To date, since 1998 there have been nine issues published.

Karla, a feminist black lesbian migrant without documents, collected some of the criticisms, which have been accumulated throughout the years, in the declaration *Por que espacios solo para mujeres?* (Why women only spaces?):

> This oppression against us does not exist only in the capitalist society, but also in those liberated spaces. The repetition of old macho thinking, the same patriarchal ideology comes along in a different face, such as an intellectual, or an activist with a political anti-capitalist, anti-authoritarian background .... The debates about sexist violence inside the social movements have been almost always pushed by women and lesbians, and not because of a simple and existing internalisation by activists who approach the necessity of a feminist political agenda while at the same time making a critical reinterpretation of their own masculinity ....
>
> It is very worrying to see the level of tolerance in the political spaces towards aggression, the difficulty of identifying the very different forms of violence against women and the lack of the capacity to act collectively. And when the normalised violence has ceased to be private and cannot been denied any more (denial is the most common response ...), justifications and excuses are put on the table. Defences and justifications make it possible to not do anything concrete. He was drunk, on drugs, just joking; she was insinuating/making advances; he is a good guy, and so on ... this is used to justify, minimise, silence or to make the sexist attitudes invisible. ... Let's form an autonomous group and put in practice the different feminist approaches. Let's struggle against the historical and daily violence .... Let us reflect and debate collectively about the issues of gender, gender-based violence, sexuality, identities, racism, class ...
>
> (*Mujeres Preokupando*, 2008)

The necessity of women-only spaces had become evident, but nevertheless women's groups have always used spaces within mixed social centres or squats in Madrid, Barcelona or Berlin.

After the experience of the women-only space in the Lavapiéx 15 squat (from April to October 1996), where the women took one floor for themselves, the women's social centre CSO La Eskalera Karakola in Madrid-Lavapiés was occupied by students, activists from the feminist movement, transsexuals, lesbians, anti-militarists and autonomous women in 1996. It became the first squatted women's social centre in Spain. The first women's squat in Spain was probably Amanacer, which existed in Valencia from 1991 to 1993 and was used as a living space. La Eskalera Karakola became a very important reference point for autonomous feminist squatters in the rest of the country, and also for the autonomous wimmin and lesbian movement as a whole.

The women there participated in or initiated various activities, mobilisations and actions, including a public sleep-out, when women went with their bedding to the Puerta del Sol (a major square in central Madrid) and denounced domestic violence (1998); torchlit night demonstrations opposing violence against women while chanting 'the streets and the night are ours too', accompanied by the campaign 'Attention, construction site. We are working against macho aggression' (1999); occupation of the Inditex company's premises in order to denounce its advertising policy (in adverts it used very thin models who represented an 'ideal' that was impossible to attain for many women, and which often led to painful effects like bulimia or anorexia) (1999–2002); various actions against the war in the former Yugoslavia and later against the war in Iraq (1999–2003); the realisation of the Noise European Summer School in Women's Studies (2001); preparations for a state-wide meeting of feminists in Cordoba (2000); annual lesbian-gay-transsexual pride events; and diverse actions alongside black women.

The women also opened the Escuela de Feminismos (School of Feminism) and La Casa de la Diferencia (House of the Difference) and started projects like Cybercentrifuga. The groups Sexo, Mentiras y Precariedad, Laboratorio de trabajadoras and Precarias a la Deriva investigated the conditions of women workers, pointed to the precariousness of their situation, and developed possible strategies of empowerment and resistance to the capitalist reality. Many other diverse groups have met at, or emerged from, the centre, including Colectivo Feministas, Las Gudos, Cazaslargas, La Eskina del Safo, Retoricas de Genero or Grupo de Teoria Queer (Group of Queer Theory), a working group against racism, Encuentro y Contraste, a workshop with migrant women, and collaborations with women's groups worldwide such as Mujeres Creando (Bolivia). Other important themes that were debated and discussed there include identities, the questioning of being woman, non-normal sexualities, the intersection of power relations and structures, the singularity of every body, the globalisation and transformation of work, queer/trans theories, and new technology (Asociación Cultural Feminista La Eskalera Karakola, 2005: 4–7; Gil, 2011: 86–98).

The belief that power relations are linked and influence each other had always played a key role in the understanding and analysis of power itself. Patriarchy, racism and capitalism (among others) are power systems that conglomerate and mutually interact. Therefore the women connected their theoretical approach and practical pronouncements with work and precariousness in capitalism, the war and globalisation, and also urban geographies and gentrification dynamics in the city and the district. They also formed groups like the Colectivo de Mujeres Urbanistas and organised workshops with women from their Lavapiés neighbourhood to rethink and map the kind of environment they really want and need.

The group was evicted in 2005 and relocated in two legalised buildings with a low rent, which caused some controversies and envy among the squatters' movement in Madrid (Martinez 2012: 20). The new location is now called Casa Publica de Mujeres (Public House of Women) La Eskalera Karakola.

La Morada, occupied by five women on 9 November 1997 in Sants, was actually the first women's squat in Barcelona, but it was not accepted by everyone on the mixed squatter scene. For its members the anti-sexist struggle was an important priority, as was 'trying to break with patterns which have been internalised since childhood in most women' (La Morada leaflet, Barcelona).

Nine years later the woman/lesbian/trans squat Mambo (an acronym for Momento Autonomo de Mujeres y Bolleras Osadas) in Barcelona achieved major significance and visibility in the one year of its existence (2006–07) and launched new and important debates. Several groups like Les Atakas (a feminist lesbian direct action group), Bloc d'Accio, Ovarika (a group of feminist reflection), self-defence groups (such as Wendo), the Theatre of the Oppressed, Girlswholikeporno, a Woman Prisoners Support Group, and women and lesbians from a number of different countries (mainly in Latin America) have met there. Besides working, exploring and performing on issues such as the relationship between art, politics and manners of visual communication, the questioning of identities, acting on macho violence or racism, they also focused on police brutality and discrimination against sex workers in their own neighbourhood, the Raval district of Barcelona, as well as initiating and hosting workshops on pornography and feminism, drag kings, sexuality and feminist theory.

In the workshop about pornography, organised by Girlswholikeporno, there was one section concerned with reflecting on and debating feminism, post-porno and queer theory, and another part involved in filming and producing their own videos. The idea behind this was to explore how women could make a porn video in a different way, showing a different kind of symbolic relation between women and sexuality, and not reproducing stereotypical and conventional heteronormative pornography. 'Women also like porno' became a slogan of that time, questioning hegemonic myths of woman's sexuality (Gil, 2011: 96–7) and contributing to self-empowerment through exploring your own desires and fantasies, in contrast to the male-dominated capitalist porn industry.

La Eskalrea Karakola (Madrid) and Mambo (Barcelona) are not the only centres that deserve mention. There were also several lesbian/gay, drag queen, queer and trans squatted houses in Berlin, all of which can be understood as emerging from the deconstructionist and queer-feminist discourses that, since the 1990s, have begun to question categories of sex and to break/split open the legality/regularity of given bipolarities of sex. All these have made the growing criticism of heteronormativity in the squatting scene more visible. The new queer politics arose from criticism about lesbian and gay identity politics as well as from the fact that bisexual and transgender people have begun to question such dichotomous and fixed identity concepts (Vanelslander, 2007).

In this context, it is important to mention that in the meantime the intersectional approach[5] of other components of domination and existing power structures contributes to a broader concept of queer and feminist theoretical discourse.

Therefore, it is not surprising that people of colour and people with precarious lives criticise the invisible normality of whiteness and middle-class positions, and demand greater attention to the complex character of identities. Critical whiteness, postcolonialism, feminism, antisemitism, antiziganism (hostility to Roma people, especially in Germany) and anarchism are just some of the political concepts and movements that have been contributing to this new understanding of complexity of power relations (see also Vaneslander, 2007).

The first Tuntenhaus[6] (House of Drag Queens) was occupied in 1981 in West Berlin, at Bülowstraße 55. The residents were evicted two years later. It was well connected with the gay scene, monthly meetings of Berlin gay groups took place there, and part of the gay film *Anderssein (Being Different)* was shot in the house.

The second Tuntenhaus, in which 30 gays lived, was very visible, glamorous and enigmatic. It was squatted in May 1990 at Mainzerstraße 4 in East Berlin, but the residents were evicted just six months later (and only 41 days after the unification of Germany), in November 1990, following three days of fierce resistance in the streets. The Tuntenhaus distanced itself from the mainstream and institutionalised gay movement, and came into conflict with it. During the annual Cristopher Street Day (Gay Pride) demonstration in 1990, some of the radical drag queens from the Tuntenhaus were thrown from the stage while reading a statement in solidarity with the relatives of the imprisoned Red Army Faction[7] members. However they were well integrated into the left gay scene and very active inside the squatting movement. Beside a second-hand bookstore with literature from East Germany and a bar named Forellenhof, the Tuntenhaus became most famous for the *Tuntenshows* (drag shows) held in its backyard.

In Mainzerstraße, where in total 11 houses had been occupied in a row and where 200 people were living, they often played the facilitator/mediator-role and became a mascot or a public symbol of the whole street: 'The Tuntenhaus, the tuntentower, the ghost house of the street, was far ahead the most beautiful, pretty, most kitsch, trash, and garish house and the biggest stumbling block for all the neighbors.' (Arndt, 1992: 44)

The third Tuntenhaus, located at Kastanienallee 86, was installed after the eviction of the second one and has been legalised. It is more a living and less a political project (Urinowa), but nevertheless some of the inhabitants have participated in various political projects like the Schwule-Antifa (Gay Antifa), the Querulanten, and the newspaper *Tuntentinte*. They have also actively participated in debates about homophobia, sexism and macho behaviour, and joined and organised mobilisations for the Rattenwagen (rat-track), the Transgenial CSD (Gay Pride), the Stöckeltreffen (meetings of drags with stiletto heels), the Tunten Terror Tour, and the Homolandwoche (a week-long meeting of radical gays at different places once a year in Germany). Every year they celebrate their famous Tunten Festival in their backyard, with lots of people in drag, shows, singing and German pop music.

The queer caravan site Schwarzer Kanal was first squatted in 1989 as a 'mixed project', and had to move two times because of gentrification measures in the Berlin-Mitte district, in the centre of Berlin.

First it had to give way to a new building for the media union Ver.di, then in 2010 it moved again because its building belonged to the Hochtief AG company. Its new location is in Berlin-Treptow, farther away from the centre. The Schwarze Kanal also plays an important role in the ex-squatting and squatted caravan site movement as well as in the autonomist queer/trans scene. It organises Queer and Rebel Days as well as the annual DIY Radical Queer Filmfestival, Entzaubert. The Schwarze

Kanal also has taken part in broader mobilisations as the Queer-Barrios at the Anti-G8 Summit Camp 2007 in Heiligendamm, the autonomous Queeruption Festival 2003, and is active in (ex)-squatter and anti-gentrification networks like WBA (*Wir bleiben alle*: We All Stay) Campaign and others (amantine, 2012).

The travelling radical Queeruption Festival, well linked with the squatting scene, took place in 2003 in Berlin and in 2005 in Barcelona, and highlighted the visibility of multiple gender and sexual identities by questioning heteronormativity, heterosexism and gender roles. Queeruption 8 in Barcelona faced some repression by the authorities, when its meeting place, an occupied factory in Hospitalet, was surrounded for almost 20 hours by the police and nine people were arrested during a demonstration which criticised the capitalist gay-mainstream commercialised culture and politics in the Eixample district (gaixample). Participants in the demonstration spray-painted slogans (*No al capitalismo rosa, Queremos ser gordas y peludas, Vull ser marika feliç, 'No eurogay gris', Coños para todas gratis, no al kapital* [*No to pink capitalism, We want to be fat and hairy females, I want to be a happy gay, No grey eurogay, Free pussies for all, Say no to kapitalism*]), threw water bombs, and caused minor damage and small confrontations at some hotels and establishments (the Castro restaurant, Zeltas, Dietrich and Hotel Axel). This demonstration, called by the Queeruption organisers 'to create an alternative to the commercial gay ambience, which is excluding others of being part of the homosexual collective for economic, ethnic or gender related reasons' (Queeruption leaflet, Barcelona), has generated many discussions within the gay-lesbian-trans movement. The nine arrested people were psychologically mistreated, beaten, insulted and threatened in a sexist, homophobic and racist manner ('Squatter and on top of that a faggot full of shit', 'Shut up or I'll put my truncheon up your arse') and tortured. They were denied water, access to lawyers or translators, prescribed medication, and had to wait 10 hours for medical attention. All the accused police officers have been acquitted of any wrongdoing.

As in Berlin, Madrid and Barcelona, many women-lesbian-trans-queer-gay squatters organise or participate in general LGBT activities and mobilisations like the annual trans march in October Stop Trans Pathologisation, and more radical activities critical of mainstream commercialisation, like the transgenial CSD (Gay pride) in Berlin and the trans march Trans-tornem a/el carrer (We come back to the streets) in Barcelona in 2012, organised by the assembly Octubre Trans Bcn, which put on various kinds of activities such as talks and conferences.

All these discussions and debates within the women-lesbian-queer-gay-trans scenes and environments alongside and about the categories gender, sexuality and identity have finally enhanced their influence and found an entry in the heteronormative reality of the squatting movements. This is also seen throughout squatted (and also subsequently legalised) places, in cities such as Berlin, Madrid and Barcelona.

The most decisive question from a feminist viewpoint and perspective will always be about domination, power and authority. That implies acknowledging the existing power conflicts and repetition of internalised roles within the squats and house projects. But many are aware of these issues, recognise the reproduction of gender roles and are developing an openness to self-reflection and criticism *(Mujeres Preokupando*, 2009). As an example, criticism arose in the Okupa Queer in Montgat-Barcelona, where several conflicts, also linked with gender, sexuality and violence, and power shifts had occurred:

> In dealing with these problems, it became obvious that the content of the word 'queer' had been understood in different ways by different people – the Okupa Queer was eventually a story of power dynamics and exclusions among different kinds of queers and other squatters.
>
> (Vaneslander, 2007)

The complexity of domination and power in relation to sex and gender – deconstructed, categorised or not – culminated in a question posed by the X_Y group:

> Is the exclusion of a person according to the category of sex not reproducing bipolarity again? Would a women's group actually have much less hierarchy, as feminist approaches to difference suggest? Or are certain manners and patterns of behaviour apart from the categorised sex of a person not more relevant instead?
>
> (X_Y, 2008)

Congruously the enhanced and broadened understanding of an anti-sexist analysis and reality was proven by a workshop on Sexualized Violence Within the Women-Lesbian-Trans Context during the Third Congress of Anti-Sexist Practices in Berlin in 2009. But of course, this does not change the fact that it is still primarily women – and also lesbian, queer and trans people – who are negatively affected by the heterosexist mainstream.[8] Therefore we can state that the area of the debate ranges between the poles of theoretical deconstruction of the gender/sex category and anti-sexist practice within the given social reality of a bipolar gender structure.

Forty-five years after the 1968 beginning of the women's, lesbian and gay movements, 32 years after the first female and gay squats in West

Berlin, and 17 and 16 years after the first female/lesbian squats in Madrid and Barcelona, debates, discussions and conflicts about sexism and patriarchal behaviour are (not surprisingly) still ongoing in the squatting world. The women of Mambo (2006–07) criticised the hostility towards their women-only space by other squatters, who did not hesitate to use insults like 'destructive separatism with the intention to weaken the movement' or 'the exclusion of men is fascism' (anonymous, 2009).

The women from La Tremenda (2005–07) pointed out that many mixed groups talk about gender as an isolated issue, giving it only relative importance, or do not consider gender as a basic struggle. The women of La Gorda (2005–08) see a lack of critical analysis within the hetero patriarchy, and experienced macho attitudes and discourses among squatters (*Mujeres Preokupando*, 2009).

For many years the former squat at Köpi 137 (Berlin), which also was criticised for not having clear anti-patriarchal guidelines, rejected any lesbian and women-only parties in its space with the argument that they did not want to exclude anyone because of their, colour, sex/gender, or origin from their space – (the main exclusion its members were referring to being that of men). The group finally agreed in 2000 to host a female/ lesbian party for the first time since 1991 (amantine, 2011: 144).

Other examples also seem to offer painful proof that sexism and sexualised violence are ongoing. In 2009 at the (later evicted) house project Brunnenstraße 183 in Berlin there were reports of sexist speech and behaviour, intimidation, sexualised and physical violence and rape. These incidents were not publicised outside the group, and those who wanted to call attention to them and make them public were threatened with violence. The organisers of a large nationwide Anarchist Congress in 2009 in the formerly squatted (now legalised) social centre of New Yorck in Bethanien had to break up the meeting prematurely, although there were around 1,000 people in attendance, because they could not guarantee an anti-sexist free space, after the group Fuck for Forest had several times crossed the boundary of what many people considered acceptable behaviour, for example by running around naked all the time (especially the men of the group), and making homophobic comments. Many of the congress participants expressed solidarity with the group. Subsequently the organisers issued a statement justifying the dissolution of the meeting, noting that 'this conflict, which started with sexist boundary-crossing and provocation, could no longer have been resolved in a peaceful way' (amantine, 2011: 150–2).

This showed once again that it cannot be assumed that an anti-sexist consensus of theory and practice automatically exists in the left-radical, anarchist and squatters environment.

In Barcelona, in 2009 and 2010, two men (one living in the Barrilonia squat – the group was evicted in 2012 – the other a neighbour) engaged in several acts of sexual aggression against at least four different women in the squat, causing major conflicts and problems between the two collectives inside the house. The social centre (including the Barrikada Zapatista group) backed up those two men and were not willing to exclude them from further activities or to condemn the acts of sexual aggression. The collective of the living space above, on the other hand, actually kicked out both men from their living area (Assemblea de Vivenda de Barrilònia, 2011). The conflict between the two groups increased because of differences over other controversial issues, and developed into a situation of 'complex war', in which members of the living spaces were finally denied access to the social centre. They were also attacked physically, insulted several times in a sexist and homo-lesbian-transphobic manner, threatened with violence, and their living space was entered twice by force and without permission by members of the social centre (Assemblea de Vivenda de Barrilònia, 2011).

Investigations by the feminist researcher Barbara Biglia in Barcelona have proven that 17.9 per cent of women participating in social movements have experienced different types of abuse in these spaces (Biglia, 2005).

Because of instances such as these, more than a few people perceive a patriarchal 'rollback' and are demanding once again that there should be more anti-sexist standards in squats, social centres and autonomous, anarchist/anti-authoritarian structures, in spite of the obvious changes that have taken place over the 45 years of the women's and lesbian movements (amantine, 2011: 67).

Both as a response to sexism, violence and macho attitudes in Barcelona and as an act of self-empowerment of women, lesbian, queer and trans people, activists have created several fanzines and booklets, such as *Tijeras para todas* – Texts about macho violence in the social movements (2009); *La Gota, que fa vessar el got* – Reflections about the sexism in social movements (2009); and *Plantemos cara a las agresiones sexistas en los espacios liberados* – Process of debates in the squat La Revoltosa (2008). One man has also written a paper in which he reflects on his own sexism and questions gender roles: *Torres mas grandes hemos visto caer*. Furthermore, meetings and *conferences jornadas sobre agresiones* (conferences about aggressions) have taken place in two squats, in 2008 in La Revoltosa and 2010 in La Teixidora. Other such conferences that have taken place since 2011 include the annual feminist autonomous workshops, actions and talks *Se va armar la gorda*, which are held around International Women's Day on 8 March.

An *Anti-Sexistische Praxen-Konferenz* (Anti-Sexist Practices Conference) has taken place annually in Berlin since 2007, and some (ex)-squats like the New Yorck in Bethanien in Berlin distribute leaflets at the entrance to parties, which explain that 'sexist, racist, antisemitic, trans- and homophobic behaviour will not be tolerated – we want a party where everyone can feel comfortable' (AG Spaß für alle, 2011).

Posters and flyers are handed out and distributed at social centres that call attention to these issues; they have also circulated in Barcelona since 2004 through the *Asamblea de Género* (Assembly of Gender): *Los espacios 'liberados' no están exentos de agresiones* (The occupied spaces are not free from aggression), and *Agresión es cuando me siento agredida/o* (Aggression exists when I feel attacked).

Some relevant examples from Madrid and Barcelona are *Falo*, a fanzine with the slogan *'liberación masculina contra el patriarcado'* (masculine liberation from patriarchy), which questions gender roles, deconstructs the image of masculinity and urges the responsibility that men have to change the patriarchal reality:

> As men we play a central role in the transformation of gender relations initiated by feminism. We should support us each other and take up the struggle against the implemented roles and sex-gender oppression as a personal commitment and as a political goal.
>
> *(Falo, 2004: 3)*

La C.U.L.O, a degenerate feminist magazine (which emerged from the feminist circle *La Manada Degenerada Feminista*), appeared in 2009 and put out two issues, questioning with enormous joy nothing less than heteronormativity. A third example, *Anarqueer* from Madrid, is a fanzine which up to spring 2013 has released four issues, discussing matters such as 'acracia and gay/lesbian/trans politics', 'transfeminism, violence and gender' and 'Kuirs [queers] from yesterday and today' among others.

A wide and broad debate about all types of gender, sexism and identity-related issues has been developing. However, although an understanding of the dissolution of sexism in everyday and 'private' life does exist and has been generally accepted and carried through to the greatest possible extent within the autonomous and anarchist squats or house projects, it is not always reflected in practice. Often this critique of sexism is included on flyers but not internalised as a recognition that has to be practised on a daily basis.

These contradictions stem from the diversity and fragmentation of actual affinity groups and squats, the lack of consistent organisations and networks, discontinuities, individualisation, the ever-recurring discussions, as well as a failure to recognise the existing knowledge. There is also a lack of knowledge in general of the history of struggles, discourses and debates within autonomous groups of women, lesbians, gay, queer and trans people (Tijeras para todas, 2009; amantine, 2012).

Although the history of development of feminist struggle and theory might differ in time in Berlin, Barcelona or Madrid, in reality the theoretical debates within the squatting scene related to sexism, gender politics, trans/queer and intersex discourses do not differ in terms of significance. While the 1968 women's/lesbian/gay movements hit West Germany straight away, its development in Spain became more complicated and delayed because of the military dictatorship of Franco (1939–75). In the present, these processes have been converging, meaning that we can find similar debates in all the places we have investigated. They may occur in different places at different times, but the questions and the theoretical intensity of the debates are very similar, with the only difference being that queer terminology is less adapted and used among the squatters in Madrid or Barcelona.

The Eskalera Karakola in particular, due to its long existence and the great participation of various groups and collectives, has played a significant role in different feminist movements and has been a part in all of the theoretical discourses and debates about queer/trans/intersex, and the intersectionality and interrelation of class, race/colonialism and gender. It has published many texts and several articles about various issues involving feminism, globalisation, violence, urbanism, the Lavapiés district, work and non-work, technology, sexualities, queer theory and transsexuality. Members wrote a foreword to the book *Otras inapropiables, Feminismos desde la fronteras* (*Other inappropriables, feminisms from the other side of the borders*) in 2004, and have published several books and articles (*A la deriva. por los circuitos de la precaridad feminina*) from the Precarias a la Deriva group, which formed part of Eskalera Karakola.

While diverse squatting movements have liberated a large number of buildings, queer/trans/feminism is slowly beginning to squat the minds of a growing number of activists. But there is still a long way to go. In fact, while the proposition 'the personal is political' is now widely accepted within nondogmatic, emancipatory, nonhierachical, autonomous and anarchist environments, we are still far from being able to make general statements or conclusions because of the diversity of the squatting movements, their contradictions, and the fragmentations of the various 'scenes' and subcultural milieux.

Despite the independent organisational structures of women's, gay, lesbian, queer and trans people's squats and their desires for a nonmixed conception of communal living and social activities, the major burden lays in how sexism is addressed in other social centres and living spaces.

Gender identity debates question gender norms, bipolarity and categories (such as man/woman). Besides female lesbian groups, there have also emerged groups who are open to trans, intersex and queer people and to other 'femininities'.

All these feminist, trans and queer debates and theories about identities, gender politics and categories are questioning the general issue of power dominance in the squatting environment as well as in society more generally.

Box 7.1 *Some Examples of the Great Variety and Diversity Within the Berlin Squatting Environment**

The Georg von Rauch-Haus, one of the very first squats, was occupied in 1971. Inhabited primarily by pupils, young workers, trainees and runaways, ten people worked periodically in large companies like AEG (General Electricity Company), maintaining contact with workers, discussing and debating with them for revolutionary change. The occupants formed apprenticeships, working as toolmakers, machinists, welders, bricklayers and so on. Thus, some of the first squatters came from a clear working-class background.

Over the last 40 years the composition of Berlin squatters has changed. While immigrants and people of colour have always been a minority portion of the squatter community, during the 1980s they squatted their own houses for the first time. In 1981, after having experienced racist/sexist discrimination in finding a new flat, seven women of Turkish descent and their children, along with a German supporter, squatted a property at Kottbusserstraße 8. The housing shortage was especially acute among young women separated from their partners. For these women the problems were immense and the difficulties they suffered severe.

In November 1980 several Turkish families moved into two squats occupied by supporters in Forstersraße 16 and 17 after having lived in a different house in poor conditions, with up to ten people in one room. Thirty-two years later, in December 2012, a group of refugees and supporters occupied a partially vacant school in Ohlauerstraße 12, naming it Refugee Strike House. These refugee-squatters occupied a public square in Kreuzberg (Oranienplatz) beginning in October 2012, living and organising in tents and mounting protests against the racist German immigration and asylum laws.

One floor of an occupied school was converted into a women-only refugee space that provided 'a free place where refugee women can meet to exchange knowledge and experiences, where they can get to discuss their rights, organise themselves and fight together against the isolation of the camps' (http://asylstrikeberlin.wordpress.com/refugee-women/).

Meanwhile, the Irving Zola Haus at Ohlauerstraße 12 was occupied, featuring a new social and political centre without barriers. While most Berlin social centres and ex-squats lack accessibility for people with disabilities, the naming of the Irving Zola squat referenced an American member of the Society of Disability Studies and editor of *Disability Studies Quarterly*. Thus a squatted house in Germany for the first time referred to an activist from the Disability Rights Movement.

In all probability, the oldest squatters in Berlin have been the grannies of Stillestraße 10 – a group of pensioners (300 retirees all together) aged from 67 to 96. They squatted in their own senior centre in July 2012 when they learned that because of budget cuts it would no longer be financed by the local municipality of Pankow. They struggled not only for their own demands but also against a thoroughly capitalist, commercialised world. As they stated in a declaration to the press:

> We don't want to leave behind a country in which a kid's music lesson, a visit to the library, or a gymnastics lesson for the elderly have become commodities, and in which everything is only valued in terms of money and in which people who can no longer afford something are simply turned into a cost factor.

After more than 111 days of squatting and several activities, and with widespread support, the politicians finally gave in and signed a contract with a long-term option for the seniors. Their struggle against closure was a total success!

* [These are only short examples showing the quantity of issues related to diversity. While the chapter focuses on gender diversity, other minority groups such as migrants are an important part of the squatters movement. These are explained in this box and are also relevant in the case of immigrant squatters in Rome: see Chapter 5.]

Notes

1 This is the feminist spelling of women, used as an expression of the repudiation of traditions that define females by reference to a male norm.

2 We refer here to West Berlin until 3 October 1990 and the unified Berlin thereafter.

3 Caldo Vegano was eventually not evicted by the police, but after an internal conflict, closed by some anarchists against the will of five people there. These anarchists were also accused of physical and psychological violence against some people from Caldo Vegano. (From Distri Maligna, April 2013, in *Equlibrio, Fanzine Anarcofeminista* no. 3, p. 5. See also the declaration of autodissolution without explanation, at http://caldovegano.blogspot.de/)

4 The name Margarida Tafanera is a homage to a woman who lived in this house in the 16th century and was one of the first witches burned during the Inquisition.

5 Seeing gender equality in relation to other social categories such as race, class, disability, sexual orientation and age. This perspective, called intersectionality, has its roots in black feminism, reflecting both racial and gendered systems of oppression. Intersectionality is still more common as a theoretical approach within research than in policy processes.

6 The Tuntenhaus (House of Drags) is a community of gays, bisexuals, queers, drags and perverts, according to their own definition: see www.tuntenhaus.squat.net/.

7 The Red Army Faction (Rote Armee Fraktion/RAF) was an urban guerrilla group active from 1970 to 1998.

8 '"When my anger starts to cry ...", Debatten zur Definitionsmacht und der Versuch einer notwendigen Antwort', in *Antisexismusbündnis Berlin 2006: Reader aus AS.ISM_2*.

References

AG Spaß für alle (2011) 'Wir wünschen uns eine Party, auf der sich jede_r wohlfühlen kann!!!' ['We want a party where everyone can feel at home!'] Berlin: self-published.

amantine (2011) *Gender und Häuserkampf [Gender and Urban Warfare]*. Berlin: self-published.

amantine (2012) '"Das Private ist Politisch" – Häuserkampf und Gender' ['"The private is political": gender and urban warfare'], in *Femina, Zeitschrift für feministische Politikwissenschaft [Femina]*. Berlin: self-published.

Anonymous (2009) 'Torres mas grandes hemos visto caer' ['Higher towers we have seen falling']. Barcelona, Spain. http://issuu.com/santstv/docs/torres_m_s_grandes_hemos_visto_caer (accessed July 2013).

Arndt, S. (1992) *Berlin, Mainzerstraße, Wohnen ist wichtiger als das Gesetz [Berlin, Mainzer Straße, Housing is More Important Than the Law]*. Berlin: Basisdruck Verlag.

Asociación Cultural Feminista La Eskalera Karakola (2005) 'C.S. La Eskalera Karakola – Memoria de la karakola' ['Memories of the social centre La Eskalera Karakola'] in *Laboratorio Urbano, Dossier Autogestionarte, independencia artistica y autogestión de espacio* [*Self-Organize Yourself, Artistic Independence and Self-Management of Spaces*]. Madrid: self-published.

Assemblea de Vivenda de Barrilònia (2011) Dossier Vivienda Barrilonia, Barcelona, Spain. http://denunciaautodefensa.wordpress.com/vivienda-barrilonia/ (accessed July 2013).

Biglia, B. (2005) *Narrativa de mujeres sobre las relaciones de género en los movimientos sociales* [*Women's Narratives on Gender Relations in Social Movements*]. PhD thesis, University of Barcelona.

Devi, P. (2012) 'Mujeres sin hombres' ['Women without men'], in W. Salamanca (ed.), *Tomar y Hacer en vez de pedir y esperar – Autonomia y moviminetos sociales Madrid 1985–2011* [*To Get and to Do Instead of to Ask and to Wait For – Autonomy and Social Mvoements in Madrid, 1985–2011*]. Madrid: Solidaridad Obrera.

Falo (2004) 'Liberacion masculina contra el patriarcado' ['Male freedom against patriarchy']. Barcelona and Madrid.

Frauencafe Moabit (1982) *Frauenbefreiung und Häuserkampf – unversöhnlich?* [*Women's Liberation and Urban Warfare – Unforgiveness?*]. Berlin, self-published.

Gil, S. L. (2011) 'Nuevos feminismos – Sentido comunes en la dispersion, Una historia de trayectorias y rupturas en el Estado Español' []New feminisms – common sense in the dispersion. A history of trajectories and breaking in the Spanish state']. www.vitoria-gasteiz.org/wb021/http/contenidosEstaticos/adjuntos/es/67/88/46788.pdf (accessed July 2013).

Martínez, M. A. (2012) 'The inevitable dilemmas of institutionalisation for urban movements: the case of Madrid's squatters', *International Journal of Urban and Regional Research* 36(5).

La Morada (1998) *La Morada, una experiencia de mujeres okupando y autogestionando un espacio* [*La Morada: An Experience of Women Squatting and Self-Managing a Space*]. Barcelona, Spain, self published.

Mujeres Preokupando (1998) Issue 2.

–– (2008) Issue 7.

–– (2009) Issue 8.

La Revoltosa (2008) *Plantemos cara a las agresiones sexistas en los espacios liberados* [*Let's Face up to Sexist Aggressions in Freed Spaces*]. Barcelona, Spain, self-published.

Sanchez, M. (2004) 'Derribando los muros del genero: mujer y okupacion' ['Destroying gender walls: women and squatting'], in R. Adell and M. A. Martinez (eds), *Donde estan las llaves? El movimiento okupa: practicas y contextos sociales* [*Where are the Keys? The Squatter Movement, Practical Issues and Social Context*]. Madrid: Catarata.

Les Tenses (1998) Col.lectiu feminista del C.S.O. L'Hamsa Infousurpa.

Tijeras para todas (2009) *Textos sobre violencia machista en los movimientos sociales* [*Texts on Male Chauvinist Violence in Social Movements*]. Barcelona, Spain, self-published.

Urinowa (n.d.) 'Kastanienallee.' Berlin. http://tuntenhaus-berlin.de/?Geschichte/Kastanienallee (accessed July 2013).

Vanelslander, B. (2007) 'Long live temporariness: two queer examples of autonomous spaces', *Affinities Journal* 1(1), affinitiesjournal.org/index.php/affinities/
article/view/3/41 (accessed July 2013).

X_Y (2008) *Wann ist ein Mann ein Mann?* [*When is a Man a Man?*]. Berlin,
self-published.

8

Unavoidable Dilemmas:
Squatters Dealing with the Law

Miguel A. Martínez, Azozomox and Javier Gil

The squatters' movement is constantly facing legal challenges. On the one hand, squatting is subjected to different legal regulations in every European country. On the other hand, legal and political treatments of squatting have also evolved over the years and according to the particular state authorities concerned. In this chapter we focus on the cities of Madrid and Berlin, in order to understand how squatters deal with the overall criminalisation of squatting and the particular threat of eviction from squats. Other European cases are also considered for comparative purposes. Squatters' resistance to the law may take place inside or outside legal institutions. Legalisation of the squats, thus, should not be regarded as the major outcome of the legal dilemmas faced by squatters. Various other strategies, benefits, side-effects and contextual explanations also need to be included in the analysis.

Introduction

October 2010: after decades of being widespread and legal, squatting empty properties for living or other purposes became illegal in the Netherlands, with a maximum prison sentence of one year, or two years if the squatters use violence or threaten to use it (Pruijt, 2012b). September 2012: in England and Wales a new law came into force that made trespassing in a residential property with the intention of living there a criminal offence (Dee, 2013). These countries were known, until then, as the last paradises for squatting in Europe (Owens, 2009; Martínez, 2012). So have they finally been lost?

The trend seems clear. Different pieces of legislation against squatters have been approved in most European countries during the last two or three decades. Squatting in West Germany was always a criminal offence, but the laws were tightened in the 1980s in Berlin. The Spanish Penal Code of 1995 included squatting, for the first time ever, in the categories of serious crime. From one day to another, the occupation of empty houses, buildings or industrial premises may turn squatters into criminals. This is the usual political reaction to the rising expansion of a radical movement. However, squatters may continue with their radical politics through means other than squatting. They can also accept some concessions and the legalisation of the occupied buildings without distancing themselves from their autonomous ways of living. [House projects like Liebig 14 in Berlin are the best example, or the former Geneva squatters turned into caravan dwellers, as seen in Chapter 2.]

The different forms of repression which follow the criminalisation of squatting necessitate different kinds of squatters' strategies to fight back. Squatting is still overtly practised in the Netherlands, the United Kingdom and Spain. Less frequently there are attempts of squatting in Germany because, even in this very repressive context, squatting still remains as a key political claim of the radical left culture, although the most recent and visible cases do not exactly fall under the category of typical 'radical left culture' occupations.

Criminalisation and repression of squatting are not the last words to be said on this subject. The persistence and resistance of the squatters' movement deserve equal attention. Variations within different countries and cities show a quite complex landscape. In France, for example, many local authorities keep close contacts with squatters (mainly with artist squatters) in order to reach agreements and legal contracts as soon as possible. In addition, many squats are initiated during the 'winter truce' with the aim of at least lasting for several months. In Denmark, where squatters face immediate prosecution, some people still squat houses in a silent manner, and occasionally there are public squatting actions for setting up social centres. These specific situations and legal contexts do not apply to other European cities. We can therefore argue that squatting flourishes even within very repressive environments, although it can adopt different forms of expression and degrees of intensity.

Second, the cases of Madrid and Berlin allow us to reflect on the legal dilemmas that squatters are obliged to face. In particular, we shall see how the practices of resistance to the criminalisation of squatting may be developed within and apart from state institutions. However, not all squatters agree with the politics of maintaining open negotiations with state authorities aimed at legalising their existing situations. The cohesion of the movement and the opportunity of its political challenges constitute two crucial factors to explain the development of such an interaction between activists and elites. When the movement appears strong and active, legalisation may not play a relevant role. Squatters then gain a legitimacy that stems from their practices, political networks and the balance of local power relationships. This temporarily prevents squatters from engaging in processes that can lead eventually to legalisation, although the flow of evictions and new occupations continues.

Legalisations have ambivalent outcomes. They can help some squatters to obtain basic resources in their pursuit of an anti-capitalist and self-managed style of living, but they can also provoke splits among different groups of activists. Thus, it seems evident that the more squats are legalised, the more difficult the practice of squatting becomes, although the case of the Netherlands prior to the recent ban on squatting coming into force indicates that this is not a general pattern all over Europe.

Squatting Rights and the Criminalisation of Squatting

Is there any right to squat the city (and the land)? Are there any legitimate 'squatting rights'? The criminalisation of squatting shows that there was a previous period when these squatting rights prevailed. Squatters also claim the legitimacy of making use of abandoned properties for the satisfaction of basic human needs. Why then has squatting become forbidden?

Squatters express a radical critique of private property, housing shortages, urban speculation, the commodification of culture and the authoritarian background of representative democracy. As such, squatting enacts a direct challenge to private owners and governments, often through the exercise of civil disobedience and illegal actions, although these may vary according to different national and local regulations, and political frameworks. Some simply end up squatting out of their need for affordable housing or to obtain a free space for social purposes. Some others enter the movement as an extension of their political will to fight urban capitalism. Some combine both motivations, while many more just approach squatted places as visitors, sympathisers or temporary activists, aiming to explore the potentialities of squatting as an experimental utopia (Pruijt, 2012a; Martínez, 2012).

Squatting may be seen as just a social reaction to the malfunctioning of the capitalist system. Neither the proprietors of land and buildings, nor state agencies, are able to manage the allocation of the whole built stock according to social needs. The failures of both the real estate market and the bureaucratic redistribution of spatial resources are employed by squatters to show society how the system actually works. Urban speculation is criticised through practical means, not only by pointing to the elites who profit from it. To take over an abandoned building is both a protest action and an effective way of solving urgent needs for those who participate. The more politicised the squatters are, the stronger is the campaign of protest against the speculators, politicians and managers who run this key mechanism of capitalism.

While squatting resembles the radical traditions that intend to overthrow the capitalist system, most of the squatters do not attempt to scale the challenges of private property (in other words, their aim is not expropriation). The 'right to the city' (RTC) is a key expression of that radical tradition. The RTC means that full citizens, as inhabitants (whether or not they hold national citizenship: Purcell, 2002), should be empowered to shape the urban space according to their needs, in a wider sense, and according to the immediate abolition of the major sources of inequality (market and for-profit relationships). This applies to those who have no access to decent housing or to urban facilities next to their house, to those who have no say in urban planning, as well as to those who do not accept the unjust distribution of wealth.

Clearly, squatters belong to the excluded and the discontented (Marcuse, 2009), although this generalisation may avoid more careful consideration of all the social conditions that have an influence on activists and supporters of squatting. To choose a place to squat, for example, is to make a decision about the areas of the city in which to participate. That is, this initial decision may be conditioned by the availability of adequate, and not totally ruined, empty buildings, but it also involves the squatters' commitment and contribution to the social production of that part of the city, with preference for the most central boroughs.

Squatting involves the appropriation of spaces in everyday life, following Lefebvre's (1968) conception of the right to the city. A spatial politics based on everyday life is manifested also in the political empowerment which squatters acquire when dealing with external enemies and with legal actions, and when they develop their experience of direct democracy and self-management. Both capabilities may also be extended to the work of establishing social networks of allies and to their participation in neighbours' campaigns, or in other social movements and struggles. The squat, thus, is the base camp, beyond its eventual functioning as a home, for all of this political embeddedness in urban politics.

The RTC has been widely criticised because of the extreme openness, ambiguity and sum of multiple struggles that the concept embraces (Attoh,

2011). While the radical and spatially based anti-capitalism attached to Lefebvre's original conception may be fruitful for calling for broad coalitions of urban movements, the fuzzy definition of the RTC may also be used by institutions and elites to add a veneer of democratic participation to their light urban reforms, charts of fashionable principles and their practices of controlled and consensual citizen participation (UNESCO and UN-HABITAT, 2009, for example; also Pisarello, 2011). Anyhow, the strength of these formulations of an 'emerging human right' (similar to the rights to a universal income, to same-sex marriage or to vote for immigrants) is that it may be enforceable within the justice system. Urban movements, then, would have a new legal resource to oppose urban speculation, privatisation, discrimination, authoritarianism and new constructions, which all destroy social diversity and the natural environment. Their weakness is that local, regional or national authorities still have enough power to channel these demands into exclusive and reformist institutions while in parallel keeping alive their war against the poor and the homeless, sex workers and undocumented migrants, skateboarders and political dissidents, among other groups. Yet the promotion of environmental justice, respect for social and cultural diversity, autonomous citizen participation and the priority of social rights over the absolute right of private property, all require urban movements to challenge, overtly and often through confrontational actions, the double-speak of governments.

In fact, in comparison with the original radicalism of Lefebvre's insight, the RTC has experienced a process of vulgarisation and domestication similar to other catch-all and umbrella expressions such as 'sustainability' (Lopes, 2010: 316). As a consequence, neoliberalism is refused but not capitalism or some forms of 'left-Keynesianism'; participatory democracy is embraced, but only as a supplement and correction of representative democracy; while complaints about gentrification never take into consideration those who never had access to the privileges of living in the city centre (Lopes de Souza, 2010: 317). Lefebvre, instead, advocated revolutionary changes, a generalised self-management and a subsequent new liveable, diverse, vibrant, accessible and just city (Lopes de Souza, 2010: 318). The same inspiration is at the core of the utopian, anarchist and autonomist traditions of many squatters, without implying any specific or dogmatic planning of the path to follow.

The criminalisation of squatting therefore, can be said to entail the preservation of capitalism and support for the elites' struggle against squatting rights. These squatting rights may be summarised as follows.

• Confronting the 'emptiness' and the vacuums of urban speculation (or the overproduction of buildings), squatting is a means to uncover and reuse that waste of common energy, space, urban infrastructures and public workforce. Private and public developers do not have absolute rights to construct wherever they want, and they should be subject to strict planning regulations. When their properties remain empty, they cause damage to society because these regulations are not observed. Squatting contributes to a reversal of that situation.

- Squatters tend to raise their voices against urban speculation. To a certain extent, squatters just claim that the conventional legal restrictions imposed on that economic practice should actually be applied. If that kind of legislation is not enforced, then squatters make visible the subordination of the law to the speculators' interests. However, the pursuits of the most political squatters go beyond that precise field of urban conflict. They use squatting as an accessible tool to criticise all forms of economic and social speculation because the entire capitalist system is rooted in speculative, and often hidden, operations which in the end are dramatically visible in the enormous divergences in wealth generated around the world.

- Squatters are sometimes accused of jumping the queue in the processes of social housing allocation. This might be true if they were actually participating in those bureaucratic processes, but usually they do not. The stock of social housing is a target of some squatters when they discover properties that have been empty for a long time, that are involved in renewal plans, or for instance when the social housing stock is subject to privatisation through housing corporations. The attitude of 'take it, do not wait for it' also suggests that squatters use direct action as a means to protest against the main problems of the management of social housing, such as the inefficiency of the system, the lack of sufficient resources, the secret character of information, and above all the unjust selection criteria. Given that the bureaucratic channels of protest tend to exclude the expressions and worries of poor people, squatters bring this issue to the front line of public concern. Again, squatting results in an effective solution to housing needs while at the same time empowering people through the provision of knowledge, skills and social support to take over an abandoned place.

- Squatters also claim the right to a fair defence and to preserve human rights when facing the threat of eviction: intimacy and privacy, physical integrity, peaceful residence, the right to education of children, the right to be rehoused immediately and to obtain compensation, the right to consultancy and notification in advance, the right to know the future use of the building, the right to the assistance of an attorney of their own choice, the right to know exactly who are the bailiffs involved, and so on (Pisarello, 2003: 68–9). Obviously, these rights are better pursued in civil tribunals, rather than in criminal courts.

As a consequence, criminalisation may be explained as a revanchist and excessive legislation against those who claim these individual and collective rights.

From Eviction Pressure to Resistance Strategies

Because in most of the places that feature in our case studies (such as Madrid and Berlin) squatting is against the law and comes under the legal status of trespassing, at some point most squatters face legal measures by owners. As a consequence, squatters also face the threat of possible eviction and even criminal conviction.

In Madrid and its surroundings, where squatting started in 1977, usually the squatters can stay at least a few weeks or months before an eviction order is issued by the court.

In the long term and as absolute exceptions, only a few squats have survived for several years without eviction, and some remain today (La Casika and the Eskuela Taller, for example), while the occupants have been evicted from several other squats after a few years (like Minuesa, Seco, the Laboratorios and Casablanca). The Squat Ateneo Libertario de Villaverde, occupied in 1980, is the longest existing squat in Madrid, having survived for more than 30 years.

In 1995 the law was modified and squatting became a criminal offence with a higher potential penalty (up to two years of prison and severe fines). However, there have been only a few convictions. Nevertheless in 1996 – in a case not directly linked to the new penal code – the harshest sentence so far was given against two squatters for an incident which took place in 1991, when some people who put up a banner in solidarity with the Minuesa squat were beaten and arrested by the police. Five years later, in a very controversial trial which included outrageously contradictory police testimonies, two people were finally sentenced to between one year (for supposedly attacking a police officer) and two years (for supposedly attacking a police officer and causing bodily harm/assault) in prison (El Acratador, 1996).

Given the pressure of potential eviction, some groups of squatters tried to negotiate alternative solutions with the local authorities, such as the legalisation of the occupied buildings. Although most of the Madrid squatters refused to be involved in negotiations, some took place as early as 1987 (by the Asamblea de Okupas) and again in 1997 (by El Laboratorio I) (Martínez, 2010). Only four squats succeeded in their intention to obtain a legal status and recognition by the state (Seco, Eskarela Karakola, La Prospe and Montamarta). These were very public cases, but there were also a few other squats which signed agreements with private owners away from the eyes of the mass media. The general attitude against negotiations and legalisations changed slightly after the emergence of the M15 movement (in May 2011), but only one squat (Montamarta), among more than 30 new ones, was able to legalise its activities, after a previous eviction and more than a year of negotiations with the city.

In contrast, in Berlin,[1] where squatting began in 1971, negotiations and legalisation have always been accessible options to avoid the pressure of eviction. To a certain extent this is nowadays widely accepted within the movement. More than 200 squats have so far been legalised. A similar situation and overall attitudes occurred in Amsterdam, where squatting dates back to 1965 and several hundred squats have turned their illegal status into a legal one.

In Berlin the regulation of the law was tightened by the conservative CDU-controlled senate in 1981, and now a recently squatted house can be evicted within days without a judicial order under the precondition of the owners' complaint – the so called 'Berliner Linie'. When no claim is presented by the owner in those first days, an eviction order then becomes necessary. This happened in the case of the New Yorck, squatted in 2005 in the Bethanien building complex. The left-wing mayor Ms Reinauer (PDS/Die Linke) tried in the first place to negotiate with the squatters, and decided not to report the case to the police. The squatters refused the conditions of the proposed agreement, as it imposed a short-term contract which would require them to relinquish the building after one year. As a consequence of the failed negotiation, the mayor herself eventually decided to proceed with the eviction. However, the police had to reject the mayor's order, as the judicial order was still missing. The court took years before deciding on eviction, and in the meantime a campaign for a referendum against the planned privatisation of the larger site of Bethanien (of which New Yorck was only a part) got under way. The following year Mayor Reinauer lost the elections and the new elected Green mayor started a round table discussion for a new negotiation process which eventually led to the legalisation of the squat (amantine, 2011).

Squatting itself, when classified as trespassing, is rarely punished heavily. The cases are either dealt with by imposing small fines or dismissed. However during the 1980/81 wave of protests the West Berlin Senate and the prosecutors used several different laws (covering the use of violence, promoting violence, resisting arrest, inciting a riot and so on), including the anti-terrorist law no. 129 (on forming a criminal organisation) to punish and crack down on the squatting movement. From 12 December 1980 to 20 October 1982, 7,809 preliminary proceedings were carried out, and there were 1,409 arrests, 172 arrest warrants, investigations according to law no. 129, and 93 prison sentences (of which 18 were to be served without possibility of release on licence) (amantine, 2012: 62).

Living under the common threat of a possible eviction led to different strategies to avoid eviction and to secure the occupied space. While in Berlin, when squatters are not evicted within the first days, judicial orders provide a fixed date for the eviction and therefore better conditions for the squatters to organise and mobilise against the eviction, in Madrid during the last decade the judges have often not communicated when the eviction is going to take place, making it much more difficult to prepare a resistance strategy. The squatters' difficulties in keeping up morale and maintaining the presence of a certain amount of people when the possibility of imminent eviction extends for weeks or even months can easily lead to exhaustion and a decline in numbers. In 2009, as an exception, the judge issued a fixed date (22 January 2009), to evict the social centre Patio Maravillas. Squatters could then easily mobilise through different media and 200 people managed to stop the eviction plan. On the other hand, one year later, in January 2010, the squatters were caught by surprise by a subsequent eviction order and were not able to resist the eviction.

In Berlin the case of the evicted house Liebigstraße 14 in February 2011 – actually a legalised house project and former squat whose inhabitants were evicted after 20 years – shows the advantage for squatters of a fixed date. For weeks the inhabitants concentrated their media campaign on a broad mobilisation of people on that specific day. The residents themselves built barricades inside the building which lasted for several hours before the police managed to enter. Their supporters used the advantage of a fixed eviction day to focus media coverage on their powerful resistance, including two demonstrations with thousands of people.

In all cases the squatters have used lawyers and legal means to protect their space and to prevent the upcoming eviction. The use of legal defence has in many cases prolonged existing occupations. In the case of the occupied Minuesa in 1988, in Madrid, countersuits and appeals used by the squatters extended the eviction for almost a year and a half after a court had ruled in January 1993 that the building had to be cleared. The squatters of Casablanca even won the legal case against the property owners. This victory gave them two and a half years (from April 2010 to

September 2012) of relatively safe use of the building, but the squatters were suddenly evicted after both pressure from the police and a new judicial sentence. In some cases in Berlin (Liebigstraße 14, Brunnenstraße 183) it took several years and many court decisions before the police could actually implement the final act of eviction.

While legal defence is widely used, the approach to mainstream media differs from city to city. Many squatters in Madrid refuse to cooperate with any of media, except their own autonomous media (independent online media, pirate radios, magazines, leaflets and so on), seeing them as forces that only defend the interests of the capitalist state. After the M15 movement of 2011, more squatted social centres allowed interviews by professional journalists, and in these cases, sometimes the squatters demanded the right to review and amend the article before it was released (this occurs in the EKO, for example). Some squats, like the Patio Maravillas during its first occupation (2007–10), were very accessible to media journalists and received generally favourable coverage. In contrast, in Berlin squatters who might share a similar critical view on the mass media do not hesitate to talk to journalists, to give interviews and to organise press conferences.

In Berlin at the beginning of the 1980s many squatters were working at the same time as editorial journalists of the alternative newspaper *Tageszeitung* (or *Taz* in brief) (founded in 1978) which is now very much affiliated to the Green Party. The Köpi squat, known for its radical verbal statements (a 'Defend Köpi' poster, for example displays a person with a slingshot ready for a militant struggle) did not have a problem in 2007, when their legal situation became unclear, in talking to journalists from *Der Spiegel*, the most famous German weekly news magazine and one of Europe's largest publications of its kind, with a weekly circulation of more than 1 million. *Der Spiegel*, ruled by social democratic principles, has been proven in many other cases to hold a very hostile attitude towards squatters, anarchists or autonomous people, portraying them as criminals and violent.

The decision to collaborate with the Berlin press, except for the right-wing and gutter press, is rather taken from case to case, differs from house to house and also depends on the specific journalist and the conditions the squatters can achieve in the individual situation to use the press for their means. A more pragmatic approach has been established and developed over the years, benefiting as well from a broad spectrum of left and left-liberal newspapers which tend to be politically more open-minded, while in Madrid any collaboration with the mainstream press is mostly rejected because of political analysis and people's experience of longstanding anti-squatting coverage.

The squatters have also developed many different kinds of resistance strategy besides the use of their own independent media (and the eventual collaborations with the mainstream media). To create attention, form solidarity and gain support within society, the squatting movement or individual squats organise demonstrations, happenings, occupations, direct action (including property damage), write flyers, produce their own booklets, and intensify contacts with neighbours and the local community. The type of action, as well as the numbers of people participating, depends very much on the creativity, diversity, variety and finally numbers and strength of the movement.

Between 15,000 and 30,000 people could be mobilised for single demonstrations at the peak of the squatting movement in Berlin in the 1980s and 1990s. One estimate was that more than 41,000 people attended demonstrations called by squatters, autonomists and anarchists in Madrid between 1985 and 2002 (Adell, 2004: 102). One of the most well-attended events was the protest against the eviction of La Guindalera on 15 March 1997, which gathered around 4,000 demonstrators. Thousands more activists and sympathisers who participated in the squats (there were more than 150 squatted social centres in Madrid and the adjacent municipalities between 1977 and 2012) should be added to those numbers. In its heyday, the compactness and multiplicity of weekly or even daily actions and occupations, combined with high levels of militancy, created not only a wide visibility for the movements' demands but also a climate of power, political strength and pressure which could increase political damage to the state and reduce the threat of eviction itself.

In Berlin in June 1981, a march was organised to the wealthy district of Grunewald, West Berlin, where many speculators, politicians and private house owners live. Eight thousand people attended the demonstration, which caused only a little damage (23 smashed windows), but an intense and furious media debate raged afterwards. The demonstrators were compared with the SA Brownshirts from the fascist era in the mainstream press, and the *Bild* newspaper associated them with terror, but in an article published in the left alternative newspaper *Taz* under the significant title 'Throwing stones is necessary', one of the demonstrators was given space to justify the incidents. He explained the interrelation between capitalism, people without homes, and the resulting public outcry which caused some stones to be thrown (amantine, 2011).

In Madrid, while in 1985 the squatters of Amparo 83 took advantage of a demonstration against NATO and collected 5,000 signatures in support of their house, in 1987 supporters of another squat, Argumosa, chose to use more radical means and to throw eggs at the mayor of Madrid, Juan

Barranco (El Acratador, 1996). Occasionally there were also riots and arrests in the demonstrations called by the Madrid squatters, but police brutality was used primarily on the days of eviction (Wilhelmi, 2002).

Besides general mobilisations during the peak times of the movement, many resistance campaigns relate to a single squat and are accompanied by a range of diverse activities. For example, in the case of the aforementioned Liebigstraße 14 in Berlin, nearly everything was tried including round table discussions with politicians. In Madrid, the Laboratorio 3 in 2003 and more recently La Osera, in 2011–12, proved to be very active in launching their own public campaigns against the evictions, although it was perhaps the Seco campaign, aiming to get a legal relocation, that was the most intense and successful.

Among other strategies, the reoccupation of a recently evicted squat or the immediate occupation of another house the same day or within the next few days is a very effective, successful and possible strategy to overcome the loss of a house. In Madrid the slogan *un desalojo, otra okupacion* (one eviction, another occupation) has proved occasionally a reality. After the eviction of El Patio Maravillas from its location at Acuerdo 8, in January 2010, a solidarity demonstration the same evening with 800 people resulted in another occupation of a different building in a nearby street, Pez 21.

Finally some squatters, especially in Berlin, have developed strategies of militant and physical resistance in order to prevent an already scheduled eviction or to retaliate in the aftermath with the intention of forcing the authorities to withdraw from continued evictions. These include the setting up of barricades inside and outside buildings, riots in the streets, confrontations with the police, direct-action attacks on capitalist corporations and state institutions as well as publicly announced threats to cause chaos or a visible amount of material damage to the city. However these strategies were never used alone: they have always been accompanied by a large squatting movement and a variety of other types of resistance.

After the eviction of the youth centre Putte in West Berlin in 1974, the Revolutionary Cells, a militant group that started up in 1973 and was active for more than 20 years, carried out an incendiary attack which destroyed the car of Peter Sötje, the city politician responsible for the eviction and the demolition of the building. In their statement the Revolutionary Cells declared 'For self-organised youth centres, let's accomplish our interests collectively and militantly.' In the 1980/1981 movement, in which within three years more then 224 occupations took place and up to 5,000 people actually lived in squats, militancy grew rapidly and was often part of the process. After riots in December 1980 and harsh repression by the state, some squatters known as Provosorischer Rat announced very openly in a declaration their intention 'to attack the police, the capitalist system, to smash windows, to make it expensive', and concluded that they intended 'to respond to any eviction with 1 million German marks extra damage and to any other conviction of arrested squatters with another 1 million German marks' (Sonnewald and Raabe-Zimmermann, 1983). Several riots, and confrontations during demonstrations and evictions, occurred as the state struck back with arrests and punishment.

The level of conflict was high, and eventually only 105 squats could be saved from eviction and were actually legalised. Ten years later, in November 1990, the 200 squatters of the Mainzerstraße in Berlin and around 1,000 supporters resisted for two days, building barricades, digging deep holes in the streets with earth-moving vehicles, throwing stones and Molotov cocktails, and using slingshots and flare guns against the police before finally being evicted by 3,000 police officers from all over Germany. The police had to utilise water cannons, tanks, heavy tear gas, live ammunition (in at least one reported occasion), helicopters and special combat units, causing injuries and 417 arrests. The 11 squats were lost but the fierce resistance as well as the tremendous critical media coverage, which exposed the first huge operation by the West German police in East Berlin after the unification of the two German states, resulted in two significant outcomes. First, the government (the Senate) of Berlin collapsed after one partner in the ruling coalition, the Green Party, quit the alliance over disagreement with the decision to evict. Second, round tables between squatters, politicians and mediators at the local district level were more easily established, and finally led to the legalisation of most squats (more than 100) in the former East Berlin.

Twenty-one years later, in 2011, during and after the eviction of Liebigstraße 14 several thousands participated in demonstrations which ended in heavy riots, smashed windows of corporate buildings (like that of the telecommunications company O2) and direct action in the streets causing €1 million of property damage. The state also had to pay a high price for that eviction since the additional police costs amounted to another €1 million. The motto of the 1980s – for every eviction, 1 million German marks in property damage – became a reality again in euros (azozomox, 2013).

Sometimes confrontation has a tragic outcome, like the death of Klaus Jürgen Rattey in Berlin on 22 September 1981. He attended a demonstration against eight evicted squats that day, and died after being chased by the police under the tyres of a public service double-decker bus which dragged him several hundred metres before stopping.

In Madrid, the level of the violent conflict was a bit lower, but in the mid-1990s in the context of the evictions of the Minuesa social centres in 1994, David Castilla in 1996 and La Guindalera in 1997, there were riots, barricades and clashes with the police that lasted several hours. There were 117 arrests inside and at least 22 arrests outside the place relating to Minuesa. Regarding La Guindalera, there were 158 arrests. In both cases, there were reports of maltreatment and torture by police (Quieres Callarte, 2008). Fifty people arrested for supposedly taking part in the riots after the eviction of La Guindalera were acquitted seven years later in 2004.

Negotiations and legalisations

Negotiations with the state have never been an easy issue for social movements, especially for those considered 'radical', like squatters and autonomists. One explanation is that any negotiation process begins with an implicit or explicit recognition of the state as a valid and legitimate political actor, and requires the squatters also to display some legitimacy. Even if squatters differ from each other – not only across cities, but within cities – most of them pursue to some degree the aim of subverting mainstream societal values and structures. Are negotiations with the state and the legalisations of squats thus simply some of the squatters' weapons of resistance when facing the law? How contradictory might that interaction be, given the state's role in the preservation of the status quo and in the repression of squatters? The coherence of the squatters' discourses and practices is thus challenged, and not surprisingly, many controversies and splits may occur within the movement after any negotiation with the authorities.

For several decades, in Madrid a large section of the squatters perceived occasional negotiations as a betrayal, as if they were selling out the movement, which would then be assimilated and incorporated into the state institutional machinery. Even so, the initiatives to negotiate and obtain a legal status for some squats gained the support of many social and political organisations, mostly from outside the squatters' movement. Some squats did not take an explicit position regarding that issue, and among those who overtly opposed legalisation, some just decided to respect different opinions. Hence the legalisation processes in Madrid did not create a deep split inside the movement, although it increased already existing divisions. The previous diversity of squatters was the result of their diverging attitudes regarding mass media, political parties and their neighbours.

In Spain and in Germany, the authorities have no initial willingness to negotiate with squatters or to legalise their situation. Instead, state authorities try first to evict squats, punish squatters and eliminate their social influence as soon as possible. A negotiation process, then, entails a provisional state recognition of squatters as legitimate political actors, in spite of their ideological anti-state and anti-capitalist principles.

On the other side, if squatters wish to enter, force or accept a negotiation, they must empower themselves. In Madrid, the primary way to achieve squatters' self-empowerment was through the creation of a network of close allies and the mobilisation of various sources of support: mass media, political parties and different moderate social organisations. In Berlin the process of empowerment followed a different path. In the early 1980s, the number of squats grew considerably until it became a serious problem for the state. Evictions became frequent but the squatters' resistance increased as well. Thus, the costs and damages after the evictions kept on growing. As a consequence, the state authorities preferred the legalisation of some of the squats, but never all of them, as the most convenient policy in order to stop the growing resistance (including, as mentioned in the previous section, diverse tactics and methods ranging from mass civil disobedience to riots, property damage and heavy clashes with the police) resulting from the evictions.

Some squats were initially not reluctant to negotiate, but after the beginning of the criminalisation of squatters in December 1980, the vast majority of the squats, including those represented by the Squats Council of Berlin, changed their mind and stated that negotiations would only take place if all the imprisoned squatters considered as 'political prisoners' were freed. It has to be mentioned that there remained a small number of squats who were not willing to negotiate under any circumstances for exclusively political reasons. At the time, the legalisation offers made by the state, which were never addressed to all squats, had created an intense debate inside the movement, which resulted in a split into several factions. Finally, while some squats signed contracts with the authorities, the rest were quickly evicted. After 1984, squatting became an almost impossible practice and it was immediately aborted by the police whenever it occurred.

Six years later, the fall of the Berlin Wall in 1989 created an ideal opportunity for a new wave of squatting in East Berlin, where over a hundred buildings were squatted. This time squatters took the initiative to obtain legal contracts to stay, and gathered the support of the majority of squats for their attempts to negotiate. The authorities of the East Berlin administration initially denied those claims. The squatters' resistance to the violent evictions and the Mainzerstraße battle in November 1990 again changed the authorities' approach. These authorities (the local authorities for various districts of Berlin) now realised they were facing a strong and empowered movement, and that the price of the evictions was too expensive in political, social and economic terms. This time most of the squatters held a common position in favour of legalisation, although not all were able to remain in the occupied buildings.

The contrast between the two cities is evident. While in Berlin the empowerment of squatters through a militant (and sometimes violent) resistance to evictions was crucial in order to open the opportunities for negotiations and legalisations, in Madrid the four legalisations of squats only occurred after long-lasting processes of bureaucratic negotiations and with strong support for the squatters' claims from various organisations. Legalisation was more a state-led initiative in Berlin, while in Madrid it stemmed from a small number of squats. Strong self-defensive resistance was not often experienced in Madrid, but most of the squatters rejected any sort of negotiation with the state. Even in the case of the legalised squats in Berlin, a militant resistance was a central resource in the squatters' repertoire of action, but once legalisation became pervasive, this became the preferred option for most of the squatters. A face-to-face confrontation with the police obviously involves a very unbalanced power relationship, so ultimately squatters are usually weakened unless they occasionally shift to alternative forms of political resistance. Even after their legalisation therefore, many of the Berlin squats kept their names as 'squats' or 'after-squats' in order to indicate their origins and purposes of self-managed collective life. In Berlin legalised squats even preserve a stronger squatter identity in the decoration of their buildings and symbols than that observed in some squats in Madrid.

Apart from the explanatory context already described, in what ways may legalisation help squatters in their anti-capitalist struggles? The first benefit for squatters is to provide them with a stable environment. When their occupation is legalised, squatters are not obliged to move so frequently. They can remain for a long time in the buildings where they live and meet, and these are buildings they fought for as a symbol against the capitalist dynamic. In spite of their temporary status (normally squatters obtained a fixed-term contract of tenancy, and not full ownership), legalised squats may be presented as successful expropriations. When a squat is evicted it is not the loss of the building that is at stake, but the cohesion of the militant group itself. Groups who made use of the building tend to become dispersed and isolated after every move: in other words, a process of political decomposition takes place. Therefore, legalisation provides a favourable background for group cohesion in the long run. Future plans may also be made without the constant threat of an eviction. Activists can also devote more resources (time, money and labour, primarily) as investments in the development of both their political projects and the maintenance of the building, although some need to do more paid work than they did previously in order to pay the rent and the bills.

Legalised squats in Madrid and Berlin have served over the years as places for fundraising and the organisation of different kinds of events and campaigns, accessible to most of the initiatives and groups belonging to the autonomist scene. These spaces became as useful for radical activism as illegal ones, although the latter are more precarious spaces. Despite occasionally receiving state subsidies, squats and after-squats promote and help independent groups, away from commercial interests and from the control of political parties and state institutions. A strong and horizontal self-management mode of organisation seems not to be destroyed by legalisation. Furthermore, legalised squats can remain as hot spots in the struggles against the processes of urban gentrification and privatisation.

While in Madrid the legalised squats function exclusively as social centres, in Berlin most of them are just used for housing purposes. After-squats or 'house projects' in Berlin may also preserve a venue for public events, very well separated from the housing spaces. Residents pay affordable rents for their individual rooms and collective supplies, but the most salient aspect of this way of living is that it enables large communities of people to share kitchens, communal spaces, food, emotions, conflicts and political engagements and aspirations. These are the kind of benefits that an apartment in the private market or the social housing stock cannot provide. To raise children in such an environment and to socialise with peers should be pointed out as two added positive values of legalised squats, in particular for younger activists, compared with the stressful vicissitudes to which illegal occupants are subjected.

Two of the projects that obtained a legal building in Madrid (Seco and Karakola) came from ruined buildings. The renovation of the squatted building was impossible so the legalisation process meant the abandonment of the building and the relocation of the project into a city-owned space. The third successful case (Prospe) was also obliged to move to a state-owned property, and only Montamarta was able to remain in the same building the group had squatted initially, which was also a city-owned one from which the members had been evicted a year before the legalisation.

Some cases of partial legalisation of squatted social centres and houses which were not publicly claimed consisted in informal agreements with private owners, but the permanence of the occupations was never sufficiently defined. These spaces served as infrastructures for the autonomist and anarchist movement, but the range of groups who made use of their premises was not at all restricted to radical activists. In this way legalised squats in Madrid may be considered as having a greater degree of openness to many other social initiatives than the legal squats of Berlin and Amsterdam. Given the limited availability of legal spaces, most of the Madrid autonomist and anarchist activists tended to launch their activities in the illegal squats. Finally, we found out that the particular strengths of the projects that provided legitimation to the groups who gained the legalisation of their squats (such as feminism, education and neighbourhood participation) prevented many other groups which could not gain such legitimacy, as well as less specific activists, from being involved there.

Legalisation may also involve other unintended consequences. First of all, negotiation processes are long and hard. Squatters have to deal with bureaucratic structures to which they are not accustomed and which they also dislike. The more they need to learn about them, the more they have to drop their current political activities. Some squatters tend to develop skills of negotiation with policy makers and managers, which increases their social capital compared with the squatters who are not involved in the negotiations (and not all can be, because the elites prefer to deal with known faces throughout the process). The negotiators also tend to be activists with a high-class educational and social background.

Legalisation also entails a certain loss of autonomy. Post-squatters are obliged to carry out changes to the building and its usage in order to adjust it to the administrative security norms: fire exits, maximum capacity of people allowed in the building, insurance payments and so on. Water and electricity supplies are also required to be completely legal, and the bills may be very expensive in comparison with the squatters' income. Although in Madrid these expenses were hardly a problem (except for Seco), some legalised squats in Berlin had to set aside a lot of money and time for those purposes. Legalisation also meant that the projects and collectives had to acquire an official status, turning themselves into legal associations. This formal obligation involves new responsibilities and hierarchical structures, although this is sometimes easily avoided in practice. Notwithstanding this, the association is in charge of the activities that subsequently take place in the building according to the terms of the contract. Any major problem could result in court cases and possible demands for eviction (this was the case, for example, of Liebigstraße 14 in Berlin). Because of their past political experience, their example of self-managed organisation and the broad social support that they still enjoy, legalised squats can retain high degrees of autonomy and prevent state interference.

Regarding the rent that former squatters pay, it is generally below the market price. This represents a solid barrier against the expansion of gentrification in the areas where the legal squats are located, but not necessarily a sufficient one. In some neighbourhoods of Berlin, squats also became symbols and active sources of resistance against undesirable urban and social changes. However, sometimes the rent is still too high for the poorest and most precarious squatters, in particular those coming from poorer countries and the working classes. In these cases, state subsidies and formal jobs are the usual means with which to pay the rent and bills of individuals. When living in a 'house project' is not affordable at all, there is still the option of occupying a *Wagenplatz*. These are mobile houses located on vacant pieces of land.

The collective expenses may also create pressure to ask any group or organisation that wants to use the space for an economic contribution. This happens even in the case of political groups and events. Thus almost no parties and concerts, for example, are completely free. Money moves up the scale of activists' priorities and leads to divisions among their social relationships. Without reaching the exclusion that commercial culture provokes, the prices for dwelling at legal squats, for accessing some events and for consuming beverages can be beyond the reach of the most deprived individuals and groups.

Finally, in many cases in Berlin, legalisation also implied that the squatters were all but forced to renovate the building under an agreement that provided for state funding as well as squatters' unpaid work. The subsidies provided depended upon this labour contribution, which was officially supervised every week until the renovations ended. This resulted in another loss of the squatters' autonomy to decide on their rhythms, processes and modes of working. In the process, the contract regulations which eased the legalisation of squats became efficient ways to try to discipline the rebellious behaviours of radical activists. In some cases this might have a significant impact, although in others it definitely did not.

Conclusions

As a conclusion we can state that any successful and effective strategy to prevent an eviction depends on many different factors, such as the strength, number and organisational level of individual squats and the movement in general, as well on the political, judicial and historical situation and circumstances of the place. According to our examinations, a crucial factor is the amount and extent of support and solidarity that the squatters can gain in their local neighbourhoods, the society at large, and (as a way to spread information about the squatters' rights) the mass and independent media. There is no such a thing as one single strategy. A combination of several strategies and tactics combined with doses of creativity and improvisation according to changing contexts seems to be an important precondition to avoid eviction. This also applies to the diverse militant strategies, since unless they are linked to other strategies, the groups that employ them remain isolated and weak.

Negotiations with state authorities and the legalisation of squats are just some of the tools that squatters can use in order to continue their political struggles and alternative ways of living. The force of previous confrontations, as we have seen in Berlin, may be used as leverage in the processes of legalisation, but some activists may be left out, and there are also side-effects such as financial dependency and legal constraints which cannot easily be removed. However, squatters can also take the initiative, as was the case in Madrid, and take advantage of different sources of social support in order to turn their squats into legal and affordable occupations.

In general, the criminalisation of squatting is a serious threat to very basic housing and political rights. Usually, the tolerance or the legalisation of squats has proven to respond better to the urban conflict about housing needs and urban speculation which is explicitly uncovered by squatters, although the criminalisation of the remaining (nonlegal) squatters may also be more intense after most of the squats are legalised, as the Berlin case shows.

Box 8.1 *The Interaction Between Spheres of Morality and of Legality*

Claudio Cattaneo

Squatted places exist because of an illegal conduct against public order. The elites find this deplorable and will never legitimise squatting. But squatters perceive the tension between the legality imposed by the state and their own morality, and evaluate the costs and benefits of breaking the law. There are two orders of costs: that of breaking the law in itself, and that of being prosecuted. The first is not a cost for squatters, but only for those people who always live obeying the law: for them, illegal behaviour is always immoral behaviour and breaking the law breaks their own moral code. If the law changes, their personal morality adapts as a consequence.

The other cost, of being punished or prosecuted by the state, bears more evident consequences: although many people condemn real estate speculation and share squatters' ideals, they would never squat for fear of the state. This is a case – probably common to most people and more likely in southern European countries – where an individual's set of moral values does not entirely coincide with the legal set imposed by the state. Reforms in legal codes or shifts in jurisprudence can lead to societal changes in moral values with respect to laws. Pressure to change the law can occur within the limits of the law, such as lobby campaigns and civil society pressure, and also in the form of civil disobedience and of other actions that might be done breaking the law. For instance the criminalisation of squatting in England and Wales was attempted at least twice unsuccessfully before its partial implementation in 2012. Katyal and Penalver (2010) show that illegal actions contribute, with their dynamism, to improving the quality of an inherently static legal system which could fall out of step with society's needs, and that therefore property outlaws are desirable.

Squatters consider the fear of the state less important than the benefits of not paying rent and of fighting against immoral laws. This occurs thanks to the internal organisation of the movement, which provides legal and social support; the prosecution costs would be higher if an individual had to bear them alone.

If both the prosecution cost and the costs of breaking the law could be reduced, different behaviour would occur. From the squatters' movements' experiences we learn that a shift of the collective imaginary with respect to the source of authority would lead to the possibility of breaking the law with less hesitation. Then, a social organisation supporting the consequences of legal prosecution could invite more people to action. This is what occurs in Spain, where people unable to pay their rents or mortgages are mutually supportive in civil disobedience against evictions, a phenomenon which is increasingly common after the institution of a platform of people affected by mortgages (PAH). In this way a defence from rampant capitalism is successfully established.

Box 8.2 *'Your Laws Are Not Ours': Squatting in Amsterdam*

Deanna Dadusc

The Netherlands has often been considered to be a safe haven for squatters. Squatting in the Netherlands has been legal and regulated since 1914, a period in which the right to housing has been considered superior to the right to property, thereby allowing the occupation of unused spaces for satisfying housing needs. In 2010 however a new law turned the occupation of empty properties into a criminal offence.

The history of squatting in the Netherlands is a history of conflicts and struggle between the squatters' movement, the police, property owners and urban authorities; in parallel with this has been a history of negotiations, formal contracts and informal agreements. These histories did not collide, rather they have mutually supported each other, and often one has been the direct outcome of the other. For many decades there has been an equilibrium between squatters and other actors, whose boundaries were constantly renegotiated, but seldom transgressed by those involved.

Changes in urban politics always led to different power balances between squatters and authorities, but squatters, in alliance with residents' organisations, also had a strong impact in influencing the directions and priorities of these agendas. In other words there has been a mutual, although conflictual, relation between squatters and authorities, where squatters were considered (and sometimes feared) as valuable political actors.

The Dutch way of regulating squatting entailed that anarchist groups often found themselves using 'the law' as a practical tool to keep a space. This, however, did not mean abandoning anarchist politics, but tactically playing with some laws in order to achieve specific goals. Urban battles, both on the street and in the courtroom, were often won by the squatters themselves, and led to important achievements in terms of squatters' power and rights.

This has not to be seen as a 'lost heaven', as the situation was strategically used by all the different parties, which, in one way or another, managed to achieve a balance that could fulfil both economic and political interests. Thus, 'tolerating' squatting often had the effect of turning a mode of resistance into a useful practice from the perspective of local governments. Starting from the Second World War, up to the 1990s, Dutch cities presented an abundance of abandoned properties and the government did not have the resources to put them into use. As a consequence it was politically and economically advantageous to have people taking care for their own needs and maximising the use of unused spaces.

Wet Kraken en Leegstand: *The Law on Squatting and Vacancy*

Around 2000, the tolerant Dutch model began to decline and the influence of right-wing politicians in both local and national politics began to grow. While in the 1980 and 1990s squatting was considered an important part of the urban landscape by the authorities, from the beginning of the new millennium squatters became an easy target for right-wing politicians who placed the 'law and order' flag at the core of their political manifesto. In October 2010, after years of proposals, discussions and resistances, squatting was turned into a criminal offence. The new legislation, named *Wet Kraken en Leegstand*, addresses both squatting and vacancy, and it employs the very term that the movement adopted from the street language: *kraken*. In this way *kraken*, an explicit political action, was turned into a crime. Under the new legal framework trespassing and squatting are punishable with a minimum of one and two years in prison respectively.

This law marks an important shift, which prioritises both the right to property and 'public order' above the right to housing. It is a law that also puts a priority on the market value of houses, rather than their use value. This has happened during a time of crisis, where in conjunction with the precarisation of labour and high unemployment rates, rental prices are getting higher, the availability of social housing is diminishing, and the amount of buildings that are left in disuse is increasing.

The new law is seldom used to convict squatters, yet it has important repercussions on the relations of power between squatters and other parties, since it aims at excluding squatters from the field of politics, and has an impact in terms of squatters' rights, owners' rights, police power and eviction procedures. As well as the law and to the discourses which promoted it, other factors have affected the possibility to squat, in particular the use of so called anti-squatting practices by property owners. Anti-squatting, also known as 'property guardianship', means filling vacant properties with temporary users who play the role of security guards, thus preventing squatters from moving in. Anti-squatting is the ultimate form of precarisation of housing: the anti-squatters have no tenants' rights, as they are legally temporary users rather than tenants, can be removed from the property with a minimum notice, and do not have rights to privacy. They do however pay an amount that is often equal to the market rent.

'Wat Mag Niet Kan Nog Steeds': *What Is Not Allowed Is Still Possible*

Today, two years after the criminalisation of squatting, the slogan and the banners have changed. Instead of looking back at what has been granted, permitted and accepted, the focus has shifted to 'What can we do?' How can new practices be invented and new possibilities opened? A new balance is still being negotiated, and after months of silence, groups of activists have started squatting again on a weekly basis. Despite the attempt to tear down their resistance, the movement is showing that squatters have not only the possibility, but also the power, to break open and resignify the discourses and practices which are criminalising their resistance.

Note and acknowledgement

1   References to West Berlin and East Berlin apply to the period before 3 October 1990; Berlin is used generally up to the present.

This chapter was edited by Lucrezia Lennert.

References

Adell, R., (2004) 'Mani-Fiesta-Acción: la contestación okupa en la calle (Madrid, 1985-2002)', in R. Adell and M. A. Martínez, (eds) ¿Dónde están las llaves? El movimiento okupa: prácticas y contextos sociales [*Where Are the Keys? The Squatter Movement: Practical Issues and Social Context*]. Madrid: Catarata.
El Acratador (1996) 'Boletin Informativo 52 Abril–Mayo 1996' ['Info-note 52, April–May 1996']. Zaragoza, Spain: Ateneo Libertario
amantine (2011) Gender und Häuser-kampf [*Gender and Urban Warfare*]. Münster, Germany: Unrast.
–– (2012) Die Häuser denen, die drin wohnen. Kleine Geschichte der Häuserkämpfe

in Deutschland [Homes are of Those who Dwell in Them: A Brief History of Urban Warfare in Germany]. Münster, Germany: Unrast.

Attoh, K. A. (2011) 'What kind of right is the right to the city?' Progress in Human Geography 35(5), 669–85.

Azozomox (2013) 'Besetzen im 21.Jahrhundert' ['Squatting in the 21st century'], in A. Holm (ed.), Reclaim Berlin. Berlin: Assoziation A.

Dee, E. T. C. (2013) 'Moving towards criminalisation and then what? Examining dominant discourses on squatting in England', in SqEK (eds), Squatting in Europe: Radical Spaces, Urban Struggles. Wivenhoe: Minor Compositions.

Katyal, S. and Penalver, E. M. (2010) Property Outlaws: How Squatters, Pirates, and Protesters Improve the Law of Ownership New Haven, Conn.: Yale University Press.

Lefebvre, H. (1968) El derecho a la ciudad/ Le droit à la ville [The Right to the City]. Barcelona, Spain: Edicions 62/Paris: Anthropos.

Lopes de Souza, M. (2010) 'Which right to which city? In defence of political-strategic clarity', Interface 2(1), 315–33. http://interfacejournal.nuim.ie/2010/11/interface-issue-2-volume-1-crises-social-movements-and-revolutionary-transformations/ (accessed 29 January 2014).

Lucha Autonoma (1996) Reflexiones sobre los Centros Sociales desde una práctica autónoma [Reflections on Social Centres from an autonomous practice]. www.sindominio.net/laboratorio/documentos/varios/debate1.htm (accessed 29 January 2014).

Marcuse, P. (2009) 'From critical urban theory to the right to the city', City 13(2–3), 185–97.

Martínez, M. A. (2010) 'Los procesos de institucionalizacion en el movimiento de okupaciones: estrategias, discursos y experiencias' ['Processes of institutionalization in the squatters' movement: strategies, discourses and experiences'], in M. Dominguez, M. A. Martínez and E. Lorenzi, (eds), Okupaciones en Movimiento: Derivas, estrategias y prácticas [Squatting on the Move: Drifts, Strategies and Practices]. Madrid: Tierradenadie.

–– (2012) 'The squatters' movement in Europe: a durable struggle for social autonomy in urban politics', Antipode 45(4), 866–87.

Owens, L. (2009) Cracking under Pressure. Narrating the Decline of the Amsterdam Squatters' movement. Amsterdam: Amsterdam University Press.

Pisarello, G. (2003) Vivienda para todos: un derecho en (de)construcción. El derecho a una vivienda digna y adecuada como derecho exigible [Housing for All: A Right in (De)construction. The Right to Decent and Adequate Housing as a Right to Claim]. Barcelona, Spain: Icaria.

–– (2011) 'Del derecho a la vivienda al derecho a la ciudad: avatares de una historia' ['From the housing right to the right to the city: avatars of a history'], in various authors, El derecho a la ciudad [The Right to the City]. Barcelona, Spain: Instituto de Drets Humans de Catalunya.

Purcell, M. (2002) 'Excavating Lefebvre: the right to the city and its urban politics of the inhabitant', GeoJournal 58, 99–108.

Pruijt, H. (2012a) 'The logic of urban squatting', International Journal of Urban and Regional Research, doi: 10.1111/j.1468-2427.2012.01116.x

–– (2012b) 'Culture wars, revanchism, moral panics and the creative city. A reconstruction of a decline of tolerant public policy: the case of Dutch anti-squatting legislation', *Urban Studies* 50(6), 1114–29.

Quieres Callarte (2008) 'Informe de la Associacion contra la Tortura' ['Report of the Associacion against Torture']. http://quierescallarte.ourproject.org/article. php3?id_article=206&id_document=3540 (accessed 29-1-2014).

Sonnewald, Z. and Raabe-Zimmermann, J (1983) *Die Berliner Linie und die Hausbesetzer-Szene* [*The Berlin Line and the Squatters' Scene*]. Berlin: Berlin-Verlag.

UNESCO and UN-HABITAT (2009) *Urban Policies and the Right to the City: Rights, Responsibilities and Citizenship*. Paris: Most2.

Wilhelmi, G. (2002) *Armarse sobre las ruinas: Historia del movimiento autónomo en Madrid (1985–1999)* [*Loving in the Ruins: History of the Autonomous Movement in Madrid, 1985–1999*]. Madrid: Potencial Hardcore.

Conclusions

Miguel A. Martínez and Claudio Cattaneo

For the social and environmental sustainability of our planet, capitalism is a serious menace. The exploitation of labour and the exploitation of nature have limits which blind capitalists simply dismiss. Continuous economic growth affects the carrying capacity of societies and ecosystems. Unsurprisingly, once the boundary limits are reached, there are reactions, crises and reverse effects for all those engaged in the growth machine, although those at the bottom of the social hierarchies experience the worst consequences.

One of the numerous initiatives of resistance against capitalism is political squatting. In this book, we have focused in particular on the squatters' movements in Europe and North America. Our perspective consists of a combination of activist knowledge and social science research. We encouraged different theoretical interpretations and their grounding in specific cities and countries, which are compared whenever possible. We believe this is a fruitful way to provide arguments that sustain squatting as an alternative practice to capitalism. The evidence collected in the previous chapters indicates that squatters also face internal contradictions and difficult obstacles in order to overcome powerful capitalist forces. Political squatting is rooted in a history several decades long, and although geographically it is spread across continents, it is still a marginal activity compared with the size of global capitalist flows and commands. Our argument, then, must be clearly contextualised: to what extent is squatting an alternative to the hegemony of capitalism?

First of all, political squatting refers to both the *illegal occupation of property* without permission and the diverse *types of activities performed* by activists and participants within squats and even closely in relation to them. Squatters oppose capitalism when they refuse the rule of private property and reject paying rent for the satisfaction of a fundamental human right such as housing. But squatters' alternatives to capitalism also include all the activities that are performed typically, although not exclusively, in and around the squatted house projects, communes and social centres.

Means and Ends

Both the practice of trespassing itself and the activities brought about by the squatters give answers to our initial questions. Furthermore, many of the contributors of this book have made visible the multiple motivations behind squatting, although the classic distinction between means and ends remains as an underlying framework. In short, for some squatters illegal occupation is not the main anti-capitalist action, so they just trespass a private property in order to develop a genuine or tentative anti-capitalist project. Squatting, then, is only a means. The end, for them, is to set up a housing project, a commune, a cooperative initiative or a social centre open to arts, politics and socialisation in a milieu of freedom, self-manage-ment and protest. To have an available, cheap or free space is crucial, but it is mostly conceived as a mere resource. Thus, should they later agree to pay rent or attain a legal agreement of tenancy, no contradiction with their other anti-capitalist struggles is observed.

Obviously, for some squatters the occupation itself is sufficiently anti-capitalist, because it challenges the plans and actions of capitalists over the built environment. Squatting, then, is an end itself. It serves for confronting urban speculation and, at least, to make visible how the elites manage vacancy for their profit while both homelessness and precarious access to housing are causing enormous suffering. Every case of squatting is able to display a hidden urban conflict, and this is valuable in itself. Of course, apart from living in a squat, the public activities hosted by the squat should be coherent with the kind of antagonist attitudes that squatting involves. But in the end, the latter are less important than the radical gesture of disobedience against the law of property.

In practice, most squatters combine the claims of both these sides – or they just do not care too much about the distinction. It would very simplistic to classify squats according to these general drivers, but it is evident that this shapes a basic level of legitimacy which obliges squatters to keep a balance between the two conceptions or to be consciously inclined towards one of them. The distinction between means and ends provides, in addition, different emphases on the anti-capitalist dimensions of squatting.

Publicly claimed squatting is an illegal action that implies a clear confrontation with the state, an attack somehow aimed at reverting the established order of a system which is considered undesirable. From the perspective of the dominant ideology it is only an infringement to the civil or the criminal code. However, it holds its own peculiarities. The taking over of abandoned properties is part of a wider struggle against private property – one of the fundamental rights in liberal democracies – its uneven distribution and the resulting social inequalities. However, as it has been argued in previous chapters, squatting goes beyond the privileging of private property before the needs of a whole population. It is also a challenge to urban speculation, to managerial and authoritarian top-down policies on housing provision, to neoliberalism and the financial colonisation of life, to the consumerist way of living, to the individualisation of social problems and, last but not least, the political alienation engendered by representative democracy. Primarily, squatting is a negation of already existing domination. But this negation is a global one, including capitalism and many other forms of domination, although the practices of autonomy and resistance are confined to the specific sites and singular conditions where we live. This idea would match what Holloway argues:

> The core of autonomies is a negation and an alternative doing. The very idea of an autonomous space or moment indicates a rupture with the dominant logic, a break or a reversal in the flow of social determination. 'We shall not accept an alien, external determination of our activity, we shall determine ourselves what we shall do.' We negate, we refuse to accept the alien determination; and we oppose to that externally imposed activity an activity of our own choice, an alternative doing. The activity that we reject is usually seen as being part of a system, part of a more or less coherent pattern of imposed activity, a system of domination. Many, not all, autonomous movements refer to the rejected pattern of activity as capitalism: they see themselves as being anti-capitalist. The distinctive feature of the autonomist approach, however, is that it involves not just hostility to capital in general, but to the specific life activity imposed by capitalism here and now and an attempt to oppose capital by acting in a different way.
>
> (Holloway, 2010: 909)

Occupied spaces in the neoliberal city stand as visible breaches of the capitalist engine. The more squatters embrace squatting as an end, the less there is room for any negotiation or co-optation with the capitalist/neoliberal counterpart. From this point of view, the ultimate goal is to delay the eviction as long as possible. While alive and kicking, every squat remains as a threat to capitalism, although not often a very dangerous one. The main shortcoming of this approach comes out when the occupation is defended from a mere ideological opposition to both capitalism and the state, apart from a concrete criticism to the urban speculation at play and from the specific activities and people who need to use the space.

However, it needs to be acknowledged that the negative approach towards capitalist institutions, even within the most radical squats (those giving priority to squatting as an end) is usually reinforced by keeping the space open for the positive creation of real alternatives to capitalism, although on a similarly small scale. The intensity of such alternatives can be pretty high when it is matched with the strong political ideals of radical squatters such as mutualism, lack of external control, absence of labour specialisation, flexibility, self-responsibility and common sense instead of clearly defined norms, spontaneous voluntarism both in performing tasks and in offering a pay-as-you-can possibility (for example for a concert fee, the price of a drink or a meal). Nevertheless, this general statement varies a lot from city to city and from squat to squat, so again, it just shows an approximation to an underlying pattern.

When squatting is considered as an instrumental tool or just a forced step given the unaffordability of urban space, the political priority resides more in the activities performed than in the anti-capitalist meaning of trespassing itself. The aim is to attack capitalism from the cultural and social side, more than from the economic and legal one. Instead of emphasising the challenge to private property, squatters focus on building up social networks of solidarity, political campaigns of protest, counter-cultural artistic expressions, a democratic social economy. The right to housing for the most needed is often included here, although it tends to be enhanced with the virtues of sharing with others the experience of living rather than just providing an individual or family shelter. Although gaining time and delaying the eviction are also important concerns in these cases, we can presume it is the political project and the activities that it catalyses that are considered, above all, to hold an anti-capitalist capacity. There is a high likelihood, then, that these squatters would easily accept an agreement with the owners in order to get the squat legalised. In the cases of homeless people or while facing the absence of affordable social spaces in the city centre, the legalisation of a previous squatting action tends to be claimed as a political victory in terms of a more just distribution of resources. The aftermath of legalisation entails new battles regarding the challenge to pay rents, bills and taxes, and to conform with other legal regulations, while keeping an eye open to strengthening the alternative project.

Another way of reconceptualising these dilemmas is by distinguishing 'formal' and 'substantive' drivers behind squatting. Formal alternatives to capitalism are valued according to their juridical form. If a law is unjust because of the constraints imposed by capitalism, then open disobedience to that specific law is a clear opposition to capitalism, especially if the opposition and living illegally can be sustained for a long time. Substantive alternatives to capitalism are those that emphasise the creation of authentic and powerful ways of living, countercultural activities, cooperative housing and work, horizontal organisation and the like. In this sense, it is the practice and the way things are done that are claimed as an alternative, no matter the legal status that they take. Again, there is blurred space in between the two ideal types, and reality is often placed at that intermediate level. Squatters' discourses and practices regarding these two approaches (either separated or combined) may also differ significantly. Therefore, self-critical analysis about the anti-capitalist value of concrete practices, means and outcomes is always welcome.

Scaling Up the Alternatives to Capitalism?

Although they have been often debated, at one of our last SqEK meetings we asked for new contributions to the following questions: *To what extent does squatting represent an alternative to capitalism? Can it be scaled up from the small-scale phenomenon it is now, and how could it – if possible – overcome capitalism?* Let us summarise here some of the answers we have collected.

Squatting can be seen as a window of opportunities open just after the phase of occupation, as Luca Pattaroni shows in his chapter. The renovating phase of the built environment is done in accordance with the ideals and desires to live in common, with no limitations imposed by regulations or landlords. When people – rather than market enterprises – are free to express their creativity and fantasy, without any commercial interest, then some real alternatives to capitalism can emerge.

There are several issues at play. Squatting in general is a creative reaction against capitalism. As Pierpaolo Mudu synthesises, 'currently squatting represents one of the few (if not the only) forms of partial "social compensation" that has been actuated against the dispossession of entire cities and environments by capitalism'. This is performed without the participation of a third agent, the state, whose role should be the redistribution of society's wealth. On the contrary 'the state is very much involved in the production of squattable empty spaces' because it is responsible for leading urban renewal planning, other planned changes in land use and even the accumulation of abandoned municipal buildings, as Pruijt remarks. Thus, it would be impossible to consider squatting in relation to capitalism but not in relation to state authorities. Modern democratic states play the biggest role in the defence of private property and in the repression of different lifestyles that challenge capitalist dynamics.

Lucrezia Lennert claims that, as long as they exist, squats represent an alternative and a threat to capitalism insomuch as they overcome, in the use of their spaces, the relations of private property and insomuch as they internally create commons as the positive expression of this overcoming, in the form of self-organisation, horizontality, communal sharing and mutual practices:

> Using the term commune can help for critically discerning the extent to which different kinds of squats are radical spaces or not, on the basis of whether or not they are creating commons as the positive expression of this overcoming. The idea of commune may also be useful for discussing squatting in relation to a wider revolutionary anti-capitalist politics.

For her, legalisation is not necessarily a 'successful' result for radical squatters whose goals are to smash the capitalist system. Thus, an argument against the legalisation of squats is that their illegal conditions provoke illegitimacy in the face of the state and capital, but not necessarily in the face of the society. If the squats are co-opted and become legal and legitimate for the elites, they lose their social legitimation as a threatening potential to the existing capitalism. Between the repressive elite and the antagonist squatters is situated the majority of civil society. Therefore, with disregard of the elites' will, the dilemma should be solved according to whether and how the social legitimation of squatting occurs in the eyes of the society at large.

Furthermore, the interpretation of legitimacy or illegitimacy depends on the nature of the 'judge' with the power to spread an interested discourse, be it the owner, the users or the court. As Miguel Martínez, Azozomox and Javier Gil argue in their chapter, squatters gain legitimacy through their practices, their social networks and the particular balance of local power relationships. In a similar line is Frank Morales's argument that connects squatters' breaking of the law with a redefinition of lawfulness:

> the 'breaking of the law' in the process of squatters' delegitimisation of the exclusivity of private property is really the primary sign of the alternative (negating) character of squatting, positing the essential break with capitalist structures while aiming to redefine what is truly lawful.

Hence the perspective changes sharply: it is private property and 'anti-life capitalism' that fall under a judgment of illegitimacy.

We are facing a power struggle with different languages of valuation expressed by different actors, which have a lot to do with legality, legitimacy and morality. For example, social centres are willing to show the provision of public services in order to gain social legitimacy against their supposed illegality and against the moral and economic issues of leaving properties abandoned for speculation, deterioration and destruction. Fighting capitalism is more than an ideological or moral slogan: it is based on the positive character of squatting, namely the activities, social networks and fellow struggles that are created and carried on around a social centre, in addition to the ideals, practices and processes of living in common developed within a commune, a house project or a workers' cooperative. This is how squats gain social legitimacy.

In a game where there is no black or white, but only a series of shades of grey, the extent to which squatting becomes an alternative to capitalism contributes to redefine the balance of power in the struggle. When people who until few years ago were dreaming of becoming private owners now turn into squatters – even though only temporarily, as a step towards the legalisation of their housing situation – we can observe that squatting ends up winning a battle and capitalism partially losing ground.

Three forces are determining the balance of power: squatters – who might be considered as uncivil actors (D'Alisa, Demaria and Cattaneo, 2013) – the civil society and the state/capitalist elites. The capability of squatters to engage with civil society is crucial. For instance in the Spanish case, where cities have experienced a sort of tsunami regarding the recent changes in land use, empty buildings were abundant and squatting has increasingly been recognised as the symbol of radical and pragmatic approaches to counter these processes. In that context, almost no political authorities explored the option of legalising squats, so that most types of squats fell under a broad range of social reactions and movements against an irrational and unsustainable capitalism.

Squatting as a Local Alternative

In Chapter 2 we have seen how home ownership can be a means for social control among other unintended effects. Once you have to pay a mortgage or rent, you cannot exit from capitalist labour markets unless the amount you have to pay is low enough. Carlsson and Manning (2010), for example, suggest a strategic exodus to a Nowtopia, which implies liberation from paid work. Considering that the whole capitalist system is rooted on the exploitation of labour as a commodity, and that the sale of people's time to the market is necessary to earn the money to pay for housing, then time becomes the central *oikonomic* element for understanding how squatting emerges as a local alternative to capitalism. In other words, squats are rich in time when time is preserved from commodification and turns into a creative labour process, without distinction between productive and reproductive work, and while improving the role of the household as a place for the production of use values.

In doing this under the veil of illegality, squatters need to be capable and self-responsible. Do-it-yourself (or do-it-ourselves) practices in self-help housing, and cooperative activities by those without any professional qualification, may cause accidents. But a decentralised self-organisation may also save diverse social and economic costs. Provided that there are plenty of abandoned places to squat, the sufficient condition for self-compliant responsible squatting to scale up is to have capable and skilled persons who undertake the role of doing things safely and without central control.

If this condition is observed, then, as Salvatore Engel-Di Mauro observes, the squatters' movement contributes to the creation of an alternative to the capitalist city which is socially and ecologically sound. This connects basic issues such as shelter, transport and food, although many global problems of capitalism cannot be addressed by localised urban struggles alone. Far from representing only an alternative in terms of housing, he remarks that the functions of squats are much more comprehensive as they 'develop radical forms of autonomy, with self-management in the reproduction of life as the primary exit strategy from the capitalist mode of production'.

If the combination of squatting with an environmentalist approach sets the ground for the emergence of powerful alternatives, the combination of squatting with feminist claims, which Azozomox presents, is one of the most far-reaching alternatives. Contrary to the pretended depoliticisation logic of capitalism, 'the personal is political'. Patriarchal domination and the social exclusion of different gender and sexual identities are intertwined with capitalist domination, and squats where only the latter is rejected tend to fail in providing a safe, inclusive and egalitarian household.

Thomas Aguilera claims that 'the answer of squatting is to demonstrate that people are able to collectively organise spaces and societies in an autonomous, ecological and non-capitalist perspective'. Squatters thus prove that people can manage their own lives without representative politics for decision making. Other 'ordinary citizens' might follow their example and not delegate their sovereignty or fit the pattern of salaried working time in order to pay for housing.

In sum, the major advantages of squatting as a local alternative to capitalism are self-determination and direct action. These constitute a decolonisation from the collective imaginary which gives authority to the state and the market. Autonomy, then, is produced not only by recalling individual freedom and independent communities, but above all through the practical experiences of collective action and decision making apart from the elites' dictates.

The second step which creates the material possibilities for setting up a local alternative to capitalism consists of a drastic reduction of the supply of paid labour, that is to say, the sale of people's life-time to capitalism. Thus, less money is put in circulation because no rent is paid and/or because most squatters typically engage in productive activities that do not account for labour time as a commodity. This is also an additional meaning of autonomy: to get rid of money as well as of the goods, services and informations that are only accessible with money. Squatters try to escape the empire of money by sharing collectively their resources, including the reclaimed urban spaces they live in. There are clear limitations to this since squatting requires, paradoxically, the existence of capitalism and its uneconomic processes for abandoned buildings to be occupied and plenty of waste and raw materials to be scrapped, elaborated and rein-vented. Capitalism produces vacancy, trash and unemployable people, but these aspects are not at the core of the growth machine. Squatters take them in a positive manner in order to put in evidence the irrational and unjust functioning of capitalism. Then, there is no essential dependency of squatters on capitalism, but just squatters' tactics to reverse the capitalist dynamics by reaching for a material autonomy. This is more likely to occur in rurban squats, and even more in rural squats, because of the closeness to nature and to the sources of primary materials, not mediated by capi-talism (Cattaneo, 2008). This is where the local alternative to capitalism reaches its greatest intensity, although it is not much visible or much applicable to society at large.

Squatting as a Global Alternative?

At a first glance, the present time does not look like as a rosy period for squatting: the historical perspective presented in the book shows that the movement has been decreasing in Amsterdam, repressed in Berlin, annihi-lated in Geneva, co-opted in NYC, less visible in Brighton and London, and so on. Although a more promising picture comes from the Mediterranean area (Rome, Madrid, Barcelona, Athens and other cities), recent crimi-nalisation in the Netherlands and England and Wales cut many lines of growing and sustaining squatting where it proved to be very efficient and socially accepted. However, as E. T. C. Dee observes, as long as there are housing needs and empty buildings, squatting will continue to flourish.

As Miguel A. Martínez, Azozomox and Javier Gil claimed in their chapter, squatters may also continue with their radical politics through means other than squatting. The examples they describe in Berlin and Madrid suggest that squatting has a strong influence in anti-capitalist politics and struggles, so that squatting practices can be scaled up to other sectors of society. The moments of severe crisis of capitalism represent the best opportunity to appreciate that influence and the renewed interests in squatting as such.

Because of the limits to the amount of empty space, squatting cannot attack the whole capitalist housing stock. The opportunity to scale up this limitation occurs when people stop paying rents to landlords and mortgages to banks. Then, the dwellers lose their legal titles to reside in their homes, but they still have the chance to keep occupying them, or to reoccupy them should they be evicted. Since 2008, this has happened increasingly, at least in Spain and the United States. More and more people became squatters, even without any previous knowledge of the squatters' movement, even in spite of the stereotypes that the mass media spread about the squatters. This leaves room for scaling up, but it enters the realm of the 'if': if *most* empty spaces were occupied combined with *most* tenants ceasing to pay their rent/mortgage, *then* capitalism would enter a far deeper crisis, and along with it so would the state, which would lack legal control over the activities performed. Surely it can be an alternative, but it is difficult to imagine how robust or sustainable it would be in any given concrete situation.

Another possible option is the creation of an alternative legality or movement institutions in a post-capitalist context. This would imply the legalisation of all squats for housing or social purposes. However, legalisation would not come alone: more citizen control from the bottom should be required to impose limits to any economic speculation, to satisfy human needs apart from the motivation of profit and capital gains, and to regulate the housing market and urban planning according to just, environmental and distributive principles. This horizon would entail a higher stability and applicability to a wider scale compared with the contentious intensity of the waves of illegal occupations. The embryonic stage of such a process is what Pierpaolo Mudu shows in his chapter: the situation for housing occupations in Rome is scaling up, with an increasing number of homeless and home seekers squatting housing and getting politicised. In some cases their housing occupations are beginning to turn into social centres too. The practice of squatting expands beyond the non-capitalist satisfaction of the housing need to cover a wider variety of needs. Moreover, political institutions, although at the margin, are also called to attend their demands and to change their policies of privatisation, and squatters amplify the housing conflict instead of staying isolated in their squats.

A third path is to consider 'entrepreneurial squatting' (Pruijt, 2012) which is generally based on a mix of professional and voluntary work, as it occurs in many autonomous squatted and nonsquatted social centres. In the context of crisis, selling-off and unemployment, this form of squatting and hybrid cooperation might spread, beginning from grassroots projects. The major reference is the transformation of factories which go bankrupt and then keep on working under workers' control and self-management. The same is attempted with some public spaces, vacant lands and former public services. There are issues of financing, economic inequalities and co-optation by the 'city branding' managers, which still deserve more careful attention in these experiments, but many squatting projects already indicate how things can be done.

As Thomas Aguilera observes:

> squatting is experimentation and innovation. These social innovations diffuse and contaminate outside the laboratory of the squatted building, outside the neighbourhood, outside the city. Thus, the relevant question is not any more whether an enlargement process to the large scale is possible, because squatters already show that it is. The question should be how to multiply places of occupation and conflicts where the daily political experiences are sources of alternative creation against capitalism.

Final Remarks

There are many different types of squatting. Their anti-capitalist outcomes depend on the interplay of their discourses and practices, but also on the specific context where they are located. We started this book based on the assumption that all forms of squatting point to some alternatives to capitalism. The thing is that the internal diversity is not always known or accepted. For example, it is usual to attend debates where some squatters accuse others of being reformist, while keeping for themselves the label of true radicals and revolutionaries. The opposite is also frequent: some squatters reject aesthetic radicalism uniquely based on slogans, attitudes, clothes and antagonistic resistance, instead of setting up long-term projects of fighting capitalism and simultaneously building up networks and movements. However, it is not so common to focus on the social class of origin of squatters, their sources of income, their styles of consumption, their real practices and their actual social connections. And more strikingly, sometimes the most time-wasting conflicts are related to the internal division of labour, the reproduction of patriarchy, personal attitudes, how to manage money or the use of drugs.

Hans Pruijt (2003) argues that squatting done by a housing movement differs from the practices of the squatters' movement. While the first conceives squatting as a tactical move and is ready for co-optation, the latter embraces squatting as both a means and a primary goal in itself. As we have argued before, diverse positions may be incorporated into either of these stances. In addition, both types of squatting have a multiplying effect which is positive for attacking different aspects of capitalism.

At the local scale, squatting provides material resources and also a political experience of self-organisation. We have named this contribution material and practical autonomy. At a global scale, squatting may defy capitalism if it is diffused and expanded. Autonomy from capitalism would be obtained through a combination of struggles and an increasing social control over crucial economic sectors such as housing. This can also entail the possibility of new institutions and political regimes where the legalisation of squats is feasible, desirable and useful for clearing the empire of capitalism. As Pattaroni and Breviglieri (2011: 164) remark, 'compromise becomes a political art, both subversive and necessary'. Thus, squats may overcome capitalism if after-squats are really low-cost, affordable and prefigurative of a cooperative way of living. Squats are commons, and not only communes. They become socially legitimate when they are recognised as examples of disobedience to unjust situations, autonomous self-organisation and shared resources for the satisfactions of basic needs.

References

Carlsson, C. and Manning, F. (2010) 'Nowtopia: strategic exodus?' *Antipode 42*, 924–53.

Cattaneo, C. (2008) *The Ecological Economics of Urban Squatters*. PhD thesis, Autonomous University of Barcelona.

D'Alisa, G., Demaria, F. and Cattaneo, C. (2013) 'Civil and uncivil actors for a degrowth society', *Journal of Civil Society 9*(2), 212–24.

Holloway, J. (2010) 'Cracks and the crisis of abstract labour', *Antipode 42*(4), 909–23.

Pattaroni, L. and Breviglieri, M. (2011) 'Conflitti e compromessi: dalla critica militante alle innovazioni istituzionali nella politica edilizia a Ginevra' ['Conflicts and mediations: from militant criticism to institutional innovations in Geneva urban policies'], in N. Podesta and T. Vitale (eds), *Dalla proposta alla protesta, e ritorno. Conflitti locali e innovazione politica* [*From Proposing to Protesting and Back Again: Local Conflicts and Political Innovations*]. Milan, Italy: Bruno Mondadori.

Polanyi, K. (1944). *The Great Transformation: The Political and Social Origins of our Time*. Boston, Mass.: Beacon Press.

Pruijt, H. (2003) 'Is the institutionalization of urban movements inevitable? A comparison of the opportunities for sustained squatting in New York City and Amsterdam', *International Journal of Urban and Regional Research* 27(1), 133–57.

–– (2012) 'The logic of urban squatting', *International Journal of Urban and Regional Research*, doi: 10.1111/j.1468-2427.2012.01116.x

Appendix

The Story of SqEK and the Production Process of This Book

Claudio Cattaneo, Baptiste Colin and Elisabeth Lorenzi

Beginning in Madrid, in January 2009, Miguel A. Martínez invited people he had met during his own research on the squatting movement to discuss the possibility of starting a research group across Europe to shape a new proposal about squatting research in a European context.

Our meeting was held mostly in Traficantes de Sueños, an activist bookstore and flexible workspace, and at Complutense University. Participants were hosted in Centro Social Seco, Patio Maravillas and other activist spaces.

In this meeting attendants presented their own trajectories and their expectations about the group, and brainstormed on how to work together, seeding the future development of a common research project and sharing their concern to remain connected and engaged with the squatting movement. We also visited some social centres, guided by the local squatters. The institutionalisation of squatting projects was our first area of network research.

The second meeting was in Milan in October 2009. Andrea Membretti and Tomasso Vitale from Bicocca University organised it, including some encounters with social centres, mostly Casa Loca, which is run and managed by the students from Bicocca, and provides services for them.

Unfortunately Andrea could not always stay with us so we were left on our own for much of the time. We held our meetings in a university room and proceeded following typical academic dynamics, making our own presentations and debating them. The meeting was not open to the wider public. On our own we visited Cox 18, one of the oldest and most well-known social centres in Milan, with a social movements archive, a bookstore and with an active social agenda. We proposed a public meeting in Leoncavallo, on the institutionalisation of social centres, but the members refused: in fact in Milan there is an old split in the squatters' movement on how to deal with this issue, and the aim of our proposal had probably been misunderstood. Instead they offered an informal meeting during a dinner. Although this was a very enjoyable and inspiring experience, we regret not having managed to organise a public event. This anecdote shows how difficult it can be to access social centres without someone from the inside to act as a point of contact.

The greatest result of this meeting was the production of the SqEK manifesto. It was written in English and translated into Spanish, Italian, French and German (SqEK, 2009 and 2011), which is very useful for formally presenting us, as a research group, in different countries.

Our next meeting was in London, in June 2010. Our hostess organised a venue and advertised the event, but again we were alone in the city. We met in the London Action Resource Centre, an anarchist centre (not squatted, but owned) which we used to sleep, cook and for our meetings and presentations. For the first time in London we were not related to a university venue.

Opening

Although our original idea was to have internal meetings (presenting and debating our work in progress), and one public presentation about squatting in different cities, by mistake the publicity for our programme had not specified this difference. So the meeting was held in a collective space, many non-SqEKers attended it, and it was great! It enriched our work and our method. But with respect to interacting with squats, we were still on our own. We visited the Foundry, whose occupants were evicted a few days later, and other places where we met squatters. However, these visits originated from individual initiatives, in little groups. In London some of us decided to work in three thematic groups, derived from the research agenda defined in our manifesto: 'database of squatting', 'networks' and 'institutionalisation'.

The next meeting was held in Berlin in April 2011. This time our hosts, Baptist Colin and Armin Khun, were with us all the time. Local people and squatters helped him in the organisation and arranged a place for us to sleep, in the Rote Insel house project, while presentations and debates took place in the New Yorck, an ex-squatted social centre in the Kreuzberg district, where we also arranged our lunches.

Since the London experience our dynamics had changed, and our presentation talks and debates were public. We had a public presentation on squatting in different countries in the theatre of the Mehringhof, a project linked to the squatting and alternative movements since the early 1980s, where we were asked for the first time why we were interested as academics in studying the squatting phenomenon, opening a very interesting debate and showing the different points of view among SqEK members.

Some time was dedicated to group working: after intense online collaborations, we could now debate face to face and present our results to the rest, such as a draft chapter on mobility among cities supported by the squatted projects (Owens et al., 2013).

Places and Spaces: Squatting Shapes the Context

Berlin was also an occasion for 'tourism on squats': we visited the Regenbogen Fabrik social centres and had a tour through the neighbourhood around the Bethanien, learning about the role of the squatting movement in shaping public space and neighbourhood identity.

The next meeting took place in Copenhagen in December 2011: coordinated by Tina Steiger, Tina Helen and Ask Katzeff, it was held in the Bolsjefabrike social centre in the Norrebrod neighbourhood, and again was open to the public. In one of the presentations, the contradiction between engaged collaborative work and academic dynamics emerged once again, and a great diversity of positions as well as a shared understanding on the role of SqEK in research were highlighted. Here, the proposal for the production of an academic book with collaborations from different SqEK members entered its final stage (SqEK, 2012) and we started to look for a publisher interested in a creative commons policy. An interesting outcome of this meeting was a tour presenting histories of successes and failures of different social centres around Norrebrod, with histories of squat relocations, evictions, and their consequent urban impact.

For our sixth meeting we crossed the Atlantic and landed in New York. Pierpaolo Mudu and Miguel A. Martínez organised a panel session at the American Association of Geographers 2012 conference, and invited SqEKers to submit papers. Those who attended received some funds to pay for the expensive trip and the conference registration because of their activities in academic institutions. This was also an opportunity for Alan Moore, Frank Morales and other activists to show what is happening in the United States and to contrast it with the European scene.

We had a reception in ABC No Rio, a legalised social centre in the Lower East Side where we also met activists in the Museum of Reclaimed Urban Space (MORUS: www.morusnyc.org), which organises tours through a neighbourhood with a rich history of guerrilla gardening as a way to squat and reclaim space in the city. Members of MORUS also joined the SqEK network. We had a public meeting in the Living Theatre, where the situation of squatting in different countries was presented with a focus on the cultural and political contrast between the European and the American movement.

We met members of the Organizing For Occupation (www.o4onyc.org) collective, which specialises in housing justice and in the occupation of foreclosed buildings for the homeless. Focusing on people's basic needs, it offered a very interesting understanding of what is a social centre in the NYC context, and helped us Europeans to understand the specific and common aspects of squatting in different continents, such as for instance the notion of occupied social centres in Italy and Spain.

Our host at the university, CUNY-GC, Amy Starecheski, offered us a space to discuss methodology with some of its students, and we also gave a public talk. In this contrast new issues emerged which had not been thought of before: the relationship between the individual and the community, what 'community' means, and how squatted places work with that, gentrification and the role of the squatting movement.

This meeting also represented the occasion to discuss face to face the possibility of writing the present book, for which the issue of analysing how the squatters' movement represents an alternative to capitalism was specified.

Our most recent meeting was held in Paris in March 2013. The local group (led by Margot Verdier and Thomas Aguilera) organised an intense programme in many different venues combining internal SqEK meetings, public presentations of our work, and even debates within the Paris squatter movement. On the first day we met in the university faculty of Sciences Po, and over the following days we moved to the LaGare XP, Le Transfo and Shaki Rail social centres, and visited several neighbourhoods, activist collectives and squats all over the city. Interesting novelties were the use of more than one venue –which the participants found useful for grasping a general knowledge of the different realities – and the occasion offered by our conference to develop the debate, internal to the Paris movement, on institutionalisation and legalisation of squats in Paris. The ideological oppositions within the French squatters were discussed a lot during the Paris meeting, especially around the question of the legalisation/ normalisation of squats all over Europe. Beside this interesting question, we as a collective decided to engage in a process of reflection about our involvement in the local squatting scene, with which some of us were already involved.

Knowing the history of SqEK meetings is also useful for understanding how the methodology of this research network is applied, and the process followed for the production of this book is a good example. It is in fact through the physical interactions that occur during our meetings that a better coordination can be achieved than when working through our email list. For instance, although the first call for contributions was sent to the list before the New York meeting, it was only after that meeting that interested authors made their chapter proposals. With the help of the publisher, an initial table of contents was drawn up, in which individual proposals were often merged into one chapter to be co-authored. The result of this invitation for authors to join forces worked very well for some chapters, but failed for some others, resulting in some authors dropping out, an occurrence that shows how our collective method, although pretty successful, has its own limitations and potentialities for further improvement.

The Paris meeting has been another moment for the revival of our process, with other authors joining in, so we included other city case studies in the form of boxes that would fit within the argument of the corresponding draft chapters which, by then, had already been completed. Moreover, during one of the presentations at the meeting we had a discussion central to the argument of this book, namely on how squatting as an alternative to capitalism could or could not be scaled up. This discussion was then be carried on via the email list, and forms part of the Conclusion. Apart from chapter authorship, this book constitutes a collective process insomuch as it has involved peer review, further comments on chapters proof reading and further discussions on the nature and the impact of SqEK, which were prompted after our Paris meeting.

References

Owens, L., Katzeff, A. Lorenzi, E. and Colin, B. (2013) 'At home in the movement. constructing an oppositional identity through activist travel across European squats', in C. Flescher and L. Cox (eds), *Understanding European Movements: New Social Movements, Global Justice Struggles, Anti-Austerity Protest*. London: Routledge.

SqEK (2009) 'The SqEK: Squatting Europe Research Agenda , v. 1.0', *ACME* 9(3), 377–81. www.acme-journal.org/vol9/SQEKeng2010.pdf (accessed March 2014).

–– (2011) 'SQuatting Europe Kollektiv SqEK: Forschungsagenda – 1.0', http://duepublico.uni-duisburg-essen.de/servlets/DerivateServlet/Derivate-26862/11_SQEK.pdf

–– (ed.) (2012) *Squatting in Europe: Radical Spaces, Urban Struggles*. London: Minor Compositions.

Contributors

Thomas Aguilera is a PhD student in political science at the Centre for European Studies of Sciences Po, Paris. He is a lecturer in political science, urban sociology, urban planning and qualitative methods at Sciences Po. He is member-coordinator of the urban research programme 'Cities are back in town'. His work focuses on public policies towards illegality, more precisely illegal housing (squats and slums) in France and Spain.

Azozomox is an activist on the anarchist/autonomous and (ex-)squatting scene, and author of the books *Gender und Häuserkampf* [*translation?*] (2011, Münster: Unrast) and *Die Häuser denen, die drin wohnen. Kleine Geschichte der Häuserkämpfe in Deutschland* [*translation?*] (2012, Münster: Unrast).

Claudio Cattaneo completed his PhD dissertation on the Ecological Economics of Urban Squatters in Barcelona at the Institute of Environmental Science and Technology, Universitat Autónoma de Barcelona, where he is a research associate. He is an active member on Research and Degrowth and is currently involved in the Can Masdeu squat in Barcelona.

Baptiste Colin is a PhD student at the Universities of Paris 7 (France) and Bielefeld (Germany), where he is working on a project entitled 'Squatting: crossed stories of Paris and West Berlin from after Second World War until the end of the 1980s. Aims, perspectives and strategies of a contested housing model.'

Deanna Dadusc is a PhD researcher and activist, living in Amsterdam. Her research interest revolves around the criminalisation of social movements, and the relations of power and resistance entailed in this process. Specifically, she is conducting research in collaboration with the squatters movement in the Netherlands.

E. T. C. Dee lives in Brighton. He makes zines and works academically on media discourses surrounding the criminalisation of squatting and the hidden history of squatting as a social movement.

Salvatore Engel-Di Mauro works, presents and writes on soil degradation and society–environment relations, among other themes such as pedagogy and decolonisation. He teaches geography at SUNY New Paltz (USA) and is finalising a study of urban garden soils in New York State. He edits the journal *Capitalism Nature Socialism*.

Javier Gil is a PhD candidate in political science at UNED (the Spanish Open University). Recently he has published several articles about the M15 movement in Spain, the political impact of social networks and political communication.

Lucrezia Lennert is a PhD researcher living in Berlin. Her research is interested in understanding radical social spaces through Deleuze's conceptual framework. In particular her work considers house projects in Berlin as 'nomadic war machines', and explores how a political philosophy of active nihilism may offer conceptual tools to radical groups and movements for dealing with evictions and other forms of state repression.

Elisabeth Lorenzi is an anthropologist working on a PhD involving the study of urban transformation influenced by social movements. She started by observing the neighbourhood movement in Madrid, and now focuses on two intertwined issues: bike mobility initiatives and the squatters' movement. In this process she considers the city as a place where many global and local processes converge as a result of the behaviour and interaction of their citizens.

Miguel A. Martínez López is a sociologist with a PhD in political science, affiliated to the City University of Hong Kong. He is an activist-researcher who has been involved in the squatters and M15 movements in Madrid. He was one of the promoters of the SqEK (Squatting Europe Kollective) network. His work deals with urban movements, anti-neoliberal struggles, autonomous social movements, citizen participation and urban sociology.

Frank Morales is an Episcopal priest who has been squatting in New York City since the mid-1980s and currently lives in a squat on the Lower East Side. The author of *Police State America* (Arm the Spirit, 2002) and co-founder of Organizing for Occupation (O4O), he has most recently taught at the New School for Social Research on the subject of 'urban homesteading'. Currently, he is writing a memoir entitled *Squatter Priest*.

Pierpaolo Mudu is a geographer who is collaborating with the Urban

Studies and Interdisciplinary Arts & Sciences faculties at the University of Washington Tacoma. He has previously worked in universities in the United Kingdom (Oxford and Reading) and Italy (Rome), and has been a visiting scholar in France (EHESS in Paris and Université de Marseille), in South Korea (Sungshin Women's University in Seoul), and the United States (University of Washington). His interests are mainly in urban and population geography. The main focus of his research is on the development of contemporary Rome as related to social movements and migrations and the transformation of public space. He has written several books and published in several journals including *ACME, Antipode, GeoJournal* and *Urban Geography*.

Needle Collective is a Brighton-based research group working on social movement theory and squatting. Its research interests are squatting, social movements, anarchism, autonomy, radical history and Brighton, with a forthcoming publication on the history of the autonomous and squatting movements in Brighton. needlecollective@riseup.net

Luca Pattaroni, sociologist, is assistant professor at the Laboratory of Urban Sociology (Lasur) in EPFL and research associate at the Institute Marcel Mauss in Paris (GSPM, EHESS). He is also chief editor of *Metropolitics* and co-director of EspacesTemps.net. Confronting political philosophy and empirical sociology, his current work focuses on the institutionalisation of counterculture and, more broadly, the dynamic interrelations between urban order, pluralism and justice. He recently co-authored a book tackling in a socio-architectural perspective the question of urban struggles and the place of difference in the city: *De la différence urbain* [*On Urban Differences*], (Geneva: Metispresse with E. Cogato Lanza, M. Piraud and B. Tirone, 2013).

Hans Pruijt studied sociology at the University of Amsterdam and obtained his PhD from Erasmus University in Rotterdam, where he currently teaches in the Department of Sociology. His interests include self-management and urban movements.

Alan Smart is a designer, scholar and critic interested in issues of production, reproduction and political economy in art, architecture and urbanism. He is currently researching relations between performance and 'non-object' art and experimental architecture and radical urban space movements in the 1960s, 1970s and 1980s, looking specifically at the Provo movement in Amsterdam and the squatter and neighbourhood occupation movements that followed it. He has taught architecture and design at the University of Hong Kong, the Sandberg Institute and Ohio State University.

Index

A

Abbé Pierre, 61
academic centres, 22
Action, 147, 148
activist research/activist researchers, 11,
    17, 20
    and 'participant observing'
        methodology, 23
after-squats, 248
    see also legalisation of squatting/
        squats, negotiation of squats
agro-ecological culture, 174
Aktie '70, 112–14
Alemanno, G., mayor of Rome, 143, 146
alter-globalisation movements, 37
alternative to the capitalist city, 170
alternative culture 65, 71
    and living differently 70, 78
alternative economy, 71, 176–8
    see also oikonomy
amantine, 193
American Association of Geographers 2012
    conference, 252
Amsterdam, 13, 15, 17, 31, 110–22, 218
    Groote Keijser, 119
    Grote Wetering, 120
    Kattenburg, 111–12
    Kinkerbuurt, 119
    Lucky Luijk, 120
    Niuwmarkt struggle, 114–15
    Oranje Vrijstaat, 114
    Prins Hendrikkade, 120
    Valreep social centre, 122
    Vetterstraat, 112
    Vondelstraat, 119–20
    Weijers building, 120–1
Anders Wonen Anders Leven Dutch
    ecological network, 184n3
anti-capitalism, 1, 4, 7, 101, 103, 111
    and ecological/radical autonomy,
        169, 175, 244, 248
    and free markets 7
    in legalised squats 226–7
    see also autonomous movement,
        commons, material alternative to
        capitalism, political squatting
Anti-Sexist Practices annual conference, 204

anti-squat companies, 122, 233–4
appropriation of ownership, 69–70
artist squatters, 159
Association of Community Organizations
    for Reform Now (ACORN), 126
Aufheben, 90
Autonomous Homeless Shelter, 97
autonomous movement, 38, 90, 127–8
    as anti-capitalist, 239
    see also anti-capitalism
autonomy in/of the squats, 184
    different degrees of,178
    in setting up the space, 69
autoriduzione (self-reduction), 139

B

Bailey, R., 86–7, 102
balance of power, 160, 232–4, 242–3
Banana Kelly, 125
Barcelona, 13, 16, 169–82, 191–200
    15O building, 170
    Barrilonia, 203
    Biciosxs, 170
    Can Masdeu, 173, 174, 176–9
    Can Piella, 173, 176–9
    Collserola Natural Park, 173, 179
    La Gorda, 202
    history of gender-related squats, 191
    Hort del Chino, 174
    Kan Pasqual, 176–9
    La Morada, 197
    La Tremenda, 202
    Mambo, 197
Barranco, J., former mayor of Madrid, 221
Berlin, 13, 14, 16, 190–200, 217–30
    anti-terrorist law no. 129, 219
    Cosimaplatz, 190
    fall of the Wall and squatting, 225–6
    Georg von Rauch-Haus, 206
    history of gender-related squats,
        190–1
    house projects, 81–2, 176
    Irving Zola, 207
    Köpi 137, 202, 220
    Liebigstraße 14, 81, 219, 222, 223,
        228
    Mainzerstraße battle (1990), 225–6

New Yorck in Bethanien, 202, 204, 218, 251
    Rote Insel house project, 251
    Scwarzer Kanal, queer caravan site, 199–200
    SqEK meeting, 251
    and squat legalisations, 218
    Tuntenhaus (House of Drag Queens), 198–9
Berlusconi, S., 141
bicycle culture, 170–2
bicycle workshops, 170–2
Bilbao, 170
    Kukutxa, 170
Black Panthers, 131
Blunden, M., 100
bona fide squatters, 30
Brighton, 13, 14, 95–9
    and history of the squatters' movement, 91–5
    Lewes Road Community Gardens, 97–8
    North Place actions, 91
    SaboTaj squat, 98–9
    Terminus Road, 93
    Wykeham Terrace bombing, 92
Brighton and Hove Squatters Association, 93
Brighton Photo Biennial, 98
Brighton Rents Project, 91, 92
Brotherton, M., 124
building developers and mass-media ownership, 149
Butler, G., 48, 49

C
capabilities, 30
capitalism, 1, 6–9, 24, 33
    as anti-life, 133, 242
    challenged by squatters, 33, 42, 62, 151–2, 177, 238
    and commodification, 6, 8
    and exhaustion of natural resources, 52–4, 183, 237
    and negative individual autonomy, 72
    as a perverse system, 7–8
    and promotion of its green side, 180
    and relationship with squatting, 6–7
    speculation, 35
    see also financial crisis, urban speculation,

caravan dwelling, 78–9, 80
Carlsson, C., 172, 183
Carlyon, T., 103
Casa Pound, 4
Cathy Come Home, 86, 103
Ceruso, F., 139
Christian Democrats in Italy (DC), 137
cities
    and co-option of autonomous environmental practices, 180
    ecological footprint of, 166–7, 184n1
    as ecosystems, 166–70
    and large-scale negative social impacts, 166–8
    and pollution, 180–2
    and power concentration, 168
    and the problem of centralised global decision making, 184
    and rural–urban split, 168–9, 172, 175
    sprawl as skin melanomas, 167–8
    and urban gardening, 172–3
Citizens Platform for the Housing Struggle, 146, 147, 148
class struggle, 29, 31
classification of vacant stock, 32–3
Cochon, G., 31
collective actions and experience, 68, 150, 156
collective autonomy, 244–5
common housing movement, 50
commons, 248
    and anti-capitalistic politics, 242
    see also anti-capitalism
communal economies, 177–9
community gardens, 49, 79, 97, 173
complexities of the movement, 91
consolidation of squats, 122
contradictions and failures, 8–9, 73–4, 112, 195, 202
    internal conflicts, 247–8
    related to negotiations and legalisations, 224
    squatting dependent upon capitalist waste, 245
    see also splitting of the movement
conviviality, 69
Copenhagen
    the Bolsjefabrike, 251
    Norrebrod neighbourhood, 251
    SqEK meeting, 252

Council of Churches, 116
counter-cultural critique
    of the consumerist society, 11
    in the creation of alternative spaces,
        62–3
counter-cultural lifestyles, 5, 29, 103–4, 189
    and caravan dwelling, 78–9
    as local contributions to a better
        world, 183–4
    and rurban communes, 177
    see also multidimensional way of
        living, legalisation of squatting/
        squats
creativity within squats, 98
criminalisation of squatting, 211–12, 230
    attempts and discourses around,
        Britain, 94, 97–100
    attempts, the Netherlands, 116
    and collective sharing of persecution
        costs, 231
    in England and Wales, 14, 85, 89,
        104–6
    in the Netherlands, 17, 32, 114, 116,
        232–4
    and police harassment, 104–5
    and preservation of capitalism, 215
    as revanchist legislation against
        squatters' rights, 217
    in Spain, 36
    see also prison sentences
crisis of capitalism, 26
    and financial speculation, 9, 34–5
    and peak oil, 53
    see also depletion of natural resources
        and the crisis, financial crisis
critical discourse analysis, 100–1
critical mass, 68, 170
critique of capitalism, 10, 14, 77, 216
    and the 'alternative culture', 65
    and dissolution into institutional
        processes, 79
    enacted and embedded, 60, 68

D
daily life in squats, 63–4, 72
decision making, 69, 184
decline, 110
Democratic Party in Italy (PD), 141
Denmark, 212
depletion of natural resources and the
    crisis, 52–4, 183

    see also crisis of capitalism
different experiences of squats, 62, 117
different relationship to the labour market,
    178
direct action, 244
    examples of, 118, 157–8, 196
Disability Rights Movement and squatting,
    207
Disobbedienti, 147
dissensual subject, 72
distribution of the sensible, 72
diversity of legislations on squatting in
    Europe, 212
Dixon, T., 105
do-it-yourself (DIY), 20, 90, 149, 174
do-it-ourselves, 244
    see also self-renovation
Douthwaite, R., 53
Droit au Logement, 61, 159–60
Duivenvoorden, E., 114
Duputell, D., first convicted Brighton
    squatter, 105
Dutch Supreme Court, 114
dynamic balance of power, 232–4

E
ecological dimension, 11, 16, 52, 168–9,
    176
economic crises and emergence of the
    movement, 36–7
Elbro, M., 95
emotional investment in squatting, 70
empty houses, 41, 111, 142
energy sustainability, 177
Engels, F., 33
enterprise squats, 117–18, 121
    and scaling-up potential, 247
environment and squatting *see* ecological
    dimension
Esping-Anderson, G., 110
eviction of squats
    and abandonment of the city, 78
    active physical resistance, 112,
        223–4, 225–6
    in Amsterdam, 112, 119–20
    Berliner Linie, 218
    in Brighton, 93
    and cost of subsequent riots, 223
    and effects on a group's cohesion,
        150, 226–7
    fixed vs surprise dates of, 219

Index

former Dutch legislation on, 114
in Geneva, 74–7
in London, 87–8
reactions after, 222–3
and use of legal means to delay, 219

F
Falo masculine liberation fanzine, 204
Fanfare van de Eerste Liefdesnacht, 118
farmland preservation, 175
festive events, 71, 118
financial crisis, 36–7
  and public policies, 38, 40, 42
  see also capitalism, crisis of
    capitalism
formal vs substantive drivers, 240–1
Forrest, R., 46–7
Foucault, M., 60
France, 212
Frankfurt am Main, 190
Franklin, A., 88
Frauencafe Moabit, 192
free meals and squats, 71
free workshops and squats, 171–2

G
gender-related movements, 16
  and alternative pornography, 197–8
  and critique of capitalism, 197, 244
  and examples of direct action, 196, 200
  and international similarity of
    discourses, 205
  and intersectional approach, 208n5
  and production of texts and debates,
    195, 203–4
  prompted by men, 204
  and queer politics, 198
  see also LGTBQ
Geneva, 13, 14, 60, 63, 176
  invention of the city, 80
  Les Grottes, 63–4, 75
  policy of tolerance towards squats,
    62, 66, 75,
  proposal of the Villa Freundler
    Convention, 70
  real estate market, 76
  repressive policy on squats, 67, 72, 75
gentrification, 48, 89, 131–2
Germany, 212
Gil, S., 192
Giuliani, R., former NYC mayor, 174–5

H
habitation phase, 72–4
Haegi, C., Geneva city magistrate, 66
Heinberg, R., 53
history of the movement, 14, 36, 61, 63–5
Hodkinson, S., 44, 50
Holloway, J., 239
home ownership, 39, 41, 45–7, 140
  exclusion from, 43
  and social exclusion, 43–4, 46–7
homeless/homelessness, 2, 86, 146
  charities, 86, 92, 97
  and the financial crisis, 153–4
  and forms of resistance, 136
  as a social problem, 101
  and squatting, 102, 154
  see also housing
homesteading, 125–7
Hoogstraten N. van, 93
house communes/house projects, 1, 7, 10,
    14, 29, 81
  examples of internal organization,
    177–8
  and state repression, 81
housing, 11, 51, 123–6
  bubble, 37–8, 40
  in caravans, 78–9
  cooperatives, 44, 45, 77, 89
  crisis, 36–43, 86, 91, 95
  and immigrants, 144–5
  and inflation, 138–9
  need, 29, 44, 87, 123
  question/issue, 11, 26, 33–43
  self-contruction, 80
  and socialist society, 43
  and squatters' 'alternative-
    oppositional' challenge, 44–5
  and urban violence, 42
  and young people, 39
  see also homeless/homelessness,
    self-renovation
Housing Action in Southwark and Lambeth
    (HASL), 106
housing alternatives, 50
Housing and Community Development
    Act, 125–6
human needs, 29–30, 213

I
idiorhythmic community, 73
illegal albeit moral behaviour, 230–1

immigrants, 2, 145–6, 152, 159, 206–7
impacts of the squatters' movement
    in Barcelona, 179
    in Berlin, 223
    in Brighton, 91, 96, 102
    in Geneva, 76, 77, 79
    in London, 89, 102
    in the Netherlands, 111, 115
    in Paris, 160
implementation of community life,
    68–9
income and rent, relation between, 141
installation phase, 68–72
institutionalization, 74, 75
intensity of alternatives, 240
internal diversity of squatters, 30–1, 189
international links, 90, 128
Italian Communist Party (PCI), 136, 138,
    139

J
Jenkins, D., 87
Jeudi Noir, 147, 159–60

K
Kabouter Movement, 114
Kirby, S., 96
Kraakkrant, Amsterdam squatters
    newspapaer, 116

L
Las Anacondas Subversivas, Madrid-based
    feminist collective. 194
lawfulness redefined. 242
Lee, M.. 130
Lefevbre, H.. 65
    see also right to the city
legalisation of squatting/squats, 11, 16–17,
    89, 119, 197
    and continuation of radical politics,
        81, 121, 212, 213, 226–7
    and continuing state repression, 81
    different attitudes towards, 218
    and effects on autonomy, 121–2
    and evictions of the non-legalised,
        225, 230
    and loss in autonomy/social
        legitimation, 228–9, 242
    and paying rents/mortgages, 50, 229
    for a post-capitalist contest, 246
    and squatting as a means, 240

and time-consuming processes 228
    see also after-squats, counter-cultural
        lifestyles, negotiations of squats
legitimation of squatting, 31–2, 63–6, 125,
    242–3
Les Tenses, Barcelona-based feminist
    collective, 193–4
LGTBQ, 4, 16
    origins of, 189
    slogan and claims of, 189–90
    standing as an autonomous
        movement within the squatters',
        190
    see also gender-related movements
Ligadura, Madrid-based feminist collective,
    192, 193
living together, 189
    principles of, 68
local vs global alternative to capitalism, 1,
    10, 17, 131, 180, 241–7
    intensity of, 245
    and need of citizen control, 246
    and plurality of manifestations, 12
    and positive multiplying effect, 248
    and self-determination,244
    and time freed from the labour
        market, 243–4, 245
London, 13, 14, 99–102
    Centre Point, 88–9
    the Foundry, 251
    and history of the squatters'
        movement, 86–91
    social centres, recently squatted, 101
    SqEK meeting, 251
    Tolmers Square, 88–9
London Squatters Campaign, 87, 90
Longstaffe-Gowan, T. 89

M
M15 movement, 38
Madrid, 13, 16, 18, 170, 192, 217–30
    Asambela de Okupas, 218
    Casablanca, 219–20
    El Laboratorio I, 194, 218
    history of gender-related squats, 191
    La Enredadera, 191
    La Eskalera Karakola, Casa Pública
        de Mujeres (Public House of
        Women), 191, 196–7, 205, 227
    La Guindalera, 221
    Minuesa, 217, 219

Index

Patio Maravillas, 170, 219, 220, 250
Seco, 227, 250
SqEK meeting, 250
Mahony, T., 90
Manning, F., 172
market logic and squats, 62, 76
Marseilles, 170
Martinez-Alier, J., 52
mass media
    effects on squatting, 88
    and homelessness, 100–1
    manipulations, 100, 112, 149
    squatters' diverse uses of, 159–60,
        219, 220
material alternative to capitalism, 178,
    245, 248
    see also anti-capitalism
May Day Manifesto, 91
Mayer, M., 158
means and ends behind squatting, 5, 15,
    125, 159, 238–40
    and need of self-critical analysis,
        241
Milan
    Cox, 18 250
    SqEK meeting, 250
minorities/diversity 11, 16
money-free alternative to capitalism, 172,
    245
moral principles, 17, 103, 230–1
Morales, F., 127
Movement for a Decent Housing, 37, 42
Movements for the Right to Inhabit
    (Movimenti per il diritto all'abitare),
    143–4, 148, 150, 151, 153–4, 159
    and its objectives 155
    and reasons for its success, 157–8
Mujeres Preokupando, Spanish gender-
    related newspaper, 195
multidimensional way of living, 12
    see also counter-cultural lifestyles
Muzio, R., 123

N
Nafeez Mosaddeq, A., 53
Naredo, J., 167
narratives built around squatters, 101, 221
National Alliance of Tenants (UNIA), 138
negotiations of squats, 217–18, 224–9
    and differences between cities, 226
    and inherent issues, 224

    see also after-squats, legalisation of
        squatting/squats
neoliberal housing policies
    Italian history of, 137–142
    in Japan, 45–7
    resistance to, 136, 141, 157
    in UK, 45–7
    in USA, 47–8
neoliberalism, 2, 3, 5, 34, 45
Netherlands, the, 211, 232–4
new left, 64
new social movement, 90
New York City (NYC), 13, 15, 16
    ABC No Rio, 129–30, 171, 252
    community gardens, 173, 174–5
    ecological autonomy from the
        capitalist city, 169
    environmental hazards, 167, 182
    Harlem, 131
    housing problems and policies, 47,
        49
    Local Storefront, 124–5
    Lower East Side, 15, 48, 49, 127–8,
        132, 175
    Morningside Heights, 124, 131
    Museum of Reclaimed Urban Space,
        130, 252
    Plaza Caribe, 124
    Rent Stabilization, 48–9
    South Bronx, 125
    SqEK meeting, 252
    and the squatters' movement, 49–50
    Tompkins Square Park, 132
    Upper West Side, 123
New York City Housing Authority, 47
North America, 2

O
occupation phase, 63–8
occupazione, 137
Occupy/M15 movement, 5, 38, 42, 101, 132
    and negotiations/legalisations of
        squats, 218
oikonomy, 184n3
    see also alternative economy
open-air squatting, 79, 174, 179
Operation Move-In (OMI), 123, 124
organization of the common space in a
    squat, 154
Organize4Occupation, 50, 130, 132, 253
ownership by use, 66

Index

P

Paris, 13, 15, 159–60, 170
    SqEK meeting, 253
partially private possession, 34, 44
peak oil,53
Péchu, C., 61
Picture the Homeless, 130
Platform of the People Affected by
    Mortgages (PAH), 16, 38, 51, 231
Platt, S., 92, 101
Poldervaart, S., 112
policy of slightly repressive tolerance, 121
Politi, R., 127
political squatting, 2–4, 85, 150, 189
    against empty buildings, 94
    against private property, 237–8, 239
    and anti-capitalist activities and life-
        styles, 237–8
    as a long-lasting transnational
        network, 8
    opposing development plans, 97–8
    relationship between politicised
        activists and desperate squatters,
        153
    as a resistance against capitalism,
        14–15, 237
    and social squatting, 27, 30, 51
    as a symbolic struggle, 35
    see also anti-capitalism
positive (and negative) character of
    squatting, 242–3
possibility of taking place, 130–1
potential to democratise the city, 184
Pound, E., 4
power of squatting, 111
Precarious Metropolitan Blocks, 147, 148
Priemus, 30
prison sentences, cases of squatters, 99,
    217, 219
    see also criminalisation of squatting
progressive socio-political practices, 12, 116
property outlaws, desirability of, 231
property owners/private property, 31–2, 44,
    94, 117, 130–1
property versus possession, 43–4, 74
Proudhon, P., 28, 33, 44
Provos, 15, 112
public cost of empty properties, 96
public opinion and support, 88, 90, 100,
    120
Puerto Rican Young Lords, 131

Q

Queeruption Festival, 200

R

radical squatters' challenge to social life, 60
Rancière, J., 72
Rattey, K. dead after eviction protests, 223
reasons behind squatting, 213
    as an alternative housing strategy, 154
    beyond housing, 5, 150–6
    deprivation-based, 150, 154
    as an end, 5, 15, 125, 238
    immediate need/for housing, 2–3,
        86, 94, 136, 138, 153–4
reclaim the streets, 5, 68
Reeve, K., 90, 102, 104
Reinauer, C., former Kreuzberg mayor, 218
Release in Haarlem, 114
resistance
    against development plans, 64, 89,
        97–8, 111–12, 114–15, 119–20,
    against domination, 239
    another occupation following an
        eviction, 222
    relation between resistance strategies
        for squats' survival, 225, 229–30,
        232
    using legal means and the mass
        media, 219–20
    using negotiations and legalisations,
        217–19
    using physical resistance, 222
    using their own means, 221–2
retired people and squatting, 207
right to the city (RTC), 2, 28, 65, 136, 159,
    175
    and the dissolution of its anti-
        capitalist ideals, 215
    and need to understand biophysical
        processes, 181
    and squatters' participation, 214
    see also Lefebvre
right to housing, 3, 11, 15, 159–60
    direct action to enforce, 157
    and political squatters' movement, 3
    and squatting as a means to, 240
    UN delegation report, 149
    versus right to property, 231–3
right to squat, 87, 114, 116, 213
    as a critique of capitalist practices,
        216

as a fair defence in civil courts,
216–17
gained after successful campaigns,
92, 94
present survival of, 103
and the reuse of empty spaces,
215–16
and visibilisation of public
mismanagement in social
housing, 216
right of use, 3–4
Rome, 4, 13, 15, 136, 170
borgate, 137
Corviale, 145
and demand for social housing,143–4
ex-Snia, 170
Forte Prenestino, 170
history of housing struggle, 137–42
Hotel Africa, 155
master plan for housing, 142
Metropoliz, 148, 149, 152, 153
Ostia, 146
Pantanella, 145
Porto Fluviale, 148, 149, 154
'Protocol on the housing emergency'
(Protocollo sull'emergenza
abitativa), 141
and public cost of social housing, 146
San Basilio, 139
San Papiers, 148, 149, 152, 153
scaling-up potential, 246
rurban (rural–urban) squatting, 16, 79,
176–80, 183
Rutelli, F., former mayor of Rome, 146

S
Saunders, P., 43–4
scaling-up of the practice, 1, 17, 180, 241–3
as an alternative way to inhabit the
city, 158
as a geographical and virtual
network, 150
past experiences, 15, 87, 94, 110, 111
potential in relation to the crisis, 15
theoretical possibilities, 246
through anti-capitalistic policies, 246
security of ownership, 70–1
self-emancipation/self-determination, 65,
67, 244
self-help housing, 125–6
self-management/self-organisation, 154

as an alternative conception of living
together, 68–70, 77, 81, 189
as a collective and comprehensive
process, 29
at local scale, 248
in the reproduction of life, 184
saving social and economic costs 244
and squats' legalisation, 227
and support against legal
persecution, 231
see also self-renovation
self-renovation (*autorecupero*), 147, 148–9,
152
as an alternative to capitalism, 151,
158
see also do-it-yourself, housing,
self-management/
sel-organisation
self-research, 20, 24
self-responsibility, need of, 244
September 11 and pollution, 182
sexualised violence in squats, cases, 193,
194, 202, 203
shadow researchers, 20
Shenker, M., 128
shrinking cities, 133
situationists, 65, 68
social centres
evolution from housing squats, 149
fascist squatted, 4
as a form of political squatting, 3,
98–9
projects which include housing, 118
and relationship with house squats,
155
and scholarship production, 23
as venues of SqEk meetings, 23
social compensation, 241
social composition of squatters, 145, 147,
153
social control, 132
social disobedience, 3
social and ecological challenges, 180–2
social exclusion, 136
social housing, 39, 41, 76, 136
and deregulation, 141
and squatters, 44, 45, 216
social housing institute (IACP), 145
social innovation, 247
social justice, 29–31
and government doublespeak, 215

social movements, 23, 86
social needs, 26–31
social struggles, 103
socio-cultural challenge to capitalism, 240
Spain, 212
spaces of resistance and living spaces,
    evolution, 79
    inclination to dwell, 73
Spanish Penal Code (1995), 212, 217
spatial deconcentration, 131–2
splitting of the movement, 76–7, 213,
    224–5
    see also contradictions and failures
SqEK, 9–10, 17–24
    as alternative to capitalism, 10, 22–4
    and collective of collectives, 10, 18
    and comparative approach, 12, 18, 22
    and contradictions, 21, 23
    and critical engagement, 19
    decision process, 17, 20, 22–4
    e-mail list, 9, 17, 23
    and knowledge production, 9, 20,
        23, 253–4
    manifesto, 251
    meetings, 9, 20, 22–4, 250–4
    network, 18, 22, 23
    research agenda, 19
    story, 250–4
    and transdisciplinarity process, 21
Squatters Action for Secure Homes
    (SQUASH), 99, 105
Squatters Network of Brighton (And Hove
    Actually)/SNOB(AHA), 95–6, 99, 105
state capitalism, 64
state and production of squattable empty
    spaces, 241
statistics on the number of squats
    in Berlin, 190, 222
    in Italy and Rome, 139, 158
    in London, 88
    in Madrid, 221
    in United Kingdom, 88, 94, 101–2
St George, P., 126
Stop Trans Pathologisation annual
    demonstration, 200
strategic alliances, 116
strategic exodus from paid work/capitalism,
    172, 184, 243
    see also work for salary
student residences (*studentati occupati*),
    156

sweat equity, 125
symptom of the housing/capitalist problem,
    95, 213–14

T
Tafanera, M., 208n4
Talocci, G., 151
technical obstacles, 129
Thatcher, M., 45
Time's Up!, 171
Traficantes de Sueños, 250
trust contract, 66, 77
Tverberg, G., 53

U
unequal gender relationships, challenge of,
    190, 192–3, 201
urban ecosystem and its depoliticisation,
    183
urban food production, benefits of, 180–1
urban gardens, 172–5
    and city resilience, 172–3
    and planning from below, 172
    and urban policies discriminating
        against, 173
    and visibility of food production, 174
Urban Homesteading Assistance Board
    (UHAB), 124
urban movement, 2, 8
urban speculation, 34, 36, 41–4, 239
    see also capitalism
urban sprawl, 41
    and destruction of farmland, 175
Urbanrise, 151–2
use value, 7, 50, 65, 76, 233
    and the household, 244

V
Veltroni, W., former mayor of Rome, 146,
    149
Vaneslander, B., 201
voluntary leave of a squat, 119

W
War (Victory) Gardens, 172
Wates, N., 89
Weatherley, M., English proponent of
    squatting criminalisation, 96, 97
welfare state, 27, 110
Wet Kraken en Leegstand, Dutch Law on
    Squatting and Vacancy, 233–4

window of opportunities and creativity, 241
women-only spaces, issues related to, 195,
    202
Women and Squatting, working group, 192
Woningbureaus de Kraker, 112
work for salary, 71
    see also strategic exodus from paid
        work/capitalism
workers control, 247

X
X_Y, 201

Z
Zappelli, D., Geneva district attorney, 75,
    76

LIFE WITHOUT MONEY
Building Fair and Sustainable Economies
Edited by Anitra Nelson and Frans Timmerman

'A timely contribution to an under-researched and under-reported area of economics: the theory of money and proposals for alternatives to the globalised capitalist financial system. I would recommend it to anyone interested in finding ways to develop an economy that functions without money.'
– *Molly Scott Cato*

Examines the failure of the money-based global economy and how we might live in more sustainable, equitable ways. A textbook and manifesto for change.

THE HERETIC'S GUIDE TO GLOBAL FINANCE
Hacking the Future of Money
Brett Scott

'This book provides a unique inside-out look at our financial system. It is not only a user-friendly guide to the complex maze of modern finance but also a manual for utilising and subverting it for social purposes in innovative ways. Smart and street-smart.'
– *Ha-Joon Chang*

Shows how activists can tap into the internal dynamics of the sector to disrupt it and showcases the growing alternative finance movement.

PlutoPress
www.plutobooks.com

FOOD FOR CHANGE
The Politics and Values of Social Movements
Jeff Pratt and Pete Luetchford

'This is a hugely rich account of the local food movement as it manifests itself across Europe, offering compelling case studies of creative alternatives outside the capitalist mainstream. The book digs deep into the social and ecological values associated with food, and fully succeeds in its efforts to bring politics back into the debate. Fascinating, inspiring and a delight to read.'
– *John Hilary, War on Want*

CRACK CAPITALISM
John Holloway

'Assuming that you want to bring down capitalism, how should you go about it? Holloway urges readers to create "cracks" in the edifice: in lieu of "alienated labour", choose to do something you think is necessary or interesting. ... Infectiously optimistic.'
– *Guardian*

Crack Capitalism argues that radical change can only come about through the creation, expansion and multiplication of 'cracks' in the capitalist system. These cracks are ordinary moments or spaces of rebellion in which we assert a different type of doing.

Clearly and accessibly presented in the form of 33 theses, this book is set to reopen the debate among radical scholars and activists seeking to break capitalism now.

 **Pluto**Press
www.plutobooks.com

THE BATTLE FOR EUROPE
How an Elite Hijacked a Continent – and How We Can Take it Back
Thomas Fazi

'There is no book as comprehensive as this. The quality of Fazi's writing and the scope of his arguments make this an exceptional work – a must read!'
– *Steve McGiffen*

'Thomas Fazi's compelling history shows how flawed institutions, a weak tax system and bank-friendly financial codes produced the Eurozone crisis, and then how that debacle was transformed, country by country, into a crisis of public debt and an assault-by-bailout on Europe's social model. Fazi thus builds a case for radical reform to save Europe from two lethal threats – the return of a vicious right-wing nationalism and the blindness of its own rulers.'
– *James Galbraith, senior scholar at the Levy Economics Institute and chair of the Board of Economists for Peace and Security*

THE NEW URBAN QUESTION
Andy Merrifield

'Merrifield is accessible, optimistic and even fun.'
– *New York Times*

A lucid and vibrant contribution to the field of urban studies, tracing the connections between radical urban theory and political activism.

PlutoPress
www.plutobooks.com

AGAINST AUSTERITY
How We Can Fix the Crisis They Made
Richard Seymour

'Essential and powerful reading.'
– *Paul Mason*

Five years into capitalism's deepest crisis, austerity has brought cuts and economic pain across the world. Why are the rich still getting away with it? Why is protest so ephemeral? Why does the left appear to be marginal to political life?

This blistering, accessible and invigorating polemic against the current political consensus provides the answers.

HUGO CHAVEZ
Socialist for the Twenty-first Century
Mike Gonzalez

'For activists and scholars alike, this is an excellent biography, which mirrors in its nuances and subtleties the complexity of the Bolivarian process and the figure of Chavez himself.'
– *Jeffery R. Webber, Queen Mary University of London*

This dramatic and intimate biography traces Chavez's life from an impoverished rural family to the Miraflores Presidential Palace in Caracas. Mike Gonzalez shows how Chavez's 'Bolivarian revolution' aimed to complete Simon Bolivar's promise of a Latin America free from imperialism.

PlutoPress
www.plutobooks.com